John Hughes was born in Sutton Coldfield, in the English Midlands, studied music at Royal Holloway College and has lived in Surrey for most of his adult life. He has earned a living in a variety of ways – selling pianos in Harrods, playing keyboards in a tribute band, as a magazine editor, in recruitment and most recently managing in the NHS.

He has written half a dozen non-fiction books and *Follow My Leader* is his second novel. The first, *Spitfire Spies*, was published by Austin Macauley in 2016. John Hughes has also produced and directed films and written screenplays, with *Home Alone, The Breakfast Club, Uncle Buck* and *Ferris Bueller's Day Off* to his credit – but that's a different John Hughes.

John Hughes

FOLLOW MY LEADER

AUSTIN MACAULEY PUBLISHERS™

LONDON • CAMBRIDGE • NEW YORK • SHARJAH

A CIP catalogue record for this title is available from the British Library.

ISBN 9781787105393 (Paperback)
ISBN 9781787105409 (E-Book)

www.austinmacauley.com

First Published (2017)
Austin Macauley Publishers Ltd.
25 Canada Square
Canary Wharf
London
E14 5LQ

Acknowledgements

My thanks to:

Rosalind Knight for kindly advising on my portrayal of her father, Esmond Knight; Steve Crook for advice about Michael Powell and his films; Archivists at the Royal Opera House, Covent Garden, for clarifying details of applause during *Parsifal*; Terry Hardy of The Max Miller Appreciation Society for giving use of the 'Cheeky Chappie' ditty official blessing; Jean Pooley for details of Reigate carnival in 1951; 'Memories of Redhill/Reigate' Facebook group members whose reminiscences have provided invaluable detail; Vera Peiffer for guidance on the German language; Barb Wells for allowing me to steal her name and who is nothing like her namesake in the story.

Acknowledgements are made to the following works referenced in this novel:

The High Window: Raymond Chandler (1942)
The Last Days of Hitler: H.R. Trevor-Roper (1947)

Prologue

Monday 30th April 1945

The woman balanced precariously, one leg on the crudely built wooden quayside, the other on the edge of the boat, her face screwed up in disgust. Her travelling companions – the man and his dog – were already on board and he was holding out a helping hand.

'Oh Wolfie, must we?' she implored. 'This thing really stinks of fish!'

'It would,' he replied tersely. 'It's a fishing boat.'

'It's vile.'

'We'll only be on here for a short while. The sooner you get on the sooner you can get off again.'

'Is all the luggage loaded?'

'Look.' He pointed towards the bow where a small mountain of cases and bags lay neatly. 'See … it's all there. Now please hurry.'

She lifted the straggling leg from the quay and stood at last on the deck. 'It's vile,' she repeated.

The skipper called out in Spanish. The ropes holding the boat at the quayside were released and thrown on board, and the revs of the gently idling engine rose in a slow crescendo. The boat eased its way out to sea. The night was nearly over and although still dark, a slight edge of light along the horizon hinted at the coming dawn. The water itself was still ink black.

As voyages went it was very brief; a ferry trip, no more. The U-boat was moored as close to shore as was safe and within minutes the silhouette of the conning tower could be seen clearly, looming ever larger until it dominated them like a giant monolith. When the fishing boat had been secured alongside, a harness was lowered from the deck of the U-boat and the man supervised the dog being strapped in and winched on board.

'Good girl, Blondi,' he said reassuringly. 'There's a good girl.' And so she was. Not a whimper could be heard as she disappeared upwards and out of sight.

A rope ladder had also been lowered.

'You have a choice, my dear,' he said to the woman. 'Winch or ladder – which will it be?'

'I'll take the ladder,' she replied with some enthusiasm, keen no doubt to escape the stench of fish. She was lithe and fit, and wore slacks and stout shoes. Soon she was making her way nimbly upwards, grabbing the rope with alternate hands and feet until she was on the deck of the U-boat.

The man – more than twenty years her senior, unfit, and hampered by formal clothing including a military jacket – followed less confidently and at a more sedate pace, though without mishap. Further along the deck, with a lamp suspended overhead to improve visibility, bags and cases were being hauled on board and dropped down the forward torpedo-loading hatch. A junior seaman had been allocated the duty of taking care of the dog and was walking her up and down, his hand gripping the lead firmly. When they reached the open hatch, Blondi's tail wagged and she pulled on the lead to try and peer inside.

'Take her down!' called out the man. 'If she's that keen, make the most of it.' His dry, husky voice did not carry, so the U-boat captain, who had come down from the bridge to greet them, bellowed out the order, repeating it word for word. They watched as the dog disappeared into the bowels of the vessel with the sailor in tow. The last of the luggage also vanished down the hatch.

The woman was shaking with nerves; the man could feel it as she held onto his arm.

'We had better get inside too,' he said.

'That's right,' added the captain. 'We should not delay any longer than necessary. You can either use the torpedo-loading hatch over there, or the bridge hatch.' He indicated the latter by pointing to the conning tower. 'The end result will be the same.'

'Another choice, my dear,' said the man. 'Which shall it be?' He could feel her shaking again. When she spoke, her voice trembled. It was dry and feeble.

'I don't think I can do this, Wolfie.'

'Nonsense, of course you can. Would you like to use the hatch along the deck, or climb up onto the conning tower and down inside from there?'

'I can't do either. I'm scared. I hate confined spaces.'

He squeezed her arm reassuringly. 'We've just been living underground for three months. This will be no different.'

She shook her head emphatically. 'That *was* different. You could walk up the steps into the gardens and stroll about anytime you wanted, even when shells were raining down.'

'I don't remember you ever doing that.'

'But you could if you wanted.'

The captain said: 'You can do that on board, come up for fresh air, though we have no garden. We shall travel on the surface whenever possible and you may come and stand on the bridge any time you choose – weather conditions permitting. It can be very bracing up there. The weather will vary a good deal as we make our way south. We will submerge only when absolutely necessary.'

She shook her head and folded her arms defensively. 'It's not the same.'

'Come, my dear,' said the man. 'Climb up onto the bridge and take a look. There's the ladder.'

She moved forward, hesitantly at first, then was up the ladder and on the bridge in moments. The man and the captain followed. In front of her gaped the open hatchway. She peered down into it, and saw what appeared to her to be a very narrow, seemingly endless dark chasm. She shuddered. Her head was spinning, her stomach churning, and she felt sick.

'I can't do it.'

'You have to!' The man's tone was suddenly harsh, his patience dwindling. 'We must continue our journey. You will be fine once we are on board and on our way. Now come on, my dear, start climbing down – everything will be all right.'

Encouraged by his words, and conscious of the edge to his tone, bordering on a command, she moved forward, twisted round to place a foot on the first rung of the interior ladder and began her descent. She gripped the sides of the shaft, took a few steps downwards and transferred her hands onto the rungs in front of her.

'That's it – you are doing well,' said the man. 'You must keep going.'

She took another few steps, which brought her head below the top of the shaft, blocking any view of the outside world. She closed her eyes to try and distance herself from reality. It was a terrible mistake. Suddenly she felt disorientated and out of control. Her insides seemed to rebel and a huge wave of nausea and panic enveloped her. Her throat was constricting, making breathing very difficult. She climbed back up at speed and leaned over the edge of the conning tower, gasping for breath.

'It's no good,' she cried. 'I can't do it. Go without me – leave me here at the Villa Winter.'

'We cannot leave you,' stated the man.

'I will be all right. You go.'

'That is not possible.' The man turned his back on her and began a conversation with the captain in a gentle whisper. After a while he turned back and said: 'We have some time to spare, my dear. Now come, let's try the torpedo-loading hatch on the deck instead – perhaps that will be easier for you. Follow me. We shall sort this one way or another.'

An hour later, after much persuasion, cajoling and, as patience evaporated altogether, plain bullying, it was apparent to both the man and the captain that there was no way the woman was going to climb inside the U-boat. By then she was sobbing her heart out and almost fainting with anxiety. The decision was made to abandon the enterprise altogether.

'I'm sorry, Wolfie,' she whimpered. 'I'm sorry.'

He was furious but said nothing. He didn't need to; his body language made his feelings clear enough. Whereas they had come on board arm in arm, there was now space between them, and no eye contact whatsoever. The luggage was unloaded back onto the fishing boat, as was Blondi the dog. The man and woman climbed back down the rope ladder and once they were on board, the boat took them the short distance back to the island.

The captain watched from the bridge. Next to him stood the First Watch Officer, his second in command.

'What a farce,' said the captain sardonically. 'What did you make of that?

'Farce is the right word. I don't know what to think. Do we hang around now, in case they want to give it another try tomorrow?'

'There is no point … it is not going to happen.'

'So, what do we do?'

'Stay here and await orders. There will be others who need a passage.'

The First Watch Officer had hoped to hear otherwise; he could not hide his distaste. 'Rats abandoning the sinking ship,' he said.

'The king of rats tonight. God knows I'd be on my way to South America if I had the opportunity, the way things are turning to shit. If our leader is taking flight the war is lost … but we have known that for a long time. It's all up for every single one of us now.'

'Well I hope orders come through soon. It's frustrating being holed up here. Not safe either.'

'We have no choice.' The captain stared at the fishing boat as it disappeared from view. 'Have you ever seen him before – the man we have made an oath of unconditional obedience towards?'

'Only in newsreels – never in the flesh, so to speak.'

'And your impression?'

'Not the charismatic figure I expected. He looks all spent … shrivelled up somehow.'

The captain nodded in agreement. 'And the woman – what did you make of her?'

The First Watch Officer thought for a moment. 'May I speak frankly?'

'Of course.'

He mirrored his commanding officer and stared out towards the boat that had now vanished into the murky darkness of the island. 'As far as I'm concerned, she can come back anytime she likes to clamber up and down our ladders. She has a nice arse.'

'They won't be coming back. Wild horses couldn't drag that woman below deck.'

'What will they do?'

The captain shrugged. 'Stay here on the island, I assume. It's as good a hiding place as any, and it would seem they have no choice, other than retracing their steps which I imagine is out of the question.' He sighed wistfully. 'And yes, I agree … she does have a very nice arse.'

Part One

Chapter 1

Monday 11th June 1951

Rowena Furse pecked her husband firmly on the cheek and watched him saunter down the driveway, struggling to light a pipe whilst juggling a briefcase and balancing a raincoat over one arm.

'Bye Howie,' she called.

'Cheerio Flossie, old girl,' he replied as he disappeared along Alders Road, heading towards Reigate station.

She closed the front door and sighed with pleasure at the thought of ten wonderful hours in which to indulge the two overriding passions in her life – gardening and opera – without a husband cluttering up the place. Gardening and opera; both the source of enormous pleasure to her, the first being the focus of her daylight hours, whatever the season, the second filling much of the rest of her time when it was too dark to be out of doors.

She loved Howard but, unlike gardening and opera, he wasn't a passion in her life. He was a good man, a very good man, and a kind, attentive husband. Most importantly he was a provider, without whom there would be no four-bedroomed house with two-hundred-foot garden, or shed amply stocked with gardening equipment; no trips to Covent Garden, Sadler's Wells and Glyndebourne; no radiogram, gramophones, record collection or music scores; and no Rover 75 P4 Saloon tucked away in the garage.

Additionally, and unwittingly, Howard had enhanced her ability to indulge her passions by failing to give her children, thus freeing her from any parental commitments. She was forty, Howard ahead of her by almost a decade and, in truth, all attempts at fertilisation had long since floundered – never to be resurrected, not even as part of VE Day celebrations when, for a sparkling and all too brief moment in time, sexual intercourse became acceptable for the normally restrained British nation. The absence of children suited Rowena. She felt no maternal instincts whatsoever, nor any interest in *that sort of thing – that* being the thing you had to endure to achieve parenthood. Howard had no real say in the matter.

She had only a vague notion of what he did up in London; something in the Civil Service, somewhere near Whitehall, but that was about all. Frankly she wasn't terribly interested. In eleven years of marriage they had hardly ever discussed how he made a living; he didn't talk about it and when she occasionally asked he gave little away.

'It would bore you to tears, Floss,' Howard would say. 'I push paper around a desk, attend meetings, draft reports … all to keep the wheels of government in motion.' And that was how it was left.

All things considered, they had much to be thankful for and were content in their life together.

Over breakfast she had explained her plan for the day's gardening as Howard read The Times and nodded and smiled on cue from behind its protecting veil. The weather was warm and sunny, a perfect May morning, and she couldn't wait to get outside to lavish affection on her herbaceous border.

The daily help, Ethel Kipling, arrived shortly after nine, called out 'Mornin' Mrs Eff', and set about clearing away the breakfast things, Woodbine fixed firmly in corner of mouth and frown fixed firmly on brow. Soon afterwards Rowena was outside, hard at it, kneeling in front of the herbaceous border, immersed in a sea of Delphiniums, Geraniums, Hostas and other hardy perennials. The borders ran the length of both sides of her neatly mown lawn, from the terrace at the back of the house to a fence that divided the garden in half lengthways. Beyond this screen was a shed, a compost heap, a small herb garden, a larger vegetable patch and, eventually, a rather modest orchard with several beehives tucked amongst the fruit trees.

The border she was tending broke halfway along its length where paving stones led to a waist-high picket gate set in an arch-shaped gap in the high hedge that separated the garden from their neighbours on that side. Beyond the gate, by a mere couple of feet, was a stark wall of wooden planking; the back of an outbuilding, possibly a shed or a summer house. Rowena didn't know for sure as she had never been next door, nor had she or Howard even seen, let alone met, the occupants during the four years they had lived there. The summer house was at the end of a long garden and the main house was in fact located in the road adjacent – Wray Park Road. The owners, whoever they were, had clearly positioned the wooden building to block the view through the gate; and to good effect.

The morning wore on and Rowena toiled away as the sun rose in the sky. She was generously built and wore a tight-fitting tweed skirt and blouse, and was soon perspiring heavily. At eleven she took a break. Before going indoors, she disappeared behind the fence, checked to make sure she couldn't be seen, pulled down her drawers and peed over the compost heap.

'You need all the moisture you can get, my dear,' she informed it affectionately.

After lunch, as she often did once Ethel had gone home and she was alone, Rowena combined her two passions and set up her portable Fidelity electric record player on a table just outside the French windows, so she could listen to music as she potted, weeded, dug and trimmed. She invariably sang along, having trained as a singer in her youth, hopeful of a career in opera. It hadn't happened, for although Rowena's vocal technique was proficient, she was wanting in musicality. Had she been sensitive about such things, her husband's pet name for her, Flossie (a reference to possibly the worst soprano of all time – Florence Foster Jenkins), might have seemed offensive; but Rowena had a refreshing lack of any such acuteness of feeling. She sang because she loved it – and that was that, no matter who heard or what they thought. Fortunately for their neighbours, known to them or otherwise, sound tended not to carry well through dense privet.

She wandered into the library, opened a large cabinet and from an extensive collection of 78 and Long Play recordings selected the *Prelude and Liebestod* from *Tristan and Isolde*. She slid it out of its cardboard sleeve onto the turntable, started the motor and gently placed the needle onto the outer edge of the black disc. From within a haze of surface noise, the first notes began to float mellifluously out across the garden. Rowena slipped her gardening gloves on and headed back to the herbaceous border.

During the next twenty minutes, Wagner's music filled the air in a long, slow, sensuous (some might say orgasmic, though not Rowena) crescendo towards one heady climax after another until Isolde had met her demise. She listened as she worked, and when it was over played it again, this time singing along to the *Liebestod*, word perfect in the German text if not pitch perfect in the notation.

As the sublime music faded away to be replaced by the gentle clicking of the needle caught in the central groove, she sat back on her haunches, surveyed the fruits of her labours and sighed a sigh of absolute contentment. Other than the distant twittering of some birds, all was peaceful.

'*Ausgezeichnet!*'

Rowena started. For a confused moment, she thought the voice had come from the record player, but it couldn't have. The source was an entirely different direction, ahead and to her right. She stood up and glanced over the border towards the gate in the hedge. There stood an old man.

'Good heavens, you startled me!' she said.

'*Entschuldigung, Fräulein.*' The voice was gruff and deep in pitch. '*Es tut mir leid.* Err … I am sorry.'

'I didn't think anyone else was about.' She strolled across to the gate. 'I do rather love listening to music while I'm gardening. I hope it hasn't disturbed you.'

The man was squeezed between the back of the wooden outbuilding and the gate. His shoulders were hunched, he held a stick in one hand and wore a hat – a rather shabby looking homburg – pulled well down onto his head. But his face was clearly visible; a nondescript face, not attractive, and his teeth were bad. He had piercing blue eyes, partially obscured behind a pair of steel-rimmed glasses. Rowena guessed he was in his early seventies.

'No, not disturbing. I love music, especially opera. I could not help but be drawn by such beautiful singing.'

'I assume you mean the singing on the record, not mine?'

The old man stayed diplomatically silent.

'It is glorious, isn't it? Wagner – *Tristan and Isolde.*'

'*Prelude und Liebestod.*'

'You know it?'

'Oh yes, naturally. I have seen much performances … many performances I mean.' The old man bowed his head coyly. 'Excuse again, my English is not good.'

'It sounds splendid to me' said Rowena. 'I speak some German, but not well. I had to learn several languages whilst studying singing at music college, to improve my enunciation. I'm a bit rusty these days.'

'You are a singer?' He tried not to sound surprised.

'Not really. I studied at the Royal Academy of Music in London when I was young. I hoped to perform professionally but, well, I didn't make the grade. I sang Isolde once in a student production ... nowhere near as good as that.' She pointed towards the record player.

'Kirsten Flagstad. You would have to be exceptional to improve on her performance.'

'You recognised her! You do know your subject.'

'Her voice is unmistakable – Norwegian not German, but a fine voice even so. I saw her perform at Bayreuth in thirty-four, just before she went to America. She sang Sieglinde in *Die Walkyre* – also Gutrune in *Götterdämmerung*.'

'How exciting, I am very envious.'

'Do you still sing?'

'Not in public. Only to amuse myself.'

'That is a pity.'

'Some people might not agree with you ... my husband for one.'

'He is not a music lover?'

'Yes, he is, that's my point, ha ha!' Rowena's laugh was loud and gauche, and very distinctive.

The old man looked quizzically at her for a moment, then he smiled.

'That was a joke, yes?'

'Very nearly but not quite it would seem. I'm Rowena by the way ... Rowena Furse.'

'It is charming to meet you too. I am Morell.' He held out his hand and bowed slightly.

Rowena shook his hand. As she leaned forward, she caught a whiff of body odour and bad breath in a startling and heady combination. 'Pleased to meet you, Mr Morell. Might I ask, have you recently moved in? I haven't seen you before.'

'Oh no, I do not live here. I am visiting a friend who invited me to stay. He has kindly put this chalet at my disposal.' He tapped the wooden wall behind him. 'I have heard him refer to it in English as a *Sommerhaus.*'

'Yes, that's about right. How kind of him. We've never seen him, your friend I mean.'

'That would not surprise me,' said Morell. 'He likes to keep himself to himself.'

'Well he does a good job.'

'He always was very efficient.'

Rowena looked back at her garden and sighed. 'Well, it has been most enjoyable talking to you, Mr Morell, and now I had better get back to my gardening. Lots to do. Shall I play some more music?'

'That would be appreciated, thank you. I will be here in the garden next door. Can I make a request?'

'By all means. What would you like?'

'More Wagner.'

'But of course!'

Morell held out his hand and Rowena shook it energetically. He bowed slightly.

'Goodbye, Frau Furse. I hope we shall be meeting each other again.'

'That would be delightful. Goodbye.'

The old man shuffled sideways round the edge of the summer house and was gone. Before settling back down to her gardening, Rowena wandered back into the house and ran a finger along her collection of records.

'Something from *Parsifal* I think,' she mused. 'That should please him.' By the time she was kneeling down in front of the herbaceous border again, Kundry's long solo from Act Two was well under way. As she listened, she reflected on her unexpected encounter.

'What a nice man,' she thought. 'If I see him again, I shall invite him to tea.'

Chapter 2

Tuesday 12th June

It was close to midnight.

High on a hill towards the south side of Reigate, Colonel Peregrine Maxwell pulled up outside the large Victorian detached house in Smoke Lane and hurried round to open the passenger door. It didn't seem quite right to him, being the chauffeur, he a retired officer in the British Army used to having car doors opened for him instead of opening them for others – and wearing a dinner jacket to boot. But he didn't care. There wasn't much he wouldn't do for this woman.

A shapely leg in a scarlet, crushed velvet evening dress appeared. Slit high up the side, it revealed a tantalising expanse of bare flesh to well above the knee. Then a hand, which he took to steady Erika von Tirpitz as she stepped out of the car. She was in her late forties, heavily made up, slim, well-endowed, and with bleached blonde hair neatly styled in cascading waves around a face that bore an uncanny resemblance to the actress June Duprez; only older. She was striking in appearance, a head turner and, in the eyes of Colonel Maxwell – whose dear departed wife of three decades had been anything but – stunningly beautiful.

She was a little unsteady on her feet, and struggled to walk round the car onto the pavement at the same time as fumbling in her evening bag for a house key.

'Nice evening, Maxwell,' she said, slurring her words inescapably. 'Thank you for dinner, most enjoyable. Fancy coming in for a nightcap?'

'Rather!'

'Mind you behave like a gentleman. Otherwise Mr Chips will have your balls for play things.'

'That's not very ladylike, Erika.'

Erika shrugged and then giggled. 'You have been warned.' She tottered towards the front door and after several failed attempts managed to insert the key into the lock. There was growling from within. When the door eventually opened, a dappled short-haired miniature dachshund, all of a foot long and six inches off the ground, ran out barking and making a level of noise entirely disproportionate to his size. He sniffed Maxwell's trouser leg and growled.

'Chippy, be quiet,' ordered Erika. 'Will you get in the house … now!'

Mr Chips did as he was bid, following his mistress inside. In the lounge, Erika took a cigarette from a box and lit it, leaving Maxwell to fend for himself. He took one from the case in his pocket. He was slightly built, little more than skin and bones, and his dinner jacket hung from him with room to spare. He had wrinkled, aquiline features, bulging eyes, and hair that may once have been cropped to military standards but was now longer and in danger of becoming unkempt. He inhaled smoke and immediately wheezed as his lungs struggled to cope.

Erika opened the drinks cabinet, clutching the doors for balance, and peered down at the bottles with the warm affection of a matriarch surveying her loved ones.

'Brandy I think. Fancy a brandy, Maxwell?'

'Rather!'

She uncorked one of the bottles and sloshed liquid into two glasses, followed by soda from a siphon, most of which missed its target. She handed one to Maxwell and slumped down next to him on the sofa with the other. Mr Chips jumped up and rested his head on her lap.

'*Prost*,' said Erika.

'Bung ho,' responded Maxwell as they clinked glasses.

'Good dinner. Worth the trek over to Guildford. Thank you for taking me to such a delightful restaurant.'

'A great pleasure.'

'My Dover sole was quite delicious – how was your Tournedos Rossini?'

'Very good.'

'And a fine wine.'

'Both bottles.'

'They should make wine bottles larger – so there's enough for two.'

'Usually there is,' remarked Maxwell. He moved his hand clumsily across and rested it on Erika's knee which was exposed by the slit in her dress. He squeezed gently. Mr Chips growled defensively. Maxwell withdrew. 'You know how I feel about you, Erika. I adore you. Everything we do together is a pleasure for me.'

'Hmm … are you by any chance having ungentlemanly thoughts, despite my warning?'

'Well, quite possibly. You can hardly blame me.'

'I've warned you about Mr Chips.' She took a large swig of brandy, then swirled what was left around in circles, staring into her glass as if becoming hypnotised by its effect. 'You know, Maxwell, we would make a strange couple, you and I – if we were ever to become one.'

'I would like that very much indeed. But what makes you say strange?'

'You, the epitome of a true blue British career soldier who fought in both wars against the Hun. Me, the Hun. You should be courting a fine, upstanding English widow with true blue blood cursing through her veins. Old brigade, like yourself. And here you are, wining and dining a German – and probably the only example in the whole of Surrey.'

'I very much doubt that.'

'Reigate then.'

'I don't think of you as a Krau ... German at all. You're not Teutonic in the slightest.'

'I have an accent that leaves no doubt as to my origins – and a name that is about as German as you can get, wouldn't you say ... von Tirpitz? It conjures up a battleship to many, or the grand admiral from whom it took its name to those who know their history better.'

'Perhaps. But I think of you as one of us, my dear – not one of them.'

'No qualms about sleeping with the enemy then?'

'Goodness, a bit late for that I think!' Maxwell snorted and pulled a school boyish face.

Erika drained her glass, stood up and pointed towards the stairs. 'Come on then ... no sleeping with the enemy tonight, but plenty of fraternising.' Her hand brushed across his trousers, pressing less than gently in the soft place between his legs. 'I want you fully alert and to attention, Maxwell. And I sincerely hope your long-term strategy has improved since the last time.'

'Well I ...'

'And the time before that come to think of it.'

Colonel Maxwell didn't know what to say to this, so he followed Erika meekly upstairs, feeling unsure of himself. Sex was not something he had excelled at, nor indeed had a great deal of experience of, during his long and mostly affectionate-free marriage. Erika, on the other hand, appeared to be very experienced indeed.

As they made their way upstairs, Mr Chips growled disapprovingly from the sofa. If it was possible for a dog to take on human gestures, he rolled his eyes as if to indicate that he knew this was not going to end well.

****

Mr Chips was right.

Fifteen minutes later, which included the time it took to undress and freshen up in the bathroom, it was all over. Erika sat up in bed smoking a cigarette and looking unimpressed to say the least.

'Not exactly the longest campaign you've waged in your career,' she declared sarcastically.

Maxwell lay next to her, a sheepish expression on his face. 'I'm awfully sorry, my dear. It's been rather a long day – I'm tired.'

'You said that last time.'

'Did I? You're younger than me – got more stamina. I think you need to take that into consideration.'

'Maxwell, as our Americans friends would say … you'd better shape up, because I need a man.' She hummed the fragment of an imaginary tune in her head. 'Isn't that a song?'

'I don't recognise it.'

'Well if not then it should be one day.'

'You know, the physical side isn't everything.'

Erika looked at him incredulously. 'What are you saying, that sex is of no consequence? Not to me it isn't.'

'Of course not, but there are many other aspects to a meaningful relationship.'

31

'Such as?'

Maxwell thought for a moment. 'Companionship, like-mindedness, empathy, all manner of things.'

'I quite agree. However, it is my belief that all those things amount to nothing if you don't underpin them regularly with a good fuck.'

'Now you're just being vulgar. It doesn't become you.'

'Pah! Downstairs, only a few moments ago – and let's face it, that's how long we've been up here in bed, a few precious moments – you said that you adored me. Now you're calling me vulgar. Make your mind up, Colonel Peregrine bloody Maxwell.'

'I do adore you. You're a wonderful woman, the woman for me. *My* woman. I don't know what to say now.'

'Well I do.'

'What's that, Erika?'

'Goodnight.'

'I say, you're not sending me on my way?'

'I am indeed. Pop your trousers on and off you go. My turn to feel tired. Let yourself out, and make damn sure Mr Chips doesn't escape.'

'This isn't a permanent goodbye I hope?'

Erika looked blandly into space. 'Call me in a few days.'

Crestfallen, Maxwell dressed himself, pecked Erika on the cheek and left. As soon as she heard a door close and a car pull away, she picked up her address book and flicked through the pages alphabetically. She halted at the letter F with a grin. F for Freddie, F for … She picked up the handset of her bedside phone and dialled a number. After a lengthy pause, a deep, sleepy voice answered with a groan.

'Freddie, it's me.'

'Mrs von T?'

'Who else?'

'It's after midnight.'

'I have a job for you.'

'Can't it wait until morning?'

'No, it cannot. You're my odd job man and I have a job for you – one that somebody else started and failed miserably to complete to my satisfaction. It will not wait.'

'Same as last time?'

'The same. Come around now please.'

'Give me half an hour.'

'Fifteen minutes.'

'Twenty.'

'Fifteen!'

The phone went dead.

Chapter 3

Wednesday 13th June

The next day was even warmer and Rowena busied herself with the herbaceous border on the side of the garden opposite the gate. Keeping them looking their best was labour intensive and they seemed to demand an inordinate amount of her time to keep them under control. She planned to work on the border all day then tomorrow focus her attention on some other essential jobs. The lawn needed mowing for a start, and the vegetable patch was beginning to feel neglected.

It was getting on towards late afternoon when she heard the voice again. She was standing back from the border, glancing along its length to assess the symmetry, Sussex trug in one hand, trowel in the other.

'Good afternoon, Frau Furse. Your garden is looking beautiful. It is clearly in good hands.'

She looked across towards the picket gate. The old man was standing in exactly the same position as before. The voice had a hoarseness about it that she hadn't noticed before, as if he had the remnants of a sore throat. She wandered over towards him. He was wearing the same clothes, she noticed, and the same homburg on his head.

'Good afternoon, Mr Morell. That's very kind of you. My garden is very important to me.'

'Yardley would love it.'

'Yardley?'

'The friend I am staying with here. He is passionate about gardening.'

'I see, I didn't know his name. My garden is my offspring in a way. I don't have children and I don't work, so my garden receives all my attention.'

'Not all I imagine. There is Herr Furse also?'

'Oh yes, him. He does receive some attention, once in a while, ha ha!'

'Martha Mödl.'

'I beg your pardon?'

'Martha Mödl. Yesterday, after our conversation, you played a recording of her singing Kundra in *Parsifal*.'

'Yes, of course.'

'Thank you for that, I enjoyed it very much. *Parsifal* is a particular favourite of mine.'

'You're welcome … and I enjoyed our chat. In fact, I was wondering if you would like to come and have tea. Your timing is perfect, I was just about to make some and it would be lovely if you joined me.'

He bowed his head and seemed flustered by the invitation. 'That is a kind thought, but I do not think I should.'

'Come now, I would very much like you to have tea with me, and to talk some more about music.'

'I am not really at liberty.'

'At liberty? That's a strange thing to say.'

'Yardley has asked me not to make it known he has a guest,' explained Morell. 'He is a very private person, as I am. He would not approve that I have even spoken with you.'

'Nonsense,' said Rowena. 'I'm sure he won't mind. Now do please come and have some tea. It will be fine. Do you like Dundee cake?'

35

'I adore Dundee cake – and every other kind for that matter.' He hesitated briefly. 'Yardley is away for a few days, so perhaps I might …'

Rowena opened the gate and gestured for him to step through. 'Well that didn't take much persuasion. I won't tell him if you won't.'

Mr Morell shuffled forwards and through the gate, leaning on his stick with every step. As he passed by, Rowena pulled the gate shut. He walked slowly but steadily. She pointed towards a wooden bench on the terrace.

'Now sit yourself down there and I'll be back in a jiffy.'

Minutes later she returned carrying a tray containing the tea things and a fruit cake, the top of which was decorated with concentric circles of almonds.

'Here we are. Milk and sugar, Mr Morell?'

'Thank you, both. Two spoons.'

'And a slice of Dundee cake – a large one. My housekeeper Ethel made it.'

He took a bite from the generous slice he'd been given, dropping crumbs down the front of his shirt, then took a sip of tea. 'That is remarkable. Your Ethel is to be complimented. She does make exceedingly good cake.'

'I keep saying to her that her talents are wasted being a housekeeper.' Rowena cut a slice for herself and sat back in the chair opposite her guest. 'Tell me, Mr Morell, I am intrigued to know more about you. Where in Germany are you from and what is your background?'

He was silent for a moment, as if considering where to begin his answer, or possibly whether to answer at all. He had taken his hat off and was wiping the back of his head with a handkerchief. Rowena could see now that he was bald apart from a narrow, cropped row of silver hair running around the back of his head from one ear to the other.

The silence was broken when Mr Morell stirred on the bench, as if to make himself more comfortable, and let out a loud fart. He looked at Rowena apologetically.

'You must excuse me, Frau Furse, I have a long-standing digestive ailment. I apologise.'

Rowena smiled awkwardly, could think of nothing to say, so just went 'Ha ha!'

'My life really began in Munich – I moved there in my twenties. I have also lived in various other places, Vienna, Berlin. I fought during the first war, then became a politician and a writer. The second war kept me very busy, and since then, like many Germans, I have been picking up the pieces – surviving as best I can.'

'Yes, I can imagine. Would I be right in assuming you are a refugee?'

He gazed intensely into his teacup. 'You could put it that way I suppose.'

'Is England your home now? Have you settled here?'

'Oh no. I do not have a home these days. After leaving Germany I have been living on Fuerteventura, but no longer.'

'Feurte what? Never heard of it.'

'One of what you call the Canary Islands … off the west coast of Africa. They belong to Spain. Franco has been good to us Germans. He was supposedly neutral during the war, but unofficially he did much to support the Reich. Now I have moved on. I have been meaning to visit your country for many years. I nearly did so during the war, but as we all know, it came to nothing.'

'And how did you spend your time whilst on Feurte … on the island?'

'Reliving my life, reading, writing, learning your language. When I left Germany, I spoke barely a word, so I decided I

37

would learn it to understand and speak the mother tongue of the victors.'

'Quite.'

'Some Spanish, also.'

'And your love of music. I must say I am impressed with your knowledge of Wagner. Did you train as a musician?'

'I have had a passion for music all my life. Great music, I mean. I saw my first opera at the age of twelve – *Lohengrin*. I was at once addicted. In my youth, when I was at the Academy of Art in Vienna, I shared an apartment with a fellow student, August, a musician. At one time, we planned to write an opera together, but with one thing and another the project never came to anything. I was busy concentrating on a career as an artist.'

'An artist as well as a musician! My goodness, you must be a multi-talented man. And you have been to Bayreuth – how wonderful.'

'I attended the Festival every summer for many years.'

'You really are fascinating. More tea?'

'Thank you.'

Rowena poured another cup each, then sat back and glanced across at Mr Morell. She felt rather in awe of him. A thought popped into her head. 'You must surely have seen Hitler then. He was an admirer of Wagner's operas, and frequented the Bayreuth Festival I believe.'

'He was often there,' said Mr Morell temperately.

'What was he like?'

'Very much like in the newsreels, only less inclined to work himself into a frenzy than they would have you believe.' He took a sip of tea. 'Frau Furse, I think it is my turn to interrogate you.'

'Ha ha! I'm sorry, I do tend to take over the conversation. Howie picks me up on it all the time. Fire away, ask me anything you like. I'm an open book.'

'I would like to know about your surname, Furse. I have never heard it before.'

'Well of course it's my husband's, not mine – a good old Devonshire one at that. His family have been land owners there for centuries. A talented lot. Howie has a cousin who's an actress, a good one, and another who paints and designs sets for the theatre and films. I adore going to the cinema, don't you? I'd say that after gardening and opera, films are my third passion.'

'I too love watching a good film.'

'Then there's Howie, sitting in an office in London pushing paper around a desk all day. Not so exciting. I'm from Devon, too, but that's a coincidence – we actually met at a Proms concert at the Queen's Hall in London before the war.'

'Were they performing Wagner?'

'Not that evening. We heard the Tchaikovsky Piano Concerto, and some Strauss I seem to recall.'

'Richard or Johann?'

'Richard. I think it was *Don Juan*. And a Mendelssohn overture – A *Midsummer Night's Dream*.'

'I have no time for Mendelssohn, but Strauss wrote some fine operas, though not in the same league as Wagner. I met him on a number of occasions. Strauss, I mean, not Wagner.'

'Goodness, lucky you!'

'Please go on,' said Mr Morell.

'Anyway, that's how I met my husband, and we discovered we had Devon in common. I'm from Seaton, just over the border from Dorset. Things gradually progressed from one thing to another, as they do, and we were married two years later.'

'And no children.'

'No, thank heavens. I'm not the maternal type, much prefer my garden. Do you?'

'No.'

'Are you married?'

'Yes ... no. I would say estranged.'

'I see,' said Rowena, sensing this might be delicate territory.

'What does your husband do for a living?'

'He's in the Civil Service, but quite what he does I couldn't say. Probably something terribly dull. He doesn't talk about his work, or if he does it's in one ear and out of the other – ha ha! To be honest, we don't have a great deal in common. He loves music, but only light stuff – Eric Coates, Haydn Wood, that sort of thing.'

'I am not familiar with those names. I enjoy some light music also. *The Merry Widow* is my favourite operetta.'

'Howard can't bear opera, and mowing the lawn at the weekend is about his only contribution to the garden. Don't say anything, but he makes an awful hash of it. I have to do it again properly when he's gone to work.'

'I will be discreet with your confession.'

'I say, are you Catholic?'

'I have detested organised religion all my life, but I had a Catholic upbringing.'

'Church of England, Howie and me. We worship at St Mark's, just down the road from here. We have a wonderful vicar there, Neville Skepper. He insists on everyone calling him by his Christian name – very progressive. I'm in the choir. More cake?'

'Thank you but no,' said Mr Morell. 'I shall leave you now to get on with your gardening. Your offspring will be feeling neglected.' He got to his feet with the help of his stick, stood still for a moment as if to find his balance, then turned to walk towards the lawn.

Rowena followed. 'This has been lovely,' she said. 'I'm so glad you came to tea. Do come again and tell me some more about your life.'

'I have enjoyed myself, thank you.'

'I know now how to entice you here again.'

'Cake?'

'Ha ha, yes – cake!'

'A real weakness. I believe in English the expression is that I have sweet teeth.'

'Almost – singular, a sweet tooth. Actually, it occurs to me that if you love cake, you must surely have been to The Old Wheel.'

'The Old Wheel?'

'Reigate's finest teashop. You haven't been?'

Morell shook his head.

'You must. The cakes are out of this world.'

'I have not seen much of Reigate. In fact, I have not seen much at all since I arrived, other than Yardley's home and garden, and the *Sommerhaus* where I like to sit and read, and sometimes write.'

'Well it's about time you did. Let me take you there.'

'A kind thought, Frau Furse, but I cannot.'

'Nonsense – of course you can!'

'Really.'

Rowena pursed her lips and frowned. 'I don't often take no for an answer, Mr Morell, so I shall work on you. I promise, you'll thank me for it when you taste their Victoria sandwich. And their doughnuts! Do you like doughnuts?'

'Very much.'

'That's settled then, I shall take you there. If you time it right, the doughnuts are just out of the oven and the jam is still warm and the inside is soft and the outside crisp. Absolutely delicious. You shall be my guest.'

41

They had reached the gate. Mr Morell opened it, then paused and leaned forwards, listening to something at the far end of the garden. 'I can hear bees.'

'That's right, I have a few hives in the orchard. I must sort them out tomorrow. Nothing like a swarm of unhappy bees to spoil your day.'

'My father kept bees. He would often come in from the hives covered in stings.'

'You can avoid that by treating them properly, and wearing the right clothing. Stings can be nasty.'

'They never seemed to bother him. Goodbye, Frau Furse.'

Rowena had been looking down towards the bottom of the garden in the direction of the beehives. She turned around to say goodbye, but the old man had gone. She closed the gate and headed back towards the herbaceous border for the last session of the afternoon.

'Mr Morell,' she said to herself as she put on her gloves, 'I adore a challenge. You are coming to The Old Wheel whether you like it or not.'

Chapter 4

Benjamin Grimshaw skipped down the steps of the Surrey Mirror building in Ladbroke Road, patted his jacket pocket to be sure his notepad was there, slipped his bicycle clips around the base of his trousers and cycled off through the centre of Redhill, past the Market Hall, up Station Road and out of town towards Reigate.

'A case of shoplifting,' the boss had said. 'No further details so get along to Knight's in Bell Street and find out the facts from the manager, name of Wells. Not exactly the most exciting assignment, I know, but a useful filler story may result. And don't go making a meal of it – be sure you're back by lunchtime.'

Every time he set off on an assignment Ben wondered if it might be the scoop he'd been waiting for; the one that would bring him the promotion from junior to fully-fledged staff reporter he so badly wanted. The one that would set him on the road to Fleet Street, like his older brother, Storm, who a few years ago had been a cub reporter on this very rag. Now he was making his mark on another Mirror – the Daily kind.

Shoplifting from Reigate's only department store, a scoop? Unlikely, unless it was the mayor, or the local Member of Parliament … or even better a famous local resident. Imagine – J. Arthur Rank, the hugely wealthy film producer who lived over by the heath, exposed as a tea leaf; now *that* would be a scoop and a half!

His shock of ginger hair ruffled in the wind as he cycled at speed, his lanky frame wavering from side to side as one foot after the other pressed down on the pedals. He stopped only at a vending machine to buy a packet of five Woodbines – raspers, he and his mates called them – and some matches. When he reached Bell Street he left his bike round the back of Reigate Garage, in the grounds of the old brewery, long since closed down, and smoked one of his raspers. Then he strolled along the pavement towards Knight's.

Mr Wells was in his forties, rather severe looking, with sharp features. He wore pince-nez, which in Ben's opinion didn't suit him at all, and had a stuffy, haughty air about him. He was, nevertheless, helpful and informative and told him everything he could. Not long after opening, one of his assistants, Barbara, had noticed a woman behaving suspiciously in the lingerie department; peering around to see if she was being observed by staff, avoiding eye contact, walking past the same items repeatedly. Classic signs of someone planning to steal. Then Barbara had been distracted by a customer wanting to make a purchase, and afterwards, when she looked around again, there was no sign of the woman – and half a dozen pairs of seamed stockings and some French knickers had gone missing from a display. Naturally he had phoned the police station immediately and reported the theft.

Half a dozen pairs of stockings and French knickers. Hardly scoop material, Ben accepted with disappointment, even if Gracie Fields herself had pinched them.

Mr Wells eyed him over the top of his pince-nez. 'By the way, how on earth did you find out about it so quickly? You were here pretty smartish. Even the boys in blue haven't been round yet.'

44

Something to do with the amount of time the boss spent buying drinks for members of the local constabulary, Ben imagined.

'Couldn't tell you, sir, I was just given the assignment.'

He asked permission to speak to Barbara, who turned out to be Mrs Wells; younger than her husband – thirty perhaps – and, in Ben's opinion, someone who would look very good indeed in seamed stockings and French knickers. She had big clear eyes, reddish-brown hair done up in a bun, and an appealing smile. She stood closer to Ben than was necessary as he interviewed her, which he liked. She smelt strongly of expensive perfume, which he also liked. Sadly, she turned out to be a poor witness and offered a less than revealing description of the thief; medium build, medium height, ordinary clothes, plain face, wore a hat. He left the store feeling deflated, though rather taken with Barbara Wells.

Outside he lit another rasper and wandered up the road, then left into the High Street. He glanced up at the Old Town Hall clock. Quarter to one; knocking on lunchtime. He was feeling peckish. Further along the street he could see the striped awning of The Dinner Gong, as if beckoning him towards it. They did a terrific pie and mash and he just fancied it. The boss could wait for the story. He threw down his nub end and went inside.

The dining room was below ground level and at the bottom of the stairs he saw a familiar face – the head waitress. Her face lit up when she saw him.

'How are you, Ben?'

'I'm well thanks, Suki.'

'And how's that brother of yours getting on in London?'

'He's well too.'

'Next time he's back home tell him to come in. It would be good to see him again.'

'I will.'

She led him to a table. 'The usual?'

Ben nodded.

'Pie and mash and a pot of tea on its way.'

He watched the neat, slender figure as it swung its way between tables to place his order. He was fond of Suki, the woman who had so nearly become his sister-in-law. She and Storm had been schoolyard sweethearts and, although they were never officially engaged, everyone expected them to tie the knot one day. They were courting for years. Then, all of a sudden, in the space of a couple of months, Storm was up in London and Suki had married someone else. Whatever had happened between them no one knew, and neither was telling. He'd asked Storm outright once and been told to mind his own sodding business.

He pulled a book from his jacket pocket – *The High Window* by Raymond Chandler – and read while he waited for his meal. It was the third novel featuring Philip Marlowe; the first two were *The Big Sleep* and *Farewell My Lovely* and he had read them both. He loved the gritty, punchy style of writing. He was just starting chapter seven: *The Belfont Building was eight stories of nothing in particular that had got itself pinched off between a large green and chromium cut-rate suit emporium and a three-storey and basement garage that made a noise like lion cages at feeding time.* If only he could learn to write like that one day.

There was a novel in him, he was certain.

Chapter 5

Thursday 14th June

Mr Morell sat hunched in the front passenger seat of the Rover, seemingly ill at ease. He had his hat pulled so far down onto his head that it obscured his face and he glanced from side to side, peering uncertainly at his surroundings.

'Relax,' called out Rowena cheerily from behind the wheel as she drove down Alders Road and turn right towards Reigate town centre. 'I'm sure your friend Mr Whatever-his-name-is won't mind.'

'Yardley.'

'Mr Yardley wouldn't begrudge your popping out for a change of scenery. He's not around anyway, I think you said?'

'He has gone away for a few days. He travels a lot – abroad, and he also has friends in Cambridge. His secretary in Germany married an Englishman after the war and they settled there. He is a lecturer at the university I believe. There are others I also need to be mindful of.'

'Well it's too late now,' stated Rowena. She turned right again into Holmesdale Road. 'There's the station … that's where Howie catches his train every morning.'

'Have you told him about me?'

'Ha ha, you make it sound as though we're having an affair! No, I haven't said anything.'

'I would prefer it if you did not. I am a private person, Frau Furse, as I have told you. I am not confident this trip to your tearooms is advisable.'

'Private? Mysterious would be nearer the mark … enigmatic even. That's it, you're an enigma. Do you like Elgar, Mr Morell? Possibly England's greatest ever composer. I love his *Enigma Variations*.'

'I could not name an opera of his.'

'He didn't write one, silly. However, he did compose some absolutely glorious choral music. *The Dream of Gerontius*, *The Kingdom* …'

'I have heard recordings of both,' replied Morell, 'but would not say they excited me especially. Restrained and introspective. There is no real passion in his music.'

'No passion? Nonsense! Anyway, nearly there. This is Reigate tunnel we're driving through – cuts under the hill and takes you straight into the town. Those doors in the sides lead to caves. They were used as air raid shelter during the war.'

'It is good of you to drive me. Perhaps you would have preferred to walk.'

'Oh, that's quite all right.'

She drove the Rover through the tunnel then left into Church Street and pulled up outside a timber-framed building with a tiled roof and old-fashioned shop front. A sign hung out into the street:

The Old Wheel Luncheon and Tea Rooms
A genuine 16th century building
Officially appointed R.A.C. restaurant
Proprietress: Miss E Milbourne

Rowena helped Mr Morell out of the car, into the shop and up some rickety stairs to the first floor. Immediately at the top hung that which gave the place its name; an old 4-foot diameter pulley wheel once used to hoist sacks of grain up from the street. The floor was sloping and uneven and Mr Morell edged cautiously to a table near the window where he sat down heavily with a sigh of relief. He took off his hat and placed it on the edge of the table. Rowena sat opposite him. The room was half full and no one took any notice of them.

'Now then, tea and cakes? You can choose from a trolley or they can bring a selection to the table if you prefer. I like the latter – has a surprise element about it.'

'Thank you, Frau Furse, I will allow you to decide.'

'All right, I'll ask for a selection.'

A pretty young girl wearing a black dress, white apron and a white lace cap came to take their order. She had shoulder length blonde hair, dimple cheeks and a butter-wouldn't-melt expression.

'Tea and a selection of cakes for two, please,' said Rowena. She looked the waitress square in the face. 'Why it's Jane isn't it … Jane Robinson, from church?'

'That's right, ma'am.'

'Haven't seen you in here before, are you new?'

'Just started a week ago.'

'I thought you worked in Knight's in Bell Street.'

A cloud seemed to descend over Jane at the mention of Knight's. 'I used to,' she began, then faltered. 'But … I didn't like it there.'

'That's a pity. Enjoying being a Nippy?'

'Not bad thanks.' Jane blushed to a deep shade of crimson and hurried away.

'Nippy?' said Mr Morell curiously.

'A waitress. Strictly speaking a waitress in a Lyons tea shop, so called because they nip around from table to table, I suppose, but I use it for any waitress. Before that I believe they were called a Gladys of all things. I prefer Nippy.'

'Gladys sounds pompous, I prefer Nippy also. This is an interesting old building.' He looked out of the window. 'I like your Reigate. A nice old-fashioned English town I think. The clock tower is well structured.'

'That's the Old Town Hall – much nicer than the new monstrosity. You probably didn't notice but it was on the left just before we entered the tunnel. Beastly object.'

'Architecture interests me. I studied it in my youth and had aspirations in that direction.'

'Another string to your bow. Whatever revelation will you come out with next!'

Mr Morell stared at her with his piercing blue eyes. He leaned forward and lowered his voice almost to a whisper.

'I like you, Mrs Furse, perhaps one day I might reveal to you something far greater than my youthful dreams of becoming an artist, or an architect, and my passion for grand opera. I have led a full and remarkable life.'

'Goodness, you're being enigmatic again.'

'The truth is that …'

'Rowena Furse! Of all people, fancy seeing you here, having tea and not inviting me.'

Mr Morell looked up to see a plump, middle-aged woman bearing down on them.

'Ruth, how lovely to see you.' Rowena stood up and they pecked each other on the cheek. 'No personal slight intended I assure you. Mr Morell, may I introduce you to my friend Ruth Kitchen? We're in the W.I. together – the Women's Institute.'

Mr Morell stood up and bowed slightly towards Ruth. 'Good afternoon, Frau Kitchen.'

'Mr Morell is new to Reigate and I'm showing him around. A refugee from Germany. He is partial to cake so I simply had to bring him here.'

'Quite right, my dear. How do you do, Mr Morell. May I join you?'

'You don't mind, do you, Mr Morell?' said Rowena.

Mr Morell bowed again slightly and said nothing. Mrs Kitchen sat down facing the window with Rowena on one side and Mr Morell on the other. Rowena called Jane over and increased the order to tea and cakes for three.

'Well this is nice,' said Mrs Kitchen. I'm glad I've seen you, Rowena, we need to put our heads together and start thinking about the carnival. It's less than a month away now and we really need to start working on our float.'

'I'm not on the committee, Ruth, you know that.'

'I know, but our self-appointed horticultural expert is and we need you badly.'

'You mean Beth Angel?'

'I do indeed,' said Ruth Kitchen, with more than a little disdain in her voice. 'There's a meeting next Monday evening … would you be a dear and come along? We can explain what we have in mind to you and you'll be able to give us some suggestions about flowers and that sort of thing. Ah, cakes!'

Jane placed the tea things on the table followed by a circular two-tier stand with an array of cakes and buns. There were scones, Bath buns, doughnuts and slices of Victoria sandwich and Dorset apple cake.'

'Thank you, Jane, they look delicious. Tell me, how's the Bishop?'

Jane blushed again, her cheeks turning bright scarlet. 'He's very well, thanks.'

'Jane's young man,' explained Rowena to the others. 'His real name is Luke but everyone calls him the Bishop – for the life of me I can't remember why.'

'He likes visiting cathedrals.'

'Ah yes, that's it – our very own Bishop of Reigate.'

Jane made a slight bowing movement and scurried away.

'Nice girl, Jane,' said Rowena. 'Sings in the choir … beautiful voice. Very popular with the congregation. Shall I be mum? Do help yourself to cakes, Mr Morell, I'm sure it must be agony sitting there staring at them.' She poured the tea as Mr Morell and Mrs Kitchen chose some cakes.

'So that's agreed, Rowena, we'll see you on Monday. The theme is hush-hush but all will be revealed then.'

'All right, Ruth, I'll be there, only too glad to help, so long as I won't be putting anyone's nose out of joint.'

'Don't worry about Beth Angel, I'll deal with her. Such a common woman – and that awful husband of hers. What's his name …?'

'Terry.'

'That's right – Terry Angel. Such an inappropriate name for a rogue. Now tell me, Mr Morell, what do you do and what brought you to Reigate?'

Morell had been sitting quietly, peering out of the window. 'I am retired and I have come to visit a friend. My first time in England.'

'Things must be pretty grim in Germany these days,' said Mrs Kitchen.

'My country has been destroyed – torn to pieces. I am glad I am not there to see.'

'I can imagine. And where do you live now?'

'Until recently I was in Fuerteventura.'

'Never heard of it.'

'One of the Canary Islands,' explained Rowena. 'Off the coast of Africa.'

'Well, you learn something new every day. And do you like our country?'

Morell nodded. 'What I have seen, yes I do. I have always felt … ah, excuse my English, it is not good, I do not know the word. Rowena, please, what is *Seelenverwandtschaft*?'

'Affinity?'

'Thank you, yes. I have always felt an infinity—'

'Affinity,' corrected Rowena.

'… an affinity with the English people. We should never have gone to war with each other, when France and Russia were both our natural enemies.'

'I don't know if I agree with you there!' exclaimed Mrs Kitchen. 'About France at any rate.'

'I have said so many times. Germany and Britain have much in common. The French were to blame for the inhuman terms of the Versailles treaty, and were determined not to release Germany from its cruel conditions. Britain was far more sympathetic and did much to work towards reducing the burden. Without your Lloyd George it would have been far worse. We learnt many things from your Empire. We were led by your example in many ways. I believe that with different … Frau Furse, *bitte, was ist Umstände*?'

'Circumstances?'

'Thank you, with different circumstances we could have ruled the world together, sharing equally.'

'And look what happened!'

Mr Morell took a bite of cake and a sip of tea. 'Things did not go according to plan.'

'All water under the bridge now, ha ha!' interjected Rowena, hoping to lighten the tone. 'This Dorset apple cake is absolutely divine.'

'What did you do during the war, Mr Morell, may I ask?' There was an abrasive, almost challenging edge to Ruth Kitchen's voice.

'Nothing I can explain to you easily. I fought for my country with my heart and soul, that is all.'

'I see. And how long will you be staying here in Reigate?'

'I am not sure. My plans are not yet complete. Some weeks at least.'

'Well if you're still around next month perhaps we can rope you into helping with the carnival. We can always do with an extra pair of hands.' Mrs Kitchen did not sound as if she wanted him to help in the slightest.

'Thank you, but I don't think …'

'Not Mr Morell's cup of tea, Ruth,' said Rowena. 'Besides, I would imagine he'd prefer to watch the carnival rather than participate – if he's still here.'

'Do come and watch. It's on the first Saturday in July. The whole town will be there. Have you introduced Mr Morell to Erika, my dear?'

'Not yet. We've really only known each other a few days.'

'You should, it might be rather nice for them to converse in their own language. I know your German is good but she of course speaks it like a native because she is one.' Mrs Kitchen wiped the corners of her mouth with a napkin and placed it on the table. 'Now, I must go, Rowena dear, I have to telephone our rabbi about Jacob. His bar mitzvah is coming soon and there are arrangements to be made.'

Mr Morell's head cocked to one side. 'You are Jews?'

'We are indeed. Not terribly orthodox, I'm afraid, but we do like to keep up with the main traditions as you would imagine. Why do you ask?'

'No reason.'

Mr Morell turned away with an air of apparent indifference and stared blankly out of the window. As he did so he farted.

'*Entschuldigung,*' he mumbled.

'Well, really!' blustered Mrs Kitchen. She handed Rowena a contribution towards the bill, pecked her on the cheek and, with a 'See you on Monday', departed.

When she had disappeared out of view down the stairs, Mr Morell said: 'I am sorry, Frau Furse, that was unfortunate.'

'It was rather. It was also very rude of you.'

'I have a problem, I told you before, and sometimes I cannot help myself. I believe in English this ailment is called meteorism. I have tried many things to try and prevent it but without success.'

'I see.'

'I am a vegetarian, which does not help matters.'

'Quite. I rather get the impression you weren't too keen on my friend.'

'I do not think she liked me either.'

'Ruth can be quite overpowering. Not to worry. Now, would you like to see a bit more of Reigate? We could wander along the High Street and into the Priory grounds. The lake is lovely. Then I will drive you home.'

'Thank you, provided you are patient with me and adopt a leisurely pace.'

'Naturally, I will be guided by you, Mr Morell. Now let me settle up.'

'No please, allow me.'

'This is meant to be my treat.'

'I insist.'

'Well if you're sure. That's very kind.'

Mr Morell paid the bill. On their way out, Rowena said goodbye to Jane (who had heard the fart and was blushing the colour of beetroot), then helped Mr Morell down the stairs and into the street.

As they were walking down towards the clock tower, she said: 'Just before Ruth joined us you mentioned you might reveal to me something greater than your youthful dreams – I think that's how you put it. Would you care to elaborate?'

Mr Morell stared ahead, focusing on the pavement ahead, tapping his stick rhythmically. 'The moment has passed now,' he said. 'Another time … perhaps.'

Chapter 6

Sunday 17th June

Police Constable Andrew Bent stood at the junction of Tunnel Road and Bell Street beckoning a row of cars to enter the tunnel that cut through the hillside above Reigate town centre. At the far end, he could see the distant figure of his colleague, PC Tobin, ready to prevent traffic from entering the tunnel from the other direction, had there been any. On Sunday evenings in midsummer there was a constant stream of vehicles making its way home towards London after a day at the coast, but little coming in the other direction. There were traffic signals in operation at all other times of the week, then on Saturday and Sunday evenings, when the flow was one-sided, they were switched off for a few hours and two constables took over on point duty.

The tunnel created a shortcut for traffic travelling north and south that would otherwise have had to circumnavigate the whole town. Tobin, who was a bit of a know-all, had told Bent it had been dug on the orders of the Prince Regent when he became King George IV. Apparently, there was a war on and a law declared that the sovereign must never be more than fifty miles from London in a time of national crisis. The king had a mistress in Brighton; fifty-two miles from London. So, he ordered Reigate tunnel to be built, which shaved exactly two miles off the journey.

'In other words,' Tobin had announced with knowledgeable pride, 'this tunnel was built for one purpose only … so the king could get his leg over.'

Bent had no idea if this was true, but it was a good story.

'Sounds apocryphal to me,' he replied.

Tobin had come back with: 'What's it got to do with the end of the world?' A know-all maybe, but easily stumped by a long word.

The traffic had petered out and PC Bent relaxed for a moment. It was only just gone seven o'clock and there would be more to come. Three hours until the end of his shift. He looked through the tunnel and saw Tobin pacing up and down, holding a hand up with three fingers in the air. He was thinking the same thing.

It was a warm evening and Bent was hot inside his button-up-to-the-neck tunic and custodian helmet. He would dearly have loved to take the helmet off and undo the top button of his tunic; but if he did, ten bob to a pound Inspector Thorne would appear as if by magic and have him on a charge, which – and Bent could hear Thorne's churlish voice saying the very words – 'would make me very happy'. He had a Merlin-like ability to pop up at exactly the moment you least expected or wanted him to. Bent remembered the inspector's less than encouraging words on his first day, this time last year: 'Your job is to learn to become a dedicated, efficient and resourceful policeman. My job is to get you the sack.' A hard man, vulgar at times, but he got results and young policemen on his patch developed into excellent coppers.

The deep-throated purr of a perfectly-tuned engine brought his attention back to the task in hand. A sleek red Jaguar XH120 roadster was making its way conspicuously up Bell Street towards him and drew to a halt in deference to the authority of his outstretched hand. Bent glanced through the tunnel; nothing was coming so he flagged the car forward. As it passed him his gaze was drawn magnetically towards the passenger. She was young, blonde, beautiful and dressed in a patterned summer frock with thin shoulder straps. Her lips were full, her hair silky and slightly dishevelled from the wind … and she was utterly gorgeous. The driver by comparison seemed totally unworthy of such a dream of a woman – older, with a receding hairline, potbelly, crooked teeth and a nose that looked as if it had been broken, often.

The car disappeared through the tunnel and as it came out of the other side, he saw Tobin turn towards him with a hand on his heart, pretending to swoon.

'Lucky bastard,' said Bent with feeling.

'Now now, that's not very nice of you, Police Constable Bent, swearing at an innocent member of the public.'

Bent winced as he recognized the dispiriting tone of Inspector Thorne, immediately behind him and only inches from his left ear. His six-foot frame was already rigid, but now he stood firmly to attention.

'Sorry, sir.'

'I should ruddy well think so.'

'Didn't see you there, sir.'

'You weren't supposed to. Jealous of that man's bit of crumpet, are you? Well you know what the attraction is … and it ain't his good looks or the size of his todger. He's stinking rich, my lad. Must be to own a Jag like that. If you had his money you'd be sitting in a car like that with a bird like that.'

'Yes, sir.'

'But you're not, and you never will be, not on Surrey Constabulary wages.'

'No, sir.'

'And what's Tobin doing up there, hopping about like he needs a drain off?'

'Don't know, sir.'

'Well I think I'll creep up on him by the donkey steps and find out. No charge this time, Bent, but only because it's Sunday and I'm in a good mood. And mind your ruddy language in future.'

'I will, sir.'

The inspector vanished as quickly as he had arrived, along the High Street where there was a cut-through that would bring him out beyond the tunnel and behind the hapless PC Tobin. Bent tried to gesticulate a warning, pointing up and over the tunnel and making what he hoped looked like the shape of a thorn with his fingers.

'Oi mister, what does that mean … stop or go?' A pimply young lad on a bicycle had pulled up and was looking at him with a puzzled look on his face. ''Urry up will yer, can I go or can't I?'

'All right off you go, sunny.'

The boy cycled off into the tunnel towards an animated PC Tobin at the far end who was making shapes in the air, mimicking Bent's attempts to warn him. As he did so, Bent saw the menacing figure of Inspector Thorne appear from the other end of Tunnel Road. Moments later, Tobin was standing sharply to attention as he got an ear bashing from his superior. It was all over very quickly and Thorne disappeared once again, leaving behind him two tense police constables to finish their shift in less than ebullient mood.

Just before ten o'clock the traffic signals were reactivated and they convened at the police box around the corner next to the Old Town Hall.

'That Thorne, he's a sly old bugger,' said Bent. 'Didn't even know he was on duty tonight.'

'I don't think he was supposed to be. He must have come on just to try and catch us out.'

'Did he put you on a charge?'

'No, but he tore me off a strip.'

'Same here. I tried to warn you he was prowling about.'

'Yes, well I always was a tad slow on the uptake. No harm done. Right, stroll back to the station to report in, then home?'

They wheeled their bikes up Church Street.

'I tell you,' said Tobin, 'I'd have rather been in one of those cars tonight, heading home after a lazy day on the beach or pottering around Brighton, than stuck doing point duty. It's so tedious. Did you see that gorgeous blonde bird in the Jag – with the ugly bloke? What a waste.'

'I did. That's what got me in trouble with Thorne – heard me calling him a lucky bastard.'

'Well you were right. She was a stunner. I'd leave my misses for her tomorrow, wouldn't you?'

'Leave your wife?' contemplated Bent. 'Yes, I think I probably would.'

'No, I meant leave your own.'

'I'm not married … as you know.'

'But you've got Meg. You're pretty serious about her, won't be long until you're down on one knee I reckon. But *if* you were married …?'

'She was gorgeous,' agreed Bent. 'Film star quality. Yes, I suppose I might be tempted.'

'No, you wouldn't, you're too much of a gentleman. The faithful, loyal type in everything, ABC, that's what you are.'

'I wish you wouldn't call me that.'

'Sorry, mate, can't help it. I love the irony of your name.'

'The joke wore off a year ago – a week after I started. No one else calls me that anymore.'

'You'll always be ABC to me. How on earth could anyone have a name so inappropriate to their calling. A. Bent – Copper.'

'A quirk of fate. Like an undertaker called De'Ath, or a doctor called Paine. Besides, the meaning of words can change over time.'

'How do you mean?'

'Well, I imagine bent hasn't always meant crooked in the sense of corrupt. Maybe fifty years ago, A. Bent, Copper, might have merely implied I had a deformity of the spine. Or it may have had an entirely different secondary meaning … trustworthy perhaps. In another fifty, bent might imply something else altogether.'

'Unlikely.'

'Take your name – Dennis. This time last year no one would have thought anything of it. Then along comes a character in a children's comic and suddenly you're Dennis the Menace to your mates – not to mention a few of our regular villains.'

'Yes, and I could do without it.'

'And I could do without ABC.'

'Point taken. That's an interesting thought, about words changing their meaning. Prick. There's another. Presumably at some stage it was just something you did to your finger with a needle. I wonder when it began to mean a man's cock.'

'Or when did cock cease to mean just a male bird?'

'And bird to mean a tasty bit of crumpet.'

'Or crumpet to mean a drop dead gorgeous woman like the one we saw earlier.'

'We could go on like this for hours.'

They reached the police station in Chart Lane and reported in to formally end their shifts. As they came out and said goodnight, Tobin reminisced again about the day trippers they had seen passing through the tunnel.

'I know I shouldn't be, but I was jealous of them you know, Andy. There was I, working hard all day on a glorious summer's day – a Sunday an' all – and there they were, lots of men and women, all smiling and jolly and enjoying themselves, making the most of their leisure time together. I was feeling glum and they all looked so ...'

'Looked so ... what?'

'I'm trying to think of the right word.'

'Well think quicker. I want to get home.'

'Gay?'

'Hmm – goodnight Menace.'

Chapter 7

Tuesday 19th June

Rowena steered the Rover into Smoke Lane and parked outside Erika's house. As she did so, a side gate opened and out bounced Mr Chips.

'Chippy, be quiet!' called Erika who appeared a moment later. She wore a figure-hugging, low-cut, patterned dress, wedge sandals and held a cigarette at a distance as if the smoke was annoying to her. The effect was of a model posing for a promotional photograph of some description.

'Rowena, how lovely. Ignore Mr Chips, he'll shut up eventually. How did it go last night at the Women's Institute – did you see off Beth Angel?'

'Ruth Kitchen did. It was awful but the upshot is that I'm in charge of decorating the float now. Beth Angel hates me. If looks could kill I'd be dead as a doornail.'

'Still, you're the right person for the job.' She turned to Mr Morell. 'This must be your friend.' She offered a hand which Morell shook warmly. She spoke in German. 'I am Erika von Tirpitz, delighted to meet you.'

'The pleasure is mine, Frau von Tirpitz. So, you have noble lineage?'

'The von?' She smiled. 'Only by virtue of the fact that I married my husband. I was born a modest Erika Vogel. Come into the garden and let's have drinks.'

They followed her along the side of the house onto a spacious terrace overlooking a small circular lawn, beyond which was a gravel area where a bottle green sports car was parked – an Alvis. The garden was small by comparison with the house. On the terrace were numerous chairs, a sun lounger and, in the corner, a table covered with an impressive collection of bottles and glasses.

'What will it be,' said Erika. 'I have wine, gin, whisky or vodka, and lots of mixers. Rowena?'

'Goodness, a bit early for me, but I might just squeeze down a G and T.'

'And you, Mr Morell?'

'Might I have some fruit juice?'

'Don't be silly, there's no alcohol in it.'

'I never drink alcohol.'

'You do when you're with me. Here, have a G and T.' She handed him a glass which he took hesitantly.

'Almost never,' said Morell sheepishly.

Mr Chips trotted up to Mr Morell and started to sniff around him. The old man bent down and patted him keenly. 'A German breed for a German lady,' he said.

'You are a dog lover?'

'Very much. I have owned dogs all my life, though never a dachshund.'

'We had several at home in Germany before the war,' said Erika. When we came to England we had to leave them behind. Then we acquired Mr Chips here a couple of years before Karl died.'

'The Kaiser kept dachshunds.'

'So I believe.'

'Rommel also. Is this little fellow named after the film, with Robert Donat?'

'That's right – *Goodbye, Mr Chips* was one of our favourites.'

'Howie's cousin was in that one,' contributed Rowena.

'Really? I don't remember you mentioning it before.' Erika took a large swig of her drink. She indicated Morell's glass encouragingly. 'Keep up, Mr Morell, I'll be pouring another one soon. I gather we are refugees alike, you and I.'

Morell took a sip, licked his lips and took another. 'That is right. However, I imagine you have been one longer.'

'Karl and I left Germany in November thirty-eight. He had never been comfortable with the direction the Nazis were taking. He was under pressure to join the party but always resisted. *Kristallnacht* was the final straw for him. He had always been an Anglophile, so we left and came here.'

'You are Jews?'

'No, but Karl always said that was the turning point within Germany. Final proof that the apple was irretrievably rotten from within, he used to say.'

'And did you agree with him?'

'In some ways, not all. It was a very difficult decision to leave for me.'

'Where did you live?'

'In Berlin, though I am from Freiberg originally. We moved to Berlin soon after we were married in 1930. Karl was a businessman.'

Morell looked at her curiously. 'Was?'

'He died four years ago, of a heart attack.'

'I am sorry.'

'And you, Mr Morell. Rowena tells me you are something of a mystery man. What brought you to England?'

'I am in transit, here only to visit a friend. I have been rootless since the war. He is helping me to make more permanent arrangements, I have matters that need to be dealt with, then a new start somewhere.'

'Would you consider going back home?'

'I do not think so. The Fatherland no longer needs me. Would you?'

Erika paused to light another cigarette. 'England is my home now, I don't think I could ever go back, apart from to visit, which I do often. I love Surrey, and Reigate in particular. Apart from a period when Karl was interned, we have lived here ever since we arrived. I have some great friends here, Rowena amongst them. By the way, I hope we are not boring you, Row darling.'

'Not at all. The whole point was for you to meet and have an opportunity to chat about Germany in German. I'm happy sipping my G and T. It's a very strong one. I'm feeling rather lightheaded already.'

Erika and Mr Morell returned to their conversation. Rowena took a sip of her drink, leaned back and her eyelids began to flutter. Mr Chips climbed up onto her lap and curled into a ball with his chin resting on her knee.

When she awoke, she was alone. Even Mr Chips had gone. The sun had moved round and was full on her, and her throat was dry. She finished what was left of her drink and stood up to find out where the others had gone. The side entrance into the house was open and she called through.

'In here, Rowena! We came inside for the comfy sofa, and so our tittle tattle wouldn't wake you.'

Rowena found Erika and Mr Morell sitting together in a capacious living room, Mr Chips on the sofa between them.

'I'm sorry, how rude of me to doze off like that. Told you it was too early for me to drink spirits.'

'Don't worry, we've been having a most fascinating and revealing conversation. Your Mr Morell has been telling me all about himself.'

'And I have been enjoying the company of this most enchanting woman.'

'Mr Morell, are you flirting with me? Are you a bit of a Don Juan?'

'Oh no. Nor am I a gardener, but I do love admiring beautiful flowers.'

Rowena giggled. 'I think I'd better leave you to it …'

'You'll do nothing of the sort. Come, I'll get you another drink. Another G and T, Mr Morell?'

'No, thank you.'

'Perhaps a wise decision, I rather think you're a bit sloshed. You stay there, won't be long.'

'Nothing more for me,' said Rowena. 'One of your G and Ts is like three normal ones.'

Erika took her arm and led her somewhat assertively out into the garden. As she poured another drink and handed it to Rowena, she lowering her voice and said: 'Fucking hell, Rowena, your friend is bonkers!'

Rowena looked at her quizzically. 'I beg your pardon? Bonkers?'

'Bonkers, crazy, insane … choose your own adjective.'

'What on earth do you mean?'

'Precisely what I say.'

'And what makes you say that?' said Rowena as she took a sip of her drink.

'Because your Mr Morell has just told me something quite outrageously ridiculous. Only a mad man would say such a thing. Mind you, he is squiffy.'

'What did he tell you?'

'He has just informed me that Morell is not his real name.'

'What is it then?'

'Adolf Hitler.'

Rowena had a mouth full of gin and tonic; rather than swallowing, she proceeded to spray it everywhere, including over Mr Chips who licked himself appreciatively.

'He said what!'

'You heard me, he thinks he's the fucking *Führer*! We were talking about Germany in the old days and he just suddenly came out with it.'

'How extraordinary!'

'Miraculous would be more to the point,' said Erika. 'Hitler died in a bunker in Berlin six years ago.'

'What does it mean?'

'It means your friend is bonkers. Or a deluded fantasist of some kind.'

Rowena looked stunned for a few moments. 'What else did he tell you?'

'That he has been in hiding since the war. Somewhere beginning with F that I've never heard of – one of the Canary Islands apparently.'

'Feurte something?'

'That's the place. He said he has had to move on now and is in transit. This friend of his, your next-door neighbour, is helping him to make arrangements.'

Rowena stared into space. 'Well I'm blowed. He hasn't told me this.'

'That's because you've filled him up with tea instead of gin. I also think he's opened up to me because he's speaking German with a German. A kindred spirit, so to speak. He said he almost told you the other day in The Old Wheel over tea, and would have done if *that Jew woman*, as he described her, hadn't interfered.'

'Ruth Kitchen. He was very rude to her.'

'I can hardly blame him,' said Erika. 'I can't bear the woman. She's a real harridan.'

'But why on earth would he confess to such a thing?'

'It beats me. If I was the greatest war criminal in history and in the heartland of his former enemy, I'd keep my mouth shut. But, of course, he isn't and it's all nonsense. He is most definitely bonkers. Having said that, there's more to him than meets the eye.'

'How do you mean?'

'His accent for a start. Bavarian, possibly Austrian even. It's quite distinctive.'

'How interesting, I wouldn't have known that. I seem to remember him telling me he spent time in both Vienna and Munich as a young man.' Rowena thought for a moment. 'Hitler was Austrian, wasn't he?'

'He was, and then he moved to Munich and spent much of his time there, in Bavaria.'

'Coincidence, that's all. Why tell such lies? I don't understand.'

'Perhaps he's trying to impress us – or he's just plain bonkers, which is more likely. I wonder if he's escaped from a home somewhere. There are quite a few round here I believe.'

'There are several.'

Rowena sipped her drink and Erika lit a cigarette. 'Perhaps it's his idea of a joke.'

'If so then hardly in the best of taste.'

'Well I shall ignore it,' declared Rowena. 'I like Mr Morell and I shall simply regard him as a nice old man who's a bit batty. Besides, he looks nothing like Hitler, there isn't any physical resemblance.'

'No Charlie Chaplin moustache you mean?'

'Exactly.' Rowena giggled. 'By the way, have you noticed he's a tad – how shall I put it politely – malodorous?'

'I have,' said Erika. 'Body and breath, can't really miss it. He's whiffy as well as squiffy.'

'Backside, too,' said Rowena, lowering her voice. 'He let one go in front of Ruth. You know – gas.'

'You mean he farted?'

'That's exactly what I mean, though I wouldn't have used that word.'

'How did she react?'

'She wasn't impressed. Nor was I.'

'If I had the courage, I'd fart in front of her. She's a harpy, a termagant!'

Rowena frowned. 'She's not that bad. He apologised to me when she'd gone. Nevertheless, it wasn't very appropriate in the middle of afternoon tea at The Old Wheel. But you know it isn't necessarily anti-Semitic to break wind in front of someone who is Jewish, surely. He told me he has a problem in … in that department. He did it in my garden, too, when we first met.'

As if on cue, they heard a farting sound from the direction of the house.

'Shush, here he comes …'

Morell appeared round the side of the house and joined them in the garden. He looked bleary-eyed. 'Frau von Tirpitz, you have deserted me.'

'Not at all, Mr Morell, we were just chatting and about to come back in.'

'Frau Furse, I am feeling tired, would you be kind enough to take me home now?'

Rowena put her glass down. 'Yes, of course. I need to get back, too. Goodness, I do hope I'm all right to drive after all these gins.'

'It has been a pleasure to meet you, Erika,' said Morell. 'I hope we shall meet again soon.'

'I hope so too, goodbye. Why don't we all have lunch together? Rowena, let's take Mr Morell to The Dinner Gong in the High Street.'

'Lovely idea.'

They walked together towards the car. Erika's dachshund trotted alongside and before climbing in, Mr Morell bent down and gave him some attention.

'Good boy, Mr Chips,' he said, patting him affectionately on the head.

Erika nudged Rowena in the ribs. 'Was that good boy or goodbye? If he's alluding to the Robert Donat film again and it was goodbye, he sounds more Brummy than Austrian.'

Rowena and Mr Morell climbed into the Rover, which moved off erratically, scuffing the kerb and zigzagging as it disappeared down the hill, Rowena battling the effects of gin and a serious fit of the giggles.

Chapter 8

Rowena lay stretched out on the sofa with her eyes closed, Puccini's music flowing over her like a fragrant balm. Howard sat opposite her, reading his newspaper. Puffs of smoke floated up from behind it at regular intervals. There was silence between them until the record came to an end.

'Poor Butterfly. She was wasted on a bounder like Pinkerton.'

'Hmm?'

'She should have taken up Yamadori's offer. He would have looked after her, and the boy, and that would have been one in the eye for Pinkerton.'

'Totally agree, old girl,' said Howard, not quite clear what he was agreeing with.

'How was work today, Howie?'

'Oh, you know, just the same old stuff as usual. Nothing exciting to report.'

He leaned forward for his coffee cup and took a sip. 'How was your day?'

'Very good. I worked in the garden in the morning. The borders are coming along nicely – all in good shape.'

'That's excellent.'

'And I spent the afternoon with Adolf Hitler.'

Howard nodded. 'Jolly good, how is he these days?'

'Remarkably well. He's living next door.'

Howard peered round his newspaper, frowning. 'Not with the Herringtons, surely?'

'The other side.'

'You did say Adolf Hitler?'

'That's right.'

'You're mistaken there, old girl. I think you'll find he's dead and gone – thank the Lord.'

'I'm sure you're right,' agreed Rowena. 'He's a nice old chap, a refugee. I've been chatting to him over the fence. Took him to meet Erika today and he just came out with it. Why would someone do that, do you think?'

'Had she plied him with booze by any chance?'

'Alcohol was involved, yes. But why tell an outrageous lie about who you are like that?'

'No idea I'm afraid, Flossie. What did Erika think, being presented to her *Führer*?'

'She thinks he's potty.'

'That's about right. How old is he, your Herr Hitler?'

'Seventies I would think.'

Howard put his newspaper to one side, got up and perused the bookshelves that covered most of one wall of their lounge, peering closely at the spines. Although slimmer than Rowena and relatively fit for his age, his eyesight was poor and he saw the world from behind thick-lensed spectacles with heavy black frames. He scratched his receding scalp with its meagre strands of hair combed over to give some semblance of cover, then selected a weighty tome and flicked through its pages. 'Here we are – born 20th April 1889 in Braunau am Inn, a town on the border of Austria and Germany. 1889, so that would make him … sixty-two now. Your chappy is too old to be Hitler, Floss.'

'Let me see?'

He handed the book over to her then picked out another, much lighter book.

'I see what you mean. He has to be a good ten years older at least. Unless he hasn't aged well.'

'He isn't ageing at all. He's dead. Here, this tells you all about it. H.R. Trevor-Roper – *The Last Days of Hitler*.'

Rowena took the book and started flicking through it while Howard returned to his newspaper. She became absorbed and read in silence for almost an hour. Then she snapped it shut.

'Well, whoever he is, he's a charming old man and I like his company. He's mad about opera.'

'Just plain mad would be nearer the mark. Perhaps he's escaped from a mental institution.'

'That's what Erika said – you could be right. Mad or otherwise, he really knows his stuff about opera. I say, I was toying with the idea of treating him to Covent Garden. We have tickets for *Parsifal* in a few weeks' time and it's one of his favourites. I thought I might ask him to come along in your place, if you wouldn't mind giving it a miss.'

'Don't mind at all,' said Howard, trying not to sound too relieved.

'Didn't think you would. I drag you up there far too often. You never complain but I know you find it all quite tedious.'

'You know me, I prefer a good tune. You go ahead and take Herr Hitler … if they'll let him in.'

'His name is Morell actually.'

'Is there any resemblance?'

'No Charlie Chaplin moustache, if that's what you mean. In fact, no resemblance at all – not that I can see.'

'Well there you go.'

'He was very unpleasant towards Ruth Kitchen in The Old Wheel the other day.'

Howard lowered his newspaper and looked quizzically at his wife. 'Would that be because she's Jewish, or because she's a total bore?'

'I wouldn't like to say.'

'My guess is he's an eccentric old man with a bizarre sense of humour who's trying to spice up an otherwise dull life – and yours at the same time.'

'You're probably quite right.'

Howard disappeared behind his newspaper again. 'Probably not even German.'

'You're probably right about that, too. He may be from Birmingham actually.'

'I beg your pardon?'

Rowena grinned to herself. 'Never mind.'

****

Terry Angel – short, squat, overweight with a hefty paunch, and in his mid-forties – sat in an armchair in the corner of his living room absorbed in the Daily Mirror. The news was grim: stalemate in the Korean war; the death toll in last month's colliery explosion at Easington now up to eighty-three; a couple of Foreign Office officials (Guy Burgess and Donald Maclean) mysteriously vanished; Aneurin Bevan rattling on about his resignation as Minister for Health. Worst of all, Workington FC had been elected to the Football League. What was the world coming to!

On one arm of his chair was an ashtray with a half-smoked Woodbine balanced on the edge, and on the other a glass of Bass Imperial Stout. His wife Beth stood opposite him doing the ironing, the board set up next to the fireplace. She talked, as was her nature, in a continuous stream broken only now and again, and very briefly, by the need for a drag on a cigarette, or to pick her teeth.

Terry Angel took it all in his stride. Over the years he had learned how to cope with living under the same roof as a woman who never stopped talking … ever. He had developed a number of techniques, chief amongst them the ability to sink for long stretches into his own cocooned world with conduits between ears and brain switched off. She quite literally would chatter from dawn till dusk.

As he told his mates in his local, The Angel at Woodhatch, when the topic of domestic strife cropped up – which was often – he would swear on the Bible that in bed at night he would frequently hear his wife fall asleep in the middle of a sentence, then wake up the next morning and finish it.

Beth – the female equivalent in appearance to her husband, only several years younger and with less of a paunch – was currently moaning about that fat cow Rowena Furse and plotting revenge for interfering with her plans for the W.I. carnival float. The job should have been hers and that Kitchen woman had connived with that Furse woman to take it away from her. Stuck up bitches, both of them. In Beth's opinion, slow strangulation – she spat out the word with such venom that it even permeated through to Terry – would be too good for them.

Time passed. Terry had read his newspaper from cover to cover and, with nothing else better to do, started to read it again. He had turned to page three when he heard his name being called.

'Terry … Terry … TERRY!'

He lowered his paper and responded with an indifferent 'Uh?'

'You're not listening to me.'

No, he thought, I am not listening to you. 'What is it?'

'Well, will you?'

'Will I what?'

'Will you take me? See, you weren't paying attention to a thing I've been saying.'

Terry yawned. 'Take you where?'

'I just told you … to the dance. Will you take me to the dance? Don't you ever listen?'

'What dance?'

'The one at the Market Hall in Redhill. We haven't been out for ages and I really fancy a dance.'

'Oh … yeh, all right.' He rustled his newspaper to indicate irritation at having been disturbed. 'When is it?'

'Saturday night of course.'

Terry grunted, took a drag of his Woodbine and drank some beer. Then he pulled a face and said: 'Oh, in that case no I can't.'

'Why not?'

'I'm working.'

'Nonsense, you're unemployed!'

'You know what I mean.'

Beth rested the iron on its cradle and stared at him accusingly. 'Out thieving?'

'Seeing a man about a dog.'

'Same thing with you.'

'Either way, I'm busy Saturday night.'

She lifted the iron and attacked a shirt sleeve. 'You never take me out.'

'That ain't true.'

'When was the last time then?'

Terry thought for a moment. 'February.'

His wife stared across at him. 'Which year?'

Terry peered trancelike at page three of his newspaper. Instead of reading about Nye Bevan's disgust at the introduction of prescription charges, he dearly wished he could see a photograph of a pretty, buxom young girl showing her breasts to brighten up his mundane, uninspiring existence. But in a national newspaper? Never.

Chapter 9

Wednesday 20th June

Rowena and Morell were having tea on Rowena's terrace again, sitting together on the bench overlooking the garden. They had talked about opera, listened to some more of *Parsifal* and chatted about various other topics. Rowena explained at length about the Women's Institute carnival float and her struggle with Beth Angel over who would arrange the flowers. The W.I. meeting on Monday had been tense and disagreeable; Ruth Kitchen was adamant that Rowena should take charge as she had such green fingers. She wasn't alone, and with the support of the majority Ruth eventually got her way and Beth Angel, her face like thunder, backed down. Mr Morell sympathised and offered some gentle platitudes, but understood that he was really only expected to listen. Once the subject had been exhausted, there was silence for a few moments, broken by Mr Morell.

'I suppose Frau von Tirpitz told you what I said about my true identity.'

'About your being Adolf Hitler? She did mention it, yes.'

'And were you shocked?'

'Not shocked, amused. I don't believe it for a minute. Hitler has been dead for years.'

'How can you be so sure?'

Rowena stretched her arms wide in a motion that indicated it was obvious. 'They announced it on the BBC – I remember it distinctly. Then it was in all the newspapers, of course, saying how he committed suicide in his bunker underneath Berlin. It's a fact. Common knowledge. They found his body, I'm sure of it, or what remained of it after it had been set on fire and burned.'

'They found *a* body.'

'And Eva Braun's, the two were found together. She had taken poison and Hitler shot himself. They were only married the day before. Mr Morell, I think you're playing games with us. Besides, you bear no resemblance to Hitler, even without that silly moustache … and you're older than him. Howie and I worked it out the other night.'

Morell stirred uncomfortably on the bench. 'You have told your husband? That is unfortunate.'

'I have indeed. If Hitler were still alive, he'd be sixty-two now. You're much older.'

'How old would you say?'

'At least seventy.'

He shook his head. 'I aged a great deal towards the end of the war – beyond my years. I was under enormous strain. Nor was I well. Nervous exhaustion. Though not with the shaking disease as some people have claimed. That was not me, but someone who looked like me.' He smiled smugly. 'It was very useful sometimes to fool the world … and be in two places at one time.'

Rowena looked puzzled. 'The shaking disease?'

'Parkinson's.'

She nodded, not quite following. 'Besides,' she continued, 'Adolf Hitler was an insane, evil tyrant – a monster, a megalomaniac. And you're such a charming gentleman. Gentle.

Innocuous. I can't imagine you hurting a fly. I think you're playing a curious game with us. Heaven knows why.'

'I am sorry, Frau Furse,' said Morell with an air of finality, 'I have enjoyed meeting you and spending some time with you. I will not be around for much longer and it is probably for the good.'

'I say, you're not moving on, are you?'

'Quite soon.'

'Well not *too* soon, Mr Morell, because I have a treat in store for you.'

Morell frowned. 'Not tea with that Kitchen woman again, I hope.'

Rowena grinned and put her hands together as if to clap. 'Ha ha! Far more exciting than that. I would like to invite you to the opera with me, at Covent Garden in London.'

'How kind. When do you have in mind?'

'Next Saturday, the twenty-third.'

'That is tempting, very much. However, I think I must decline. Pottering around Reigate is one thing ... going up to London is a different matter.'

'Come now, I thought you'd relish the opportunity to see something of this country while you're here. You can hardly spend all your time tucked away in deepest Surrey, doing nothing and seeing even less.'

Morell appeared contemplative and was silent for a while. 'It is not that simple I'm afraid, Frau Furse. I have others to consider, and my position is delicate.'

'Nonsense! Besides, you haven't asked me what they are performing.'

'What are they performing?'

Rowena leaned forward and half-whispered in his ear. '*Parsifal.*'

Morell's eyebrows raised and he stared at her as if in disbelief. 'Surely not! Now *you* are playing games with *me*.'

'I assure you I am not.'

'It is very tempting. How would we get there?'

'I can drive us up.'

'Alas I have to decline. It is a very difficult decision to make, but I really cannot.'

'Wouldn't you like to know who is singing?'

'I think you are about to tell me.'

She leaned forward again and pronounced each syllable with a break in between. 'Kirs ... ten ... Flag ... stad.'

Morell looked stunned. 'As Kundry?'

'As Kundry.'

He gazed blankly into the distance, speechless for a good half a minute. 'I do not have evening dress with me.'

'Don't worry, I can sort out something for you. Howie's a bit bigger than you but I'm sure Ethel can make a few adjustments. She can sew as well as cook.'

'If I agree to come, I insist on paying for the tickets.'

'That won't be necessary, really.'

'Frau Furse, money for me is no object. I must insist.'

Rowena shrugged. 'Very well, as you wish.'

Morell sat back in his chair with a smile of unbridled contentment lighting up his face. 'What time would you like me to be ready?'

Chapter 10

Saturday 23rd June

They set off in the Rover in the early afternoon and drove up the A23 which took them all the way to Lambeth, then a short hop to the Thames and over Waterloo Bridge. Rowena parked on the Embankment and they stood for some time gazing across at the river at the strange array of weird and wonderful exhibits that was the Festival of Britain. Then they strolled along the Strand and across into Covent Garden, up Southampton Street and eventually into Maiden Lane. Rowena had booked a table at Rules for an early supper. By the time they reached the restaurant, Mr Morell looked weary and was leaning heavily on his stick.

'Are you all right there, Mr M? Was that a bit too much of a walk for you?'

'I will be fine. I just need to rest.'

'I hope you like it here. It's the oldest restaurant in London apparently.'

'So, the Luftwaffe missed it. Yet another of Göring's many failures.'

'Mr Morell! That is a terrible thing to say!'

'*Entschuldigung.*'

They sat down at a table on the ground floor and ordered; a steak and kidney pudding with oysters for Rowena and scrambled eggs with vegetables for Mr Morell.

'Is it far from here to the opera house?' he asked as he drank some tea.

'Not at all, just a few minutes' walk. Curtain up at six so we're in plenty of time. How are you feeling?'

'Very good. I am refreshed by the oldest scrambled eggs in London.'

'I must say you look rather dapper in Howard's dinner jacket. How's the fit?'

'Large, but it will suffice, thank you.'

Mr Morell paid the bill and they made their way around the edge of Covent Garden market and up Bow Street, arriving outside the opera house with a quarter of an hour to spare. They took their seats and glanced through the programme.

'The conductor is Karl Rankl,' observed Morell. 'An Austrian.'

'Yes, and it says here he had to leave Germany when the Nazis came to power.'

'A Jew?'

'No but his wife was.'

'He did the right thing.'

'They returned to Austria and stayed until thirty-seven when they went to Prague.'

'Ahead of the *Anschluss* … another wise decision.'

'Then they fled to London when Germany invaded Czechoslovakia.'

'We already had the Sudetenland. It was a matter of time.'

'And here he has done a grand job building up a fine opera company virtually from scratch. He's a jolly good conductor … I've seen him many times.'

'Let's hope he does not recognise me.'

'Now don't start that again, ha ha! You needn't worry, he'll have his back to you all evening. Adolf Hitler indeed.'

'Do you know about applauding during *Parsifal*?'

'I do. In fact, it's mentioned here in the programme: *In accordance with the wishes of the composer there will be no curtain calls and the audience is requested to refrain from applause.*'

'What, entirely? Let me see.' Mr Morell read the sentence. 'Pah, that is such misleading nonsense. The whole business about the composer not wanting any applause is a misunderstanding that began on the first night. Wagner loved applause. He meant none after Act One and Act Two. Of course you should applaud at the end. If no one else does, I will alone.'

'Oh dear, I think you mean it, too.'

At six o clock exactly, Rankl took to the podium and the performance began. Three Acts, two intervals and more than four hours of divine music later, it was all over. The curtain came down and the audience sat in absolute, reverent silence … until it was broken by an elderly man in the centre of the stalls whose faint clapping seemed to reverberate magically around the inside of the opera house. Heads turned to identify the heathen. There were mutterings from some die-hards who were shocked and appalled. Then the woman next to him started clapping, too. Others followed, and soon the house was ringing with genuine, if rather cautious, applause. There were no curtain calls, and eventually the audience fell silent.

Rowena said: 'Let's get out of here quick, before the opera police come and arrest you.'

'I was merely doing what Wagner wished. I am right and the Royal Opera House, Covent Garden, is wrong.'

'Nevertheless, I suggest making ourselves scarce. Did you enjoy it?'

'Wonderful!' he declared, reverting to German in his excitement. 'Flagstad was magnificent as you would expect. Parsifal had a fine voice, too. An impressive production all round. Thank you, Frau Furse, I have had a most enjoyable day. Now I feel tired.'

'In that case, why don't you wait here and I will go and fetch the car? It's a bit of a walk and I'll get there much quicker on my own.'

'If you wouldn't mind, that would suit me very well.'

They made their way into the foyer. Rowena left Mr Morell sitting on a chair and hurried back down Bow Street and along the Strand. It was a beautiful evening, still warm, and her head was full of musical moments from the performance. There wasn't much traffic so she managed to weave her way back up to Covent Garden without difficulty. She parked right outside the imposing columns of the opera house and walked through the main doors into the foyer.

'Here we are, Mr Morell,' she called. She looked across to where she had left him. The chair was empty.

Mr Morell was nowhere to be seen.

****

Rowena had only been gone a few moments when Morell sensed someone standing in front of him. He looked up and saw a tall figure with a shock of white hair, big bushy eyebrows and a ruddy complexion staring down at him. To his left and slightly behind stood a woman in full evening dress.

'I say,' barked the man. 'Aren't you the Johnny who started the clapping?'

'I am.'

The man leaned forward, grabbed Morell's hand and pumped it up and down. 'Jolly good show. Bloody thing went

87

on far too long, most operas do, but it's bad form not to show appreciation in the usual manner.'

The woman tugged at his arm impatiently. 'Come on, Clive, let's go, and please mind your language.'

'This is the one, Gladys, he started the clapping. Jolly good show.'

'How do you do,' said Mr Morell.

'Likewise.' She smiled cursorily at him.

'Gladys … that is also a name for a Nippy?'

'Well, really!'

The man called Clive peered at Mr Morell. 'I say, haven't we met before? You look familiar, I'm sure our paths have crossed somewhere. Were you at Passchendaele?'

'I was, but not on the same side of the lines as you.'

Clive's eyebrows lifted a good inch higher than they were before. 'Good grief, a Kraut! Should have realised from the accent. Gladys, he's a bloody Kraut!'

'Yes, dear, and you've been listening to a bloody Kraut's music all evening. Now do come along.'

The couple bustled their way out of the doors leaving Mr Morell feeling unsettled and exposed. It wasn't a good place to sit, he decided. He stood up and went out into the street. People were milling about in all directions. Clive and Gladys were just a few paces ahead of him, so he crept around the corner of the opera house into Floral Street where it was dark and there were fewer people. He was feeling nervous, and his bladder was suddenly telling him it was time to be relieved. He looked along the street but could see nowhere that might be a possible source of that relief. As he walked along the pavement, he noticed a sign ahead of him – Stage Door. He peered inside; a man was sitting in a side office behind a glass screen. Morell stepped aside as a couple carrying instrument cases came out and

88

hurried off, chattering away, oblivious to their surroundings. The urge to urinate was getting stronger. Overpowering.

'Excuse me,' he said, addressing a circular hole in the glass. 'I am sorry to interfere but I have just been to *Parsifal* here and now I need to use the toilet, please.'

The stage doorman frowned. 'Sorry, sir, this ain't a public convenience.'

'I know; however, my need is great. I would ask for … what word is it … clemency?'

'Can't break the rules for one. Unfair on all the others.'

'Where please then is the nearest …?'

'Try the pub on the corner. Out of the door and left, only a short walk.'

As Mr Morell turned towards the door, he felt himself bump into someone behind him.

'*Entschuldigung.*'

The man looked at him, smiled with amusement, and addressed him in German.

'Ah we speak the same language. My apologies also.'

Mr Morell stared into the face of Karl Rankl. 'Maestro,' he said. 'I have just seen your magnificent performance of *Parsifal* and was asking to use the toilet here, but regrettably I have been denied.'

'This is not a public area,' explained Rankl. 'However, perhaps I may be able to pull a few strings for you – a fellow Austrian I think?'

'That is right.'

'Where from exactly?'

'Near Linz.'

'A lovely town. I am from Gaaden, not so far from Linz. You look familiar – have we met before?'

'That is unlikely.'

'Reginald,' said Rankl, 'please allow this gentleman to use our facilities as a favour for me?'

The doorman nodded disapprovingly and pointed down the corridor. 'Second on the left.'

'Thank you, Herr Rankl,' said Morell your kindness is greatly appreciated.'

'My pleasure. Good evening.'

Rankl disappeared and Mr Morell shuffled down the corridor and into the gents. He bypassed the urinal, entered one of the cubicles, shut and locked the door, and let out a long, satisfying and seemingly endless fart. Then he urinated. As he did so, he heard the door of the gents open and two voices in mid-conversation.

'… I know, but not a bad performance tonight.'

'Not bad. Not good, but not bad. Intonation was ropey in places.'

'Tempi variable, too.'

'He's good but you can really tell the difference when a guest takes charge.'

'We need Beecham.'

'He wouldn't come, not after the things he's said about the current regime. He'd be good though.'

'Or Kubelik.'

The door of the cubicle opened and out came Mr Morell, passing behind the men standing at the urinals. 'Kubelik,' he stated, 'is a Czech … and Czechs are no good. Stick with Rankl. He is a good man and a fine conductor.'

One of the men glanced over his shoulder and looked him up and down frostily. 'Really? And what do you know about it?'

'I have seen the greatest conductors perform, over many years – at Bayreuth.'

The second man shook his penis and buttoned up his trousers. 'I suppose you're Adolf Hitler then.'

'I am.'

'In that case I'm Hermann Göring.'

'Don't be foolish, Göring is dead.'

'So is Hitler.'

As he opened the door to leave, Morell muttered: 'That's what you think.' He hurried out into the corridor, past the doorman in his office, whom he thanked, and back into the street. He felt flustered. The man in the toilet had called him foolish, which he hated. But he was right; foolish to say such things to a complete stranger. Preoccupied, he turned left instead of right – away from the foyer of the opera house – and walked without any thought of time or where he was heading. He zigzagged around the market, finding himself in one unfamiliar street after another.

Soon he was completely lost.

****

An usher remembered seeing an old man sitting on the chair talking briefly to another man and a woman, but he couldn't say where he had gone. Rowena went out into the street. She searched in all directions but there was no sign of Mr Morell. When she had given up any hope of finding him, she walked across the road to Bow Street Police Station to report a missing person. The duty sergeant's advice was to leave some details, not to worry and to go home; he would turn up safe and sound eventually.

She went back to the car and waited anxiously until midnight, just in case, then drove back to Reigate. When she got home, she immediately phoned Erika.

'Rowena darling, it's one in the morning, I'm in bed … and not alone.' As if to confirm this, a loud snore could be heard down the telephone line.

'Who with?'

'No one you know.'

'I'm sorry, Erika, but I'm very worried and needed to talk to you.' Rowena explained what had happened.

'So, let me get this straight. You've mislaid Adolf Hitler in the middle of London?'

'Don't be so emotive, Erika! Mr Morell, not Hitler. What shall I do?'

Erika yawned. 'Go to bed and have a good night's sleep, that's what I'd do.'

'That's not helpful at all. I'm worried about him. Where on earth could he have got to?'

'Perhaps he got lucky and has been whisked away by an adoring Valkyrie.'

'It was *Parsifal* not *The Ring*. Erika, you're no comfort whatsoever. I took him up to London as a treat and I ended up losing him and abandoning him there. I feel awful.'

'Abandoning? Now who's being emotive! Not your fault … he'll find his way back, mark my word. Bad pennies always do. Go to bed.' The phone went dead.

Rowena tried to do as she was bid, but she tossed and turned, her mind racing with all the possibilities of what might have happened to Mr Morell. Sleep did not come.

Chapter 11

The telephone bell in the police box startled PC Bent. He was leaning against the side, smoking a cigarette, having just finished his stint on duty at Reigate tunnel; a short break before cycling off on his rounds. It was getting on for midnight and the busier he kept himself the quicker the six remaining hours would pass. He didn't mind doing the night shift so long as there was something happening all the time; there was nothing duller than being marooned at one of his points with nothing to do.

He stubbed out what was left of his cigarette and picked up the receiver.

'Bent, is that you?'

He recognised the voice of Sergeant Baldwin.

'Yes, Sarge.'

'Have you got anything on?'

'No, all quiet here. Traffic signals are back on, PC Tobin has set off on his rounds and I was just about to do the same.'

'Lucky I caught you then. Change of plan, my son. Pedal over to the station, would you? I've got a job for you.'

'Right away, Sarge.'

Bent closed up the police box and climbed onto his bike. It took barely five minutes to reach Chart Lane, where Sergeant Baldwin was standing on the pavement outside the station waiting for him, a canvas bag in his hand.

'Ah, just the man. Not the most exciting task I'm afraid, Bent, but can you bike this over to Redhill nick for me? Sergeant Cartwright is expecting it.'

'I will indeed, Sarge. What is it, a key piece of evidence in a forthcoming trial or something?'

'Of those two categories, this fits firmly into the second … or something. None of your business, now hop it and get back over this way as soon as you can.'

PC Bent slung the bag over his shoulder and set off along the A25, the direct artery joining Reigate with Redhill. Barely ten minutes later he was approaching Redhill town centre, cycling down Station Road, then turning left at the Market Hall towards London Road. There was no one about. As he rounded the corner, he saw to his right, opposite the railway station, the imposing facade of the Odeon cinema, where his girl Meg worked as an usherette. She'd been there tonight but would be long gone by now. He cycled on to the police station opposite the football ground. To his surprise, Sergeant Cartwright was also standing outside waiting for him.

'Evening, Bent. That my special delivery?'

'It is indeed, Sarge.' He handed over the bag. 'Must be precious to warrant a reception committee.'

'Very precious. Well I don't want to take you away from your duties any longer than necessary, my lad. Thank you for bringing it over – now off you go back onto your own patch.'

PC Bent cycled off, wondering what was inside the bag that deserved such special attention. The content felt hard and lumpy, definitely not paperwork or files of any sort. Quite heavy. He had no idea. Instead of heading back towards Reigate, he pulled up outside the Odeon, for no other reason than its association with Meg. He leaned his bike against the railings that led to the steps in front of the cinema entrance. A quick cigarette before heading back would do no harm.

He lit up, then climbed the steps to see what was showing. A new comedy, *The Lavender Hill Mob,* starring Alec Guinness who in the posters was hugging Stanley Holloway with glee. *YOUR BIGGEST LAUGH IN* YEARS! it declared; then something about a great gold robbery. Produced by J. Arthur Rank, Bent noticed, raising his eyebrows … Reigate's most famous resident. The film looked good; he must come over and see it when he had a chance, maybe take Meg if she wasn't fed up with it by then. As he stood there, he suddenly felt the need to relieve himself. He glanced behind him. An elderly man with a walking stick was crossing the road from the station, heading towards the cinema. Other than that, there didn't seem to be anyone else around. Bent edged round the side of the building until he was completely hidden from view and proceeded to pee up against the wall, his cigarette clamped firmly between his lips, his eyes squinting to avoid the smoke.

When he'd finished, he took the last few drags of his cigarette before wandered back round to the front of the cinema. He noticed a figure cycling past, none too steadily, from under the railway bridge and along Station Road into town. It was the same old man he'd seen a moment ago, he was sure. The bike looked familiar. He looked across at the railings. His was no longer there.

****

'Sorry sir, no more trains to Reigate now until morning.'

Mr Morell had looked at the ticket collector in disbelief. 'But how am I to get home?'

'Can't help you there, sir. It's a good half an hour walk, I can tell you that much. Longer for you I'd imagine.'

'Is there a taxi?'

'Not at this time of night.'

Morell stood outside the station and looked around him. Redhill was deserted. He looked across the road towards the town centre, then to his left at the Odeon cinema, then to his right, across the station forecourt. He didn't even know which direction Reigate was.

He crossed the road and sat down on the steps of the Odeon, reflecting on his journey so far. By luck rather than judgment he had found his way into Trafalgar Square where he stopped a couple and asked them for advice on how to get to Reigate. They suggested taking a taxi to Victoria Station, and kindly flagged one down for him. Purchasing a ticket and finding the right platform had been confusing but he'd managed. With minutes to spare he had just caught the last train to Redhill.

From his seat on the Odeon steps he looked around again. He noticed a bicycle leaning against some railings. There was no owner to be seen. Would he be able to ride it? At least twenty years had passed since the last time. He stood up, wandered over and, with a bit of a struggle, managed to climb on. Wobbling perilously, with his stick somehow tucked under his arm, he set off to the right, under a railway bridge, only to be confronted by a hill; too steep for him to tackle. He turned around and decided to try the other direction, which looked flat and took him through the middle of the town. He cycled back past the Odeon.

Out of the corner of his eye he saw a figure step out from the side of the cinema, stub out a cigarette, gaze towards him, then start running.

'Oi that's my bike. Stop thief!'

Mr Morell had no intention of stopping. He peddled harder, passed the Market Hall on his right, crossed the High Street and continued on up Station Road. Behind him he could hear the crisp sound of boots hitting solid ground as the man chased after him. Then the shrill pierce of a whistle.

'Shit,' puffed Mr Morell, 'a policeman!'

As the shops petered out, the road began to incline gently, enough to slow him down. Worryingly, the footsteps were getting closer and he could hear the man's breathing. There was another blast on the whistle, longer this time and much louder. The policeman was almost alongside him now, and for a few moments their eyes met. Morell stared into his face and the policeman stared back. The policeman lunged forward to grab either the bike or the thief. The whistle started to blow again but came to an abrupt halt with an upward glissando and a grunt as Morell poked his stick firmly into the man's stomach.

'Oof!' groaned the policeman as he toppled sideways.

Mr Morell glanced over his shoulder; the policeman was spreadeagled on the road and didn't look as if he would be getting up in a hurry. He rode on, past a church, over a railway bridge and round several bends before stopping by a war memorial to catch his breath. He felt exhausted. To his relief he saw a signpost for Reigate. He was heading in the right direction. When he had recovered, he rode on.

Twenty minutes and several more stops later, he was cycling sedately into Reigate along Church Street, past The Old Wheel tea rooms and right into Tunnel Road. He felt relieved to be back on familiar territory. He cycled over the level crossing by the station, into a side street and was soon at the junction of Wray Park Road and Alders Road. Ideally, he would have preferred to reach his summer house via Rowena's garden, to avoid being seen; but it was pitch black and he couldn't be sure of finding his way. Instead he cycled directly to Peter Yardley's where he knew the side gate would take him onto the path leading down to the end of the garden.

He dismounted and started wheeling the bike up Wray Park Road. It then occurred to him that taking a stolen police bike home with him was not a wise move. Ahead, in front of a large house set back from the road, was a row of dense bushes. He pointed the front wheel at the narrow space between two of them and pushed hard until the whole bike was out of sight.

'OW!' came an agonised cry.

'*Entschuldigung.*'

'What you think you're playin' at?'

'I am sorry, I did not think there would be anyone there.'

'Well there is. Ooh my leg! I think it's broken.'

Morell could not see the figure in the bushes. 'Who are you?' he asked.

'None of your business.'

'What are you doing in there?'

'None of your bleedin' business either.'

'Goodnight then.'

'Piss off!'

Mr Morell walked away and minutes later was climbing into his bed in the summer house. All his life he had suffered from chronic insomnia, but tonight he fell asleep almost instantly, with barely a second thought as to who on earth might be hiding in a bush at that time of night.

****

Sunday 24th June

'And what ...' spluttered Inspector Thorne from behind his desk as he glared at PC Bent and Sergeant Baldwin, both standing rigidly to attention in front of him, '... in the name of Hades were you doing outside the Odeon in Redhill in the first place!'

'He'd gone there on an errand for me, sir,' explained Sergeant Baldwin, sounding edgy and not a little obsequious.

'I'll thank you to let him speak for himself, Baldwin.'

'Sorry, sir.'

'Well, my lad?'

'I was on an errand for the Sarge, sir,' explained Bent.

'To the Odeon?'

'No, sir, to Redhill police station.'

'And what was that errand precisely?'

'Delivery of a bag, sir – to Sergeant Cartwright.'

'And what was in the bag?'

'Don't know, sir, I wasn't told and I didn't look.'

Thorne raised his eyebrows. 'Do you expect me to believe that? I'd have stopped and had a gander if it had been me.'

PC Bent said nothing.

'What was in the bag, Baldwin?'

'Something I needed to get to Sergeant Cartwright, sir. Something of a private nature.'

'Well it's been the cause of the theft of a police bicycle so it's no longer private. Come on … out with it.'

There was a pause as Sergeant Baldwin shifted from one leg to the other and winced at what was to come. 'Football boots, sir.'

'Football boots?'

'Yes, sir. Tens – we have the same foot size and I promised to lend them to him for a Sunday league match, today. Only I forgot to do it until he phoned and reminded me last night. So you see I had to get them over to him. Last minute thing, sir. Shouldn't have done it – sorry, sir.'

'Shouldn't have done it? Too bloody right you shouldn't have done it. You mean to tell me you wasted valuable police resources and time getting Bent here to cycle all the way over to Redhill on a night shift to deliver some sodding football boots to a sodding colleague?'

'Sorry, sir.'

'I should bloody well think so.'

'Very sorry, sir.'

'And now we've lost a bike, to boot.'

Baldwin smirked. 'To boot – very good, sir.'

'Shut up!'

'Can't tell you how sorry I am, sir.'

'Well shut up then.'

'Yes sir, sorry sir.'

Inspector Thorne turned his attention back to PC Bent. 'This doesn't explain what you were doing skulking around outside the Odeon, which is not exactly en route between Redhill and Reigate nick. Explain yourself, Bent.'

'I stopped for a fag, sir. A cigarette.'

'I know what a fag is thank you. Does the word have any other meaning?'

'Not at present, that I'm aware of.'

'Why the Odeon of all places?'

'Because it was only a little out of my way, and … well, my girl works there and I thought it would be nice to stop off.'

'Do you have a bit of a sentimental nature then, Bent?'

'I think I must have, sir.'

'And what were you doing down the side of the Odeon to the extent that you left your bike unattended?'

'Just wandered down there … no particular reason.'

'Come on, lad, I wasn't born yesterday. Your girl wasn't by any chance with you and you weren't by any chance round the side of the Odeon slipping her a length?'

'Good grief!' said Bent, genuinely shocked at the suggestion. 'No, I was not!'

'Sir.'

'No I was not, sir.'

'So, what were you doing? Last chance to tell me the truth before I put you on a train to Guildford on a charge.'

'I needed the toilet, sir.'

'Aha, so that's it. You were pissing in a public place, were you? At least I bloody well hope you were pissing and not the other thing.'

'Most definitely not, sir!' said Bent, even more shocked.

'And while you were doing that your bike was being pinched by a mystery man who popped up out of nowhere.'

'Yes, sir. Not a complete mystery, I think he almost certainly got off the last train from London. It had just gone through Redhill.'

'And you gave chase?'

'I did, sir, but lost him just before Reffel's Bridge.'

'What sort of age was this villain?'

'Elderly I'd say. Seventy perhaps.'

'And he outpaced you?'

'No, sir. I caught up with him and was about to apprehend him when he poked me in the stomach with a stick. I lost my balance and fell.'

'Did you get a good look at this aged master criminal?'

'I did, sir.'

'Good enough to identify him?'

'I think so, yes.'

'And how did you get back to Reigate?'

'I walked, sir. Took a while as I bruised my knee.'

'Anything else you'd like to tell me while we're at it?'

'Yes sir. About the thief.'

'What about him?'

'He was wearing a dinner jacket.'

Inspector Thorne slumped back in his chair, a look of bafflement on his face. 'Well what a shower – what a class A shower you are. I don't know what to say, really I don't. Actually, yes, I do … Baldwin, don't you ever waste my manpower on petty private errands like that again, hear me?'

'Yes sir, sorry sir.'

101

'And Bent, don't you ever agree to courier footy boots, or anything else for that matter, for anyone – is that abundantly clear?'

'Yes sir, sorry sir.'

'AND do not make a habit of being caught short and getting your todger out in public places – at least not while you're on duty.'

'Yes sir … I mean no sir.'

'Right, that's all I have to say to you. Now get out – and for God's sake STOP apologising!'

'Sorry sir.'

'OUT!'

Chapter 12

'Mr Morell ... are you there?'

Rowena tapped again on the glass of the summer house door. No response. The curtains were drawn but hadn't met properly across the door and she could see inside. It was dark. There was no sign of life. She tapped again. Still no response. Then she heard something, a quiet muttering; from where she couldn't tell. Eventually a bedraggled figure in a dressing gown shuffled towards the door.

'Oh, Mr Morell, I am so relieved to see you! I've hardly slept all night, I was so worried. I'm sorry I lost you. What happened? I came back for you but you had gone.'

'Come in, Frau Furse, it is better you are not seen. Would you like some tea?'

Rowena stepped inside and sat down on a wicker chair.

'No thank you, I won't stay, but I just needed to know you were safe.'

Morell pulled back some curtains and the room flooded with light. He stood by the window, looking across the garden.

'Yes, I am safe. I did not like sitting in the foyer, so I went outside, then I needed to find a toilet, which I did at the stage door, thanks to maestro Rankl.'

'Karl Rankl the conductor? You talked to him?'

'He allowed me to use their facilities – a kind man. Then I came out, took a wrong turning and was lost, but eventually managed to board a train from Victoria.' He didn't mention stealing a bicycle to get from Redhill to Reigate.

'How extraordinary. Well done for being so resourceful. Really, Mr Morell, I feel dreadful for letting you down like that. Such a miserable end to an otherwise lovely evening.'

'All is well that ends well. I am fine, and thank you for taking me to see *Parsifal*. I enjoyed it so very much.'

'And well done for initiating the applause.'

'Someone had to. I don't know how much longer I will be here, but if you are contemplating any more trips to the opera in the near future I would be pleased to accompany you.'

'That would be delightful. I'm not sure what else they are doing. That was the last performance of *Parsifal*. I'll have a look and see.'

Rowena stood up as if to leave. 'Meanwhile, tomorrow I am having lunch with Erika and she has specifically asked if you would come too.'

'I would be delighted. I think your friend Frau von Tirpitz is a very charming lady.'

'You and most other men. She attracts the opposite sex like magic. Colonel Maxwell, for example, is completely smitten by her.'

'Who is he?'

'Retired army. He lives on Reigate Hill, not too far from here. He's fallen for Erika hook, line, and sinker, bless him. They socialise quite a bit together although I'm sure Erika isn't serious about him. He's quite a bit older than her … a widower. Gets very possessive about her.'

They talked for a while longer, then Rowena left and Mr Morell went back to bed. It was Sunday morning and he had nothing in particular to do all day.

Beth Angel had plenty to do. A dozen things in fact and she was not averse to letting her husband know the finer details of every one, from peeling the potatoes properly (getting into all the eyes to remove the black bits) to mowing the lawn (keeping the columns dead straight). Her husband sat for most of the morning in his armchair, legs stretched out in front of him, ears switched off, reading the Sunday Pictorial. Occasionally he dozed, but Beth never noticed.

At one o'clock, the two 'little' Angels, Beryl and Peg, were rounded up from the street outside, forced to wash their hands, and dinner was served; roast beef, Yorkshire pudding, carrots, peas and immaculately peeled roast potatoes, with rhubarb crumble and custard for pudding. Beth did most of the talking whilst the others ate in silence.

After dinner, Terry Angel knew what to expect next; a diatribe about how his wife was the only one in the household who did a stroke of work, and all the others were lazy good for nothings and how ungrateful they all were. For the sake of some peace and quiet, and with great reluctance, he offered to mow the lawn.

'Make sure you get them lines straight,' bleated Beth. 'And empty the grass box regular or there'll be cuttings everywhere.'

He took the lawn mower out of the garden shed, attached the grass box and set off down the centre of the lawn, his eyes focused on the back door of the house as a point of reference. It was the first time that day he had put pressure on his legs, and he suddenly felt pain shoot down his left shin. He winced. This wasn't going to be easy.

'What's wrong with your leg?' called out Beth who had been watching with a critical eye from the back porch.

'Some idiot barged into me with his bike last night,' said Terry Angel. 'Caught me right on the shin.'

'Are you sure you didn't fall over drunk and bash it? You were late enough getting home.'

He ignored her and pressed on with the mowing. It wasn't so bad once he got into his stride. His lines were straight and true, so Beth, with nothing currently to complain about, turned away and went back into the house.

'You should have taken me out dancing like I asked,' was her parting jibe. 'I bet I'm right. Bashed it falling over drunk.'

'I'd like to bash you,' mumbled Terry Angel to himself, knowing he'd never dare.

****

Monday 25th June

The next morning, Mr Morell spent more time than usual getting dressed, and at midday, as agreed, appeared in Rowena's garden.

'Where are you taking me this time?' he asked as they climbed into the Rover.

'The Dinner Gong – a nice restaurant in the High Street. We walked past it the other day after tea at The Old Wheel. It's actually in a basement, beneath Mason's, the ladies fashion store.'

At twelve-thirty they pulled up outside the restaurant to see Erika standing waiting for them underneath the striped awning. Mr Morell stepped out and shook her hand.

'How lovely to see you again, Frau von Tirpitz.'

She smiled warmly. 'And you, too, Mr Morell.'

They made their way down a long staircase to the restaurant; it was busy, but Suki the head waitress recognised the two women as regulars and managed to find them a table towards the back in a quiet corner. They ordered lunch and some drinks; coffee for Rowena and Morell, gin for Erika.

Erika lit a cigarette and looked across at Mr Morell. 'So, here we are again. I must say, Mr Morell, you took me by surprise the other day when you announced your true identity.'

'I was drunk. I imagine you did not believe me.'

'You can understand why.'

'What about you, Frau Furse, do you still not believe me?'

'Of course not!' declared Rowena vehemently. 'You're Mr Morell, a charming gentleman whose company I enjoy. That's all.'

'So, if I were Adolf Hitler it wouldn't bother you?'

'You're not, so it doesn't.'

There was a pause in the conversation. The expression on Morell's face might conceivably have reflected a hint of disappointment, as if he had been willing them to believe him. His head lowered and he stared at his coffee cup.

'What I don't understand is this,' said Erika. 'If you are who you say you are – and I don't believe for a moment you are – why are you telling us? Surely you wouldn't want anyone to know, that you survived the war and are here in England.'

'As I said before, I had drunk too much – I am not used to it. Perhaps also I have my reasons.'

'I would like to hear them.'

The soups came; vegetable for Morell and mulligatawny for Erika and Rowena. When the waitress had left them and Morell had taken a few tentative sips and winced as it burned his mouth, he put his spoon to one side. When he spoke, he spoke in German.

'That would take some time. I am not intent on announcing it to the world. I told you because I like you both and want to be completely honest with you. In truth, I have nothing to hide. I fear nothing. The war is over and what went before, with all

107

its mistakes on both sides, should be laid to rest. I am an old man who would simply like to listen to sublime music, read, eat cake, relax and enjoy the rest of my life for however long it may last. I am in transit to a safe place. What I have said all along is clear now, that the real enemy of Germany and Britain alike is Russia, and always was. I have never had time for that senile drunkard Churchill, but when he said that an iron curtain has descended across the continent, from Stettin in the Baltic to Trieste in the Adriatic, he was right. The so-called Allies have broken up Europe in such a way that should never have been allowed. The Russians are the real demons in the world. If luck had been with us, we would have annihilated them in forty-one. The Czechs are no better. Or the Poles – I never understood why Britain took a stand over them and went to war. We are alike, the British and the Germans. We modelled ourselves on the British Empire and the ruthlessness with which you built and administered it. That is why I held back from wiping out the British army at Dunkirk, and postponed any invasion plans. I had no interest in doing so. Already my thoughts were turning towards the east. In truth, they had never left it.'

Erika inhaled and shrugged her shoulders. She also spoke in German. 'That's all very well, but nothing you say convinces me that the man sitting next to me eating soup is Adolf Hitler. You could be any one of a thousand Germans who could, if they wished, say the same things. I, too, am German, and have similar feelings about the British ... and the English in particular. I feel at home here amongst English people. Perhaps you are right about the Russians. But Adolf Hitler? I think you are a little deranged there, Mr Morell. Besides, you'd be taking a huge risk wandering around claiming to be the greatest war criminal who ever lived.'

'I have never been afraid of taking risks, no one could ever deny that of me. Of course, there is always the possibility I am simply a mad man – a lunatic who has escaped from an insane asylum.'

'I know you are not,' said Erika.

'How can you be so sure?'

'Because I have spent some time over the last few days contacting all the asylums in Surrey – Springfield Asylum in Tooting, Brookwood in Woking, Cane Hill in Coulsdon – I've spoken to them all. Currently, there's a Napoleon Bonaparte and a couple of Jesus Christs unaccounted for, and a Mahatma Gandhi would you believe! But all the Adolf Hitlers appear to be present and correct.'

Mr Morell shrugged. 'That rather strengthens my case. What can I do or say to convince you I am the real thing?'

'That's easy,' said Rowena. 'By telling us something that proves unequivocally you are who you say you are. Something that only Adolf Hitler could possibly know.'

'And how would you know it was true?'

'Hmm, good question. I don't have an answer to that.'

Mr Morell broke off the end from a bread roll and popped it into his mouth, then tried his soup again. It had cooled down somewhat and he ate a few spoonfuls.

'Very well,' he said, wiping his mouth on his napkin. 'I shall help you. I can indeed tell you something only Adolf Hitler would know, and you yourselves are able to corroborate.'

'This I'm looking forward to!' said Erika eagerly.

'Same here,' agreed Rowena.

Mr Morell paused for effect. When he spoke, Erika froze.

'Frau von Tirpitz … we have met before.'

****

'More thieving in Knight's, young Grimshaw,' called the boss across the office as he put the phone handset back onto its

109

cradle. 'Get over there, dear boy, and bring me the facts. More silk stockings and French knickers walking out of the door, I'll be bound.'

'*Ladies' under apparel* is what you changed it to in the piece,' remarked Benjamin as he slotted his notebook into his pocket and prepared to leave.

'Only in deference to the delicate sensitivities of our conservative readership. One day in the future we shall be able to print the sordid details in full in our local rag, but unhappily those liberal times are a long way off, I fear.'

Benjamin wondered how someone so verbose in his own speech could be so tight a sub-editor. Storm had said the same.

'Was that your source on the phone just now?'

'It was indeed.'

'Who were you talking to?'

'A little birdie. And it's whom, not who, with to at the beginning. When not encouraging us to fight on the beaches and Lord knows where else, dear Winston is on record to the effect that ending a sentence with a preposition is something up with which he will not put. I happen to be of the same opinion.'

'Which little birdie?'

'Never ask me that again, dear boy. Never. Sources are confidential. They are sacrosanct.'

When Ben was almost out of the office door he heard: 'And try and get a better description of the culprit this time. One that doesn't sound like a half-finished water colour of a female of indistinct appearance and indefinite age.'

'Bollocks,' replied Ben, low enough in volume not to be audible; or so he thought.

'I heard that!' thundered the boss's voice.

As he approached Knight's department store, Ben saw Mrs Wells, Barbara, in the window. She was rearranging a display, moving items of a tea service around on a large tray. When she noticed him, she smiled her appealing smile and looked towards the display with a quizzical look as if to ask his opinion. He pointed at the teapot and indicated it should be moved a little to the left, which she did. He nodded approvingly and gave the thumbs up. She smiled again and withdrew from the window.

Had her fingers lingered along the spout a little longer than necessary … or had he imagined it?

'Thank you,' said Barbara when he was inside the shop. 'Easier with two.'

'Most things are,' said Ben.

Barbara grinned at him, then winked. 'Is that so?'

He felt himself colouring up. 'I didn't mean …'

'That's all right, I'm not easily shocked. I suppose you've come about this morning's theft.'

'I have. Is Mr Wells about?'

'Not at the moment, but I can tell you all about it. It was me who saw her again. Same woman as before.'

'What did she take?'

'Bed linen. Some very nice sheets and pillow cases.'

'Not, um, ladies' under apparel this time then?'

'No French knickers or silk stockings if that's what you mean. I read your article in the Mirror. Dear me, all very stuffy. Ladies' apparel indeed.'

'That was the editor, not me.'

'Well anyway, it was bed linen this time. She was wearing different clothing and a hat pulled down to cover her face, but I knew as soon as I saw her it was the same woman. She's a fast mover. I went straight into the office at the back to fetch Tunbridge – that is, my husband, Mr Wells – that's my pet name for him.'

Benjamin was scribbling in his notebook.

'For goodness sake don't print that!'

'Don't worry, I won't. Then what happened?'

111

'By the time we came back out she was gone.'

'Description?'

'Medium height, medium …'

'Hang on,' Benjamin interrupted. 'That's what you gave me last time. Can you describe her in more detail? It would help in trying to identify her.'

'That's what the police said. Well, she was about my height, which is medium. Podgy. Couldn't see her hair because she had a hat on – but that was sort of maroon in colour, old-fashioned, popular in the twenties, not nowadays.'

'What else was she wearing?'

'A heavy coat,' said Barbara. 'Charcoal grey, much too heavy for June. She must have been boiling. I suppose that was to try and disguise herself.'

'Did you see her face?'

'Only for a moment, and that was in profile. Quite a big nose, and a bit chinless. Not exactly an oil painting.'

'That's really helpful – I'll make sure we publish as much as we can to try and catch her this time.'

Out of the corner of his eye, Ben noticed Mr Wells appear from his office. He stood there for a moment, surveying the store. A pretty young assistant was returning some rolls of fabric to a shelf nearby. Mr Wells ambled past her and Ben saw his hand surreptitiously ruck up the back of her dress and squeeze her bottom. The girl started, but said nothing and carried on with her work.

'That sort of behaviour goes on a lot round here,' said Barbara impassively.

'Doesn't anyone ever report him?'

'Their word against his – and he's a good liar. So, they just leave. I expect she'll be handing in her notice soon.'

'It would make a good story.'

112

'Please no!' She grabbed his arm and squeezed it tight. 'You wouldn't, would you?'

He wouldn't, but he chose not to say so. 'How do you feel about it, Mrs Wells?' asked Ben awkwardly.

'Barbara … in fact call me Barb. You're Benjamin, is that right? Do you prefer Ben or Benjamin?'

'I don't mind. Most people say Ben.'

'Well I prefer Benjamin. How do I feel about my husband groping young girls? Keeps him from groping me, which is a blessing. All that business between us is finished. We work well together, but our domestic set up is a sham.' She looked him straight in the eyes. 'It can be very frustrating sometimes, if you know what I mean.'

Ben felt himself colouring once more. 'Anyway, thanks for the information … Barb. A few more questions about what she actually stole and I'll be off.'

'Fire away, I'm all yours.'

When he came out of the store onto Bell Street, Ben had a rasper alight in seconds. His hands were shaking. A scoop, but not the kind he was expecting; Mrs Wells was giving him the come on! And he liked it. He didn't care that she was married. Clearly, she wasn't happy, and things weren't happening for her in the bedding department (he chuckled at his own analogy). Storm had put him right about that once. Married women were fair game, so long as you didn't get found out. All he had to do now was work out a way to arrange a tryst. It should be easy enough to make up an excuse to pop in and see her again; some sort of follow up about the shoplifting.

He strolled around the corner to The Dinner Gong. All this titillation had given him an appetite, and pie and mash was on his mind.

****

113

Rowena looked at Erika, then at Mr Morell, then back to Erika, who had gone quiet, and pale.

'Erika, did you ever meet Hitler?'

Erika sat rigidly for some time, then nodded slowly. 'Actually, yes I did. I was introduced to him once, at a dinner I attended with Karl.'

'At the Kaiserhof Hotel in Berlin,' said Mr Morell.

'That's right.'

'In thirty-four.'

Erika stared at him in disbelief. 'How on earth did you know that?'

'Because I was there and I remember you. How could I forget such an attractive and beguiling young woman!'

She continued staring at him, her spoon put down, her soup forgotten and going cold. 'Well that is remarkable.'

Nobody around the table spoke. The soups were taken away and main courses brought on, but appetites had diminished. When she spoke, Erika's words came hesitantly, as if composing her sentences in advance as she went along, not certain of what would follow.

'Ah but there were hundreds of people there. I met a lot of men that evening. It proves we were at the same dinner perhaps, but nothing more.'

'It has made you think,' said Mr Morell.

'Yes, it has done that.' Erika thought for a while. 'No. You could have been one of many men there. We sat on a table with a number of businessmen and their wives, then we mingled with others. Karl was keen to establish contacts. We met quite a few other National Socialist party officials as well as Hitler. You could be any one of them. We went to many such dinners. No, I am not convinced.'

'And you don't look like him,' added Rowena. 'And you're too old.'

'I have aged beyond my years, that is true. As to looks, they change with time. I have virtually no hair now, no moustache, and my skin is wrinkled which it never used to be.' He tapped his spectacles. 'My eye sight is poor, also.'

'I say,' said Rowena, glancing around conspicuously. 'A few heads are turning. I think perhaps we ought to keep our voices down – and perhaps speak in English?'

****

The restaurant was almost full but after a short wait Suki managed to squeeze Benjamin in at table towards the back of the restaurant.

He sat down, ordered, then took out *The High Window* and read another chapter as he waited for his lunch. He dearly wanted to visit Los Angeles one day, maybe work there, as a reporter. A stringer even, a freelance chasing stories about the rich and famous. That would be a dream come true. Storm would be proud of him, and that would make him feel like a million pounds ... or dollars.

He was aware of some people on the next table. They were talking in a foreign language; German, he was fairly certain. One of the women was quite a looker, if you liked heavily made up older women. He grinned to himself as a moment ago he had read a couple of sentences that might have been written about her. *From thirty feet away, she looked like a lot of class. From ten feet away she looked like something made up to be seen from thirty feet away.* The other woman looked ordinary, overweight and squeezed into clothes a size too small; he wondered if she had any stolen stockings stuffed inside her handbag. And there was an old man, hunched over and with a walking stick next to his chair. He, too, looked very ordinary. Mind you, there was something about his features. If you stuck a little moustache on

115

him, he might pass for Charlie Chaplin's dad. Ben chuckled to himself at the thought.

His meal arrived and he tucked in, taking large mouthfuls then reading a paragraph or two between each. As he scraped the last bits of mash from his plate and was wondering if he had room for pudding, his ear seemed to tune in to the conversation across the way. They were speaking English now. Gradually he found himself hearing every word.

He forgot about pudding, and instead pulled out his notebook and pencil.

****

Mr Morell sat back in his chair and wiped his mouth with a napkin.

'I will try my best in English. I learnt a little in my youth, and have studied it more so in the years since the war, but I am lacking practice.'

'Your English seems to improve at will,' observed Erika. 'Something I would like to ask you, Mr Morell. The friend you are staying with next door to Rowena, is he also German – a fellow Nazi perhaps – and would we know him?'

'I do not wish to speak of Yardley. His position in many ways is more delicate than mine. He has been good to me and that is all I will say.'

'Does he know you've been socialising in Reigate, telling the locals you're Adolf Hitler?' asked Erika.

'He has not been here to tell. He is away on his travels. However, he returns soon. Tomorrow I believe.'

'And will you tell him?'

'No.'

'You say you don't want to put him at risk, yet here you are doing just that.'

116

Mr Morell frowned, none too pleased.

'What is he doing to help you, this Mr Yardley?'

'He is making arrangements for me to relocate, to move somewhere safe.'

Rowena took over. 'So how did you trick the world into believing you – and presumably your wife Eva Braun – both committed suicide in the bunker in Berlin?'

Mr Morell pursed his lips, searching for the words. 'Frau von Tirpitz, in English what is *Täuschung*?'

'Trickery. Sleight of hand.'

'Thank you. It was a trick.'

'And on the subject of Eva Braun, are you still married to her? Where is she?'

'We are estranged. She has remained on Fuerteventura.'

'I see.' Rowena paused, not knowing what to ask next.

The meal over, conversation moved on to lighter things. Mr Morell insisted on paying the bill, again, and they climbed back up the stairs to street level.

'What shall we do now?' asked Rowena. 'It's not even two o'clock yet, any ideas?'

'It's looking a bit cloudy. How about the cinema – do you like films, Mr Morell?'

'I enjoy good films, yes.'

'Let's wander down and see what's on. There's The Hippodrome just around the corner in Bell Street, or The Majestic a little further on in Bancroft Road. Not far. You might as well leave the car here, Rowena.'

They strolled round to look at both cinemas.

'Well,' said Rowena, 'it's either *Strangers on a Train*, a gripping thriller from the master of suspense Alfred Hitchcock at The Hippodrome, or *Old Mother Riley's Jungle Treasure,* a comedy at The Majestic. I know which I'd prefer – some light relief after our rather serious conversation over lunch.'

'Do you have any preference, Mr Morell?'

'No, I am happy for you to choose.'

'Well that settles it then. Comedy wins.'

As they stepped inside The Majestic, they failed to notice a young man with ginger hair walking past the cinema behind them, gazing hard as if to make a mental image of the curious trio.

****

Benjamin stared at his notebook and perused the words he had scribble down in the restaurant. All very strange. What did it mean? Something, but he had no idea what. Worth pursuing though, he told himself.

When they had left, he followed immediately afterwards, tailing them down the street towards The Majestic. Having watched them disappear inside, he doubled back to where he had left his bike, flipped on his cycle clips, and pedalled hastily out of town towards Redhill. He dismounted outside the Surrey Mirror building and hurried inside. As he walked into the newsroom, a voice bellowed.

'Benjamin Grimshaw, where the bloody hell have you been! How long does it take to cover a minor case of shoplifting, for God's sake?'

'Sorry, boss, I stopped off for some lunch afterwards.'

'Well get typing.'

'Boss, listen, I was in The Dinner Gong just now in Reigate and I overheard a conversation at the next table.' He flicked open his notepad and handed it to the boss. 'What do you make of all this …?'

The boss sat down at his desk, slid a pair of spectacles onto his bulbous nose and perused the words jotted on the page in front of him. He read them several times, then dropped the notepad onto his desk.

'Well my lad,' said the boss, 'looks like you're onto something here.'

'Do you think so?'

'Undoubtedly. Put all those bits of the jigsaw together and what have you got?'

'I'm not sure.'

'I'll tell you. You've discovered probably the greatest criminal mass murderer in history, whom we all thought shot himself in a bunker under the rubble of Berlin six years ago, the personification of evil itself, having a lunchtime tête-à-tête in The Dinner Gong.'

'Do you think so?'

'I shall hold the front page.'

Benjamin's eyes widened. 'You're kidding me!'

'Yes, I'm kidding you.'

Benjamin's eyes narrowed instantly. 'Bollocks.'

'Ah you're revered brother's favourite expression as I recall … clearly it runs in the family. But who am I to judge when he is now in the employ of Lord Northcliffe, no less, on a national up in Fleet Street and I'm seemingly doomed to remain on a turgid local for the rest of my born days. Bollocks indeed. I would suggest you're either the subject of a practical joke, young lad, or you might possibly have overheard a group of amateur thespians rehearsing a play of obscure origin. Home grown I expect. Lord knows there are enough amateur theatrical groups in the area, each with its own budding R. C. Sherriff eager to find an audience.'

'But they were speaking in German – surely that must mean something?'

'Part of the subterfuge, I imagine.'

Ben fell silent, his brow beetled as he mulled over this latest disappointment.

'No,' he said, more to himself than the boss. 'There's something to this. I'm sure of it.'

'Well if you know better than I, feel free to cast your net and see what you haul in, but in your own time, not mine. Now, type up this shoplifting story for me pronto, Benjamin Grimshaw, and let me see some copy or I'll dock your wages.'

Chapter 13

Two hours later, copy submitted, cub reporter Ben Grimshaw was out and about again, loitering in Bancroft Road opposite The Majestic. When people started to emerge at the end of the main feature, he kept a beady eye open for the two women and the man he'd seen going inside earlier. He had one foot on a pedal ready to move fast if necessary.

The crowd wasn't huge; it was a midweek matinee after all. He watched closely, never taking his eye off the entrance and the gentle trickle of people flowing into the street. When the trickle dried up, there was still no sign of them. He waited a few minutes longer; perhaps one or more had needed to visit the ladies or gents on the way out. Still they didn't appear.

Surely they weren't going to stay and watch the film again? They didn't seem the type. Or they may have gone into the café for something to eat; they did a nice omelette in there. Unlikely, surely, after a hearty lunch in The Dinner Gong. What to do now – stay or go? He didn't know. A rasper might help resolve his quandary.

****

Erika, Rowena and Mr Morell emerged from The Hippodrome onto Bell Street, shading their eyes as they grew accustomed to daylight again.

'Well, I enjoyed that very much. Hitch really knows how to pile on the suspense. The scene where Bruno drops the lighter down the storm drain and can't reach it had me on the edge of my seat. What did you think, Mr Morell?'

'I enjoyed it also. An interesting concept – two men exchanging murders to remove any identifiable motive from the killings. It might have succeeded had not one of them been such a weak character. Far more enjoyable than the little we saw of Old Mother Riley. I did not understand a word.'

'Oh dear, we should have thought of that before going in. Never mind, we jumped ship in good time and all was well in the end, even if we did have to pay twice.'

Rowena said: 'Can I give you a lift home, Erika?'

'Very kind, but no thank you, it's only a short walk.'

They said their goodbyes. Erika headed off along Bell Street in one direction and Rowena and Mr Morell in the other, back towards the Rover which was still parked outside The Dinner Gong.

****

Ben fed the rasper between his lips and was about to strike a match when, out of the corner of his eye, he glimpsed a familiar figure appear where Bell Street and Bancroft Road met, waiting to cross … the good looker of the two women. Where the hell had she come from! He slipped the cigarette into his pocket and cycled to the junction of the two roads to take a better look. By the time he got there she had crossed and was heading along Bell Street, away from the town centre in the direction of Cockshot Hill. He glanced the other way, up towards Reigate tunnel and caught a glimpse of the other woman and the old man disappearing round the corner into the High Street. They must have changed their minds and gone to The Hippodrome instead.

Bollocks – who to follow? Whom even! Two were better than one, he judged, and haired up Bell Street as fast as he could pedal and into the High Street. He saw them approach a car parked immediately outside The Dinner Gong. The woman opened the passenger door and helped the old man to climb in.

****

'Alfred Hitchcock is a wonderful film maker, don't you agree?' said Rowena as she drove off. 'He's made some wonderfully exciting films. *The Thirty-Nine Steps* is one of my favourites. Robert Donat again – Mr Chips no less. The man not the dog, ha ha!'

'I miss owning a dog.' said Morell. 'When I am settled I shall have one. I prefer larger breeds – German Shepherds especially. I have owned several over the years.'

'I like dogs as well,' agreed Rowena, 'but prefer not to have one myself in case they spoil my garden. Here we are, nearly there, shall I drive you to your door or would you prefer to sneak in the back way as usual?'

'Kindly drive me straight home, I am feeling ... *ach was ist verwegen*?'

'Reckless? Bold?'

Ja ... reckless is good.'

****

Ben cycled past the car parked outside The Dinner Gong and pulled into the curb about fifty yards or so ahead of them.

123

He leaned backwards as if to check his rear wheel. The car was pulling away and towards him. A Rover 75 – nice. He made a mental note of the registration number.

Now for the hard part; keeping up with a sporty saloon motor on a bike. At the end of the High Street the Rover turned into London Road. Ben followed. Fortunately, the woman was driving slowly, chatting with the old man, and he managed to keep pace as London Road became the Broadway. There they pulled away from him, but only as far as the level crossing where, as luck would have it, the gates were closed. He caught up with them, keeping a car's length away. When the gates opened, he was close behind. They turned right just past the crossing, into Holmesdale Road. A series of subsequent turns kept the speed down and made the next stretch easy. When the car turned into Wray Park Road and slowed down as it approached a house on the left, Ben pulled up and dismounted, flipping the bike over so the wheels were pointing skywards. With one eye, he fussed over the rear tyre, checking for a possible puncture; with the other he took in the scene outside the house. Two cars, it seemed, had arrived at the same time. The old man got out of the one he'd been trailing and a short squat man got out of the other. As they did so, the woman made a three-point turn and drove back towards him, swerving to avoid his upturned bicycle. She turned into Alders Road, and out of sight.

****

As the Rover approached the house, another car turned into the driveway just ahead of them, having come down Wray Park Road from the other direction. A short, plumpish man with a round, fleshy face got out from the passenger side and stared at them as Rowena pulled up.

'Shit,' said Mr Morell. 'This is unfortunate timing. Pardon my language, Frau Furse.'

'Oh dear, are you going to be in trouble?'

'I have a little explaining to do.'

'Is that Yardley?'

'Yes, back sooner than expected. Not to worry, I will deal with it. Thank you for a most enjoyable afternoon. We shall have tea and cake again soon, I hope.'

'I hope so, too.'

'And another trip to the opera?'

'If you're permitted.'

'I will be. There is only one leader around here.'

'Ha ha!'

'Did you manage to discover if there is anything else worth seeing at Covent Garden soon?'

'I had a quick look. How about *The Pilgrim's Progress*? It's by Vaughan Williams – another of our finest composers.'

Morell pulled a face. 'I think not. I know some of his music. Like Elgar, too English for his own good. Did someone once say that listening to the Fifth Symphony of Vaughan Williams was like staring at a cow for forty-five minutes?'

'I've never heard that.'

'Well if no one has said it yet, they will one day.'

'Talking of staring,' said Rowena, 'your friend Mr Yardley is making me feel rather uncomfortable.'

'He can be very protective, too much so on occasions. Goodbye, Frau Furse.'

'Goodbye.'

Morell climbed out of the car and approached his friend.

'Yardley,' he called. 'Good to see you back, and earlier than expected …'

Both speaking in German, Rowena observed as she made a three-point turn and drove away, swerving slightly to avoid a young man attending to his upturned bicycle at the side of the road. A puncture it would seem. As she passed him, he stared back at her. His red hair was distinctive and looked vaguely familiar; but she couldn't place him.

****

Ben couldn't hear the men's conversation, but the tone was evident; they were disagreeing about something. Both were gesturing at each other and pointing down the road in his direction, though not at him. They hadn't even noticed him. He flipped his bike over again, climbed on and cycled past the house slowly, glancing across as he did. He noticed a third man near the porch, watching him intently. The two men were walking towards the house now and had their backs to him. He could hear their voices, though not what they were saying. He wouldn't have understood even if he'd been standing right next to them. They too were speaking German.

Strange.

****

Monday 2nd July

It was one of Hewson's irritating personal quirks – and there were many – that he insisted on using cover names even when in the secure environment of MI5 headquarters. Another was his habit of tapping out someone's cover name in Morse code on the heating pipe that led from his office along the side of the main office, his bizarre means of summonsing them for a meeting.

Hewson was, naturally, a cover name. So was Perriam. Perriam had been sitting at his desk studying a surveillance report when he heard the pipes ring out his unique identifier. He closed the file, locked it in his top drawer and headed across the room through a maze of desks, mostly unoccupied at present.

'Perriam, come!' said Hewson gruffly from behind a wall of cigarette smoke. He, too, had a report in front of him. Perriam recognised it from the cover as one of his own; hence the summons. He sat down and glanced across his boss at the view through the window beyond. Had the office been on the other side of the building he would have enjoyed a delightful expanse of the Thames flowing gently towards Lambeth Bridge. As it was he had nothing more to feast his eye on than grey stone and another window.

'Who is he?'

Another irritating habit; talking to you as if you were a mind reader.

'Who is who?' asked Perriam patiently.

'This chap! This German!' Yet another was to speak as if everything he said was a eureka moment.

'You mean the old man staying with Yardley?'

'Who else! Who the bloody hell is this mysterious new neighbour of yours?'

'His name is Morell ... Theodor Morell.'

'Also known as Adolf Hitler?'

'He has made that claim, yes.'

'To your wife!'

'That's right – and to her friend who is also German.'

'You've met him?'

'Not yet.'

'Believe him when he says he's Hitler?'

Perriam shook his head. 'I've spoken with Yardley who claims he is an old business colleague he's known since before the war. Possibly a Nazi, but we have no way of knowing.'

'What's he doing here then, popping up out of nowhere?'

'In transit, it would appear. On his way from Europe to start a new life. Probably in South America.'

'Sounds like a Nazi. Perhaps we should quiz him.'

'Oh, I don't know, if he is he must be a pretty low ranking one. Hardly worth it. By all accounts he's a rather unassuming chap, according to Rowena.'

'*Mrs* Perriam?'

'Indeed.'

'So, what's it all about then, this "I'm Hitler" business? D'you think he's cracked?'

'Quite probably. When I put it to Yardley, he simply laughed. Delusions of grandeur, he claims. Napoleon syndrome. The man's insane ... but harmless.'

'What does Mrs P make of him?'

'She thinks the same. She's rather fond of him and doesn't believe for a minute he's Adolf.'

Hewson stabbed a finger at the report. 'You say in here there's no physical resemblance.'

'Apparently not – and he's older than Hitler, by all accounts. It doesn't add up.'

'Time you found out for yourself!'

'Indeed. I shall make a point of meeting Mr Morell.'

'Very good. Hitler? Preposterous! Keep an eye on things, but frankly I can't see there's anything to be inordinately concerned about. Yardley has given us no trouble whatsoever since he's been our guest.'

'Will do.'

'Theodor Morell ... the name of Hitler's personal quack as I recall.'

'That's right.'

'So, is it he?'

'Definitely not. Morell was grossly fat – several times the size of this chap by all accounts. Besides, he's dead.'

'So is Hitler.'

'It's as good a cover name as any. I don't think we can read a great deal into it.'

Hewson nodded and threw the report onto his desk dismissively. 'That's all!'

'Yes, sir,' said Perriam as he stood up. By the time he had reached the door, Hewson was tapping away on the heating pipe to convene his next meeting.

Chapter 14

Tuesday 3rd July

Rowena hadn't seen Mr Morell for more than a week. As she worked in her garden, she occasionally glanced in the direction of the side gate, hoping to see him standing there; but there was neither sight nor sound of him. It was on the following Tuesday that he eventually showed himself again.

'Good afternoon, Frau Furse.'

'Mr Morell, how nice to see you. I thought perhaps you might have moved on.'

'Not yet. There have been complications.'

'Either that or I thought you might have been grounded by your friend Mr Yardley.'

'What is grounded?'

'Like a plane, ha ha! Not allowed out … *Ausgangsverbot*. I thought you might have got into trouble after I dropped you back home last week. Mr Yardley looked peeved.'

'There was a lively discussion. I explained I have made some new friends here in Reigate in his absence, that I have told them who I am, and naturally they don't believe a word of it and think I am insane. Now *he* thinks I am insane too … and not for the first time in our association. We understand each other and all is well. Nevertheless, I thought it prudent to keep myself to myself for a while.'

'Well it's good to see you. Tea?'

'With cake?'

'But of course.'

As they sat together on the terrace, Rowena said: 'So what have you been doing with yourself?'

'I have been reading, and also listening to some music, and writing …'

'How interesting. What are you writing, may I ask?'

'My life story – my autobiography.'

'I would very much like to read it one day.'

'Perhaps you will, one day.'

'Mr Morell, may I ask you a question and if so can I ask for an honest answer?'

'Of course.'

'Joking aside … who are you, really?'

'My name is Morell.'

'And what is your first name?'

'Theodor.'

'So, you are not Adolf Hitler.'

'No.'

Rowena picked up a book from the table in from of her and opened it where a bookmark had been inserted. 'Not Professor Theodor Morell by any chance – Adolf Hitler's private physician?'

'That is possible.'

'In which case, I've been reading about you.'

'Which book is that?'

'It's called *The Last Days of Hitler,* by H.R. Trevor-Roper. It belongs to Howard.'

'I have read it. Full of inaccuracies. I think most people he interviewed told him what he wanted to hear rather than the truth. He believed it all. Very amusing in places.'

'If you're Theodor Morell, then Trevor-Roper isn't very complimentary about you. She skimmed down the page. '*A quack ... a gross but deflated old man, of cringing manners, inarticulate speech, and the hygiene habits of a pig.* That doesn't sound like you.'

'As I said, full of inaccuracies.'

She pointed to a place on the page. 'Apparently, you died in May 1948. That seems to be clearly documented.'

He nodded. 'That cannot be denied.'

'So, you're not Theodor Morell.'

'That's the name you will see on my passport.'

'But you're really Adolf Hitler.'

'Dear Frau Furse!' exclaimed Morell, slipping into German. 'What does it matter! I am Morell, I am Hitler – both dead according to the history books. I'm a high-ranking member of the National Socialist party who escaped capture and trial after the war and have been leading a quiet life ever since. I am an insane fantasist who likes to believe he has been someone of note towards the end of his life. I'm a music lover, an animal lover, an art lover – we haven't talked much about art yet, we should do. An old man who loves cake and the company of likeminded people. Does it matter who I am?'

'It matters to me to be told the truth.'

'You want the truth? All right then, I am Adolf Hitler.'

'Oh, you're impossible!'

Morell took off his spectacles and rubbed the bridge of his nose. 'You are not the first person to say so.'

As if in protest, Rowena continued speaking in English. 'Let's talk about something else.'

Morell sat quietly for a while, as if choosing a different topic. 'Tell me about the carnival – I have been reading about it in the local newspaper. It takes place this coming weekend I believe. How are your preparations coming along with that dreadful Kitchen woman?'

'She is not dreadful at all, she's a very nice person,' said Rowena indignantly. 'If anyone is dreadful it's Beth Angel who's been trying to poke her nose in at every turn. Nevertheless, I have it all planned and it's going well. They want garlands of flowers everywhere. I'll be working all Saturday morning getting it ready. You will come and watch the procession, won't you? It starts at three in the afternoon in Earlswood, the other side of Redhill, and should reach Reigate about an hour or so later. I shall be riding on the float.'

'Excuse me, what is a float?'

'Oh, I'm sorry, it's a lorry or a van that takes part in the carnival procession, decorated in some way, and with a theme of some kind. The W.I.'s theme this year is *Nature's Bounty* so we'll be surrounded by fruit and veg all the way – and flowers of course.'

'I think this needs to be seen to be believed.'

'You'll come? Wonderful! Perhaps I can arrange for Erika to pick you up.'

'That would be a treat. How is she?'

'Not bad, spending most of her time fending off Colonel Maxwell. I think she thinks he's about to propose marriage.'

'And what will the answer be?'

'A resounding no, there's no doubt about that. She doesn't really care for him and, frankly, she's using him. I've given her a good ticking off for playing with his emotions … using him to take her out for dinner and up to town for shows. Poor thing, he's going to be heartbroken when he finds out. He knows about you, by the way, and is convinced you're a threat of some kind.'

'I hope he does not appear at my door with *Rache* in mind. He'll encounter more than he bargained for if he does.'

'*Rache* … retribution? I don't think it'll come to that.'

'Does he know my true identity?'

'Well if he does I wish he'd let me know because I haven't a clue! I don't think so, no.'

'Is it wise for me to be seen with Frau von Tirpitz at the carnival, under the circumstances?'

'Why not? It will do old Maxwell good to see Erika has other men in her life. He might go a little purple in the face but that's his look out.'

Mr Morell nodded his approval. 'How will we plan this – will you talk to Erika? I have no way of contacting her.'

'Leave it with me.'

'I hope she collects me in that impressive car I saw parked at the end of her garden. An Alvis TB21 I think.'

'I'm sure she will. Do you like cars?'

'Very much, I have owned some beautiful motors in my time. All German.'

'Well the Alvis is a British car of course.'

'Built in Coventry.'

'So I believe.' Rowena hesitated. 'Coventry, hmm … let's not go down that road.'

There came a rattling at the side gate.

'Ooh eeh! Rowena, are you there?'

'Talk of the devil. Erika my dear, do come through! Look who's here. We were just talking about you. Your ears must have been burning.'

Erika appeared with Mr Chips in tow. 'Mr Morell, how do you do? If I'd known you were here, I'd have come sooner. I've just had the most awkward lunch with Colonel bloody Maxwell. Couldn't wait to get away. That man is driving me absolutely bonkers.'

'Bonkers?'

'Mad, crazy. He simply has to go. He just tried to propose to me – on the top of Reigate Hill, down on one knee, the whole business! He looked so ridiculous down there, looking up at me like a little puppy dog, I could barely stop myself from giggling.'

'I presume you said no.'

'Of course I did.'

'Not good.' Rowena frowned. 'Erika, you know my feelings about this. You really have got to stop playing him along. Tea?'

'Got any gin?'

'Tea only I'm afraid.'

'If one must. You're absolutely right, Row, I must break away from him. Now I see clearly what has to be done. You said you were talking about me. All nice things I assume?'

'We were talking about the carnival. Mr Morell would like to see the procession and I said I'd ask if you wouldn't mind taking him on Saturday.'

'I'd be thrilled. Good excuse to avoid Maxwell. Shall I come and pick you up, Mr M?'

Morell smiled appreciatively. 'If you would not mind. Outside Frau Furse's house would be preferred.'

'What time does it start, Row?'

'The procession leaves Earlswood at three, then wends its way up the Brighton Road into Redhill, left into Station Road, up to Reffel's Bridge, then Shaw's Corner, along Blackborough Road and eventually into Reigate – ending up on the heath where the floats are to be judged by the mayor. The whole thing stops for a breather somewhere along the way, so if you want to catch it in the centre of Reigate I'd say four-thirty would be about right.'

'Shall I pick you up at one, Mr Morell? We can have a spot of lunch at The Dinner Gong and still have plenty of time to spare.'

'Thank you, I would like that very much. I shall be ready.'

135

'Then,' added Rowena, 'in the evening there's a funfair on the heath.'

Erika grimaced. 'Perhaps we can give that a miss, maybe have a spot of dinner instead – if you can stand the excitement of two meals with me in one day, Mr Morell.'

'I would like to try.'

'That's settled. Meanwhile I need to sort out Colonel bloody Maxwell.'

'And how do you intend doing that?' asked Rowena.

'Well, I suppose there is the straightforward way – refuse his proposal and tell him I don't want to see him anymore. We're not compatible and there's simply no future in it.'

'Sounds like a good plan.'

'Or there's a less direct way.'

'And that is …?'

'Let him think he's got competition. He gets hugely jealous if another man even looks at me. If he believes I'm seeing someone else, he'll probably combust spontaneously.'

Rowena shook her head. 'I prefer the first option.'

Erika took a sip of tea and grimaced. 'I'm a bit of a coward when it comes to things like this I'm afraid. What do you advise, Mr M?'

Morell pursed his lips. 'I am not one to offer advice on such matters. Always in my life I have tried to go with my instincts. Perhaps you should do the same.'

'Thank you, I might just do as you say. Now come on, Row darling, this tea is all very well, but it tastes like horse piss. Where's the gin?'

Chapter 15

Saturday 7th July

The weather on the day of the carnival was dull and overcast, but dry. When Erika approached the house in Alders Road in the Alvis, Mr Morell was waiting for her. He climbed into the passenger seat and she reversed around the corner and pulled away at speed. Mr Morell felt himself being pressed back into his seat and he grabbed his hat so as not to lose it in the slipstream.

'You don't mind being driven fast I hope?' said Erika brightly. 'I only do fast.'

'Oh no, fast is good. I love being driven at speed.'

'In that case let's whizz up to the top of Reigate Hill and back – we're in good time. You can get up a bloody good head of speed on the way down.'

At Reigate station, she turned right and accelerated up the hill, chatting freely, looking across at her passenger more often than keeping her eyes on the road ahead, which did not seem to worry Mr Morell.

'How is your complicated love life since we last spoke, Frau von Tirpitz?' he asked.

'Well I've had a talk with Maxwell, said thanks but no thanks to his proposal of marriage and that I want some time to myself. He didn't like it one bit, seems to think he owns me and

137

has some divine right over me. He is such a pompous old windbag. Rowena is right of course, I've only myself to blame for getting mixed up with him in the first place, and for all the wrong reasons.'

'Is he in love with you?'

'He believes he is but he isn't really. He's attracted to me and wants to own me – add me to his collection of trophies. Possession is the key with him. He doesn't know what love is. That poor wife of his must have had the patience of Job when she was alive.'

'When did she die?'

'About ten years ago. He's very well off and has a lovely house, quite near here on the hill in fact.' She pointed a finger vaguely in the direction ahead of them. 'I say, changing the subject – though not entirely as Maxwell told me this – you see that pub on the left, The Yew Tree?'

'I see it.'

'Well behind it are some houses and apparently during the war one of them was Monty's headquarters. You know, General Montgomery of Alamein.'

'Oh … him.'

'Yes, quite. 21st Army Group I think Maxwell said, and he would know. Apparently, there's a veritable rabbit warren of caves and passageways dug into the hillside beyond. Built by Welsh miners during the war, by all accounts.'

'Montgomery accepted the unconditional surrender of German forces on Lüneburg Heath, just days after my supposed death. I never forgave Dönitz for agreeing to that, though he had the good sense not to do it in person. It was beneath him to negotiate with a mere Field Marshal.'

'There really was no choice by then, surely. It was all over. Germany had no fight left.'

138

'Nonsense!' said Morell sharply. 'We should have gone on fighting until the tide turned. I will not accept …'

'Now now,' interrupted Erika. 'You're being Adolf again. So why then did you flee? Wasn't that the action of a defeated man, a leader who had led his people and his country down a one-way road to disaster?'

Morell was looking flushed and angry and opened his mouth to reply. But Erika cut him off. 'Don't answer that, no doubt you had your reasons. Look, this is the top of the hill. A quick turnaround and … here we go. Tally-ho!'

Erika pressed her foot firmly down on the accelerator and away they hurtled down the hill, picking up speed at an alarming rate. Mr Morell's anger dissipated almost instantly; he pressed his hat onto his head with one hand and waved his stick in the air with the other. A grin lit up his face and his eyes shone. In just a few moments The Yew Tree passed by in a blur and before he knew it they were at the bottom of the hill, bouncing over the level crossing and slowing down as they approached the tunnel leading into the town.

'Good?' said Erika, beaming with pleasure.

'Yes good. Very good!'

'Now let's eat and drink and be merry. If time allows after lunch let's go up the hill again. I drive even faster with gin inside me.'

A quarter of an hour later they were sitting in The Dinner Gong. Erika had reserved a table, which was just as well as it was extraordinarily busy. The High Street was adorned with buntings and many of the shops had special window displays. They were on their dessert (bread and butter pudding) and Erika on her third G & T when they heard heavy footsteps on the stairs from the street. They broke their conversation to look across. Rowena's face appeared at the bottom, scouring the dining room anxiously until she saw them.

'Thank goodness! My dears, I am so glad I caught you. We need you. The carnival needs you!'

'What on earth is the matter? said Erika, gesturing for Rowena to take a seat next to her at the table.

'Yes, what is wrong?' asked Morell.

'Well,' began Rowena, her voice breathless and at its dramatic best. 'There's been a bit of an accident, or rather an altercation. I've been helping put the carnival procession together all morning over at Earlswood – finishing off the W.I. display and sorting out every other last minute detail. I've been up to my eyes in flowers, fruit and veg. I must say it's looking rather splendid, even though I say it myself.' She paused for breath. 'Anyway, the float in front of us belongs to The British Legion. Their theme is *Great Leaders of Our Time*, and they have ex-servicemen dressed up as Lloyd George, Winston Churchill, Eisenhower, Montgomery. Even General de Gaulle … not quite sure how he qualifies, ha ha! Oh, and Winston has Clemmie with him. They have a lot of people squeezed into a small area on the back of their lorry, all with props and barely any room to move – in fact too many to be honest. Well, to cut a long story short, when they all climbed on together to arrange where they'd be positioned, tempers started to fray. I could see it all from where I was situated behind, on the W.I. float.'

'What happened? asked Erika.

'Not quite sure how it began but there was some obvious jockeying for the best spots and a lot of grumbling and moaning going on. Then it would appear that General de Gaulle brushed against Monty and knocked his beret askew. Monty said something in response – I think he accused him of doing it deliberately – and de Gaulle didn't take kindly to that in the slightest.'

Mr Morell nodded in understanding. 'I believe De Gaulle can be touchy at the best of times.'

'It's the Gallic temperament. Well, to everyone's surprise de Gaulle quite unexpectedly took a swing at Monty, a real haymaker. But Monty saw it coming, ducked and instead, de Gaulle caught Mrs Churchill smack on the nose!'

'Oh my Lord!'

'There was blood everywhere. Winston was furious.'

'I can imagine.'

'He was sitting at an easel, pretending to paint. He stood up, leaned over to take a swipe at de Gaulle, missed him entirely and almost flattened Lloyd George.'

'Good heavens. What happened next?'

'Winston swung his arm back to try for another punch, lost his balance and toppled backwards off the side of the lorry. What a kerfuffle! The only one who got off lightly was Eisenhower.'

'Was Winston all right?'

'Fortunately he landed on the grass verge. No serious injury, but he was shaken up and, more to the point, flatly refused to get back on the float – and I quote – "with that bloody Frog".'

'Jesus,' said Erika. 'You couldn't make this up!'

'Meanwhile Clemmie has been whisked off to hospital with a suspected broken nose.'

'Did you follow all that, Mr Morell?'

'I did,' he said, sniggering with his head bowed low. 'So much for post-war entente amongst the victorious Allies.'

Rowena leaned forward, looking serious, as if she had come to the crux of the matter. 'Which means the British Legion are two down. They're very badly organised and have no one lined up in reserve. So, I said I knew a couple of people who would help in their hour of need, and dashed over here.'

'You don't mean us, surely!' gasped Erika.

'I do indeed. You'll be good sports won't you, and help them out, in their hour of need?'

'But I don't look anything like Clemmie ... and Mr Morell looks even less like Winston!'

'Nonsense, tie your hair back, wrap a scarf around your neck, pop a hat on, smile a lot, and you'll do. They have all the props. Besides, it's Winston everyone will be looking at. Get Mr Morell here into a siren suite, pad him out a bit – quite a bit actually – pop a cigar in his mouth, have him give the Victory sign once in a while, and no one will tell him from the real thing.'

'I don't think so,' said Erika.

'Oh, come on, chaps, do lend a hand. What about the Dunkirk spirit ...'

'That means nothing to me,' said Morell flatly.

'They'd be so grateful – and so would I. Finish your lunch quickly, settle the bill and hurry yourselves over to Earlswood Road. Erika, you know where that is don't you – just off the Brighton Road?'

'I know.'

'It's ...' she looked at her watch, 'ten past two now. The procession leaves at three. You can just make it.'

'What do you think, Mr M?' said Erika. 'Shall we give it a whirl? Could be fun.'

'Frau Furse, Frau von Tirpitz, are you seriously expecting *me*, of all people, to parade on the back of a lorry through Redhill and Reigate, in front of hundreds, possibly thousands of people, dressed up as Winston Churchill?'

'Is that a problem?'

'Is that a problem!'

'Oh, come on, Adolf, if that's who you really are,' gushed Rowena. 'If you're going to play games with us then we can do the same. I'm off, got to get back. I expect to see you both in

142

Earlswood in half an hour – I won't take no for an answer. We're about halfway along the procession. Look out for the fruit and veg. If you see a float with a Red Cross pub sign and a young girl sitting in the stocks, you've overshot – that's St Philip's Youth Club doing *Olde Reigate Towne*. They're immediately behind us. Don't let me down.'

Erika and Mr Morell sat in silence; she looking across at him, he avoiding eye contact. 'I don't think we have any choice. I wouldn't want to let Rowena down, and I'm sure you wouldn't either.'

Mr Morell said nothing and sat completely still, staring into space.

'Mr Morell?'

There was no reaction.

'Right, one more quick gin and let's be off.' She waved for attention and the head waitress hurried over. 'Suki darling, can you do a Gin and IT for me? You can? Make it a large one, would you?'

Mr Morell stirred. 'What is that … a Gin and IT?'

'Gin with sweet vermouth and bitters. It's a nice drink, has a bit of an edge.'

'Kindly order two.'

Chapter 16

The carnival procession – consisting of twenty-three floats of varying shapes and sizes from large flat-backed lorries to the small delivery vans of local tradesmen – set off from Earlswood Road on schedule at precisely 3 p.m., snaked its way at walking speed onto the Brighton Road and trundled towards the centre of Redhill. Crowds of people lined the pavements, waving and cheering and throwing coins into buckets held out by those on the floats, most of whom were in costume of one sort or another.

To Rowena's huge delight, and relief, from her position on the W.I. float behind, she could see Mr and Mrs Winston Churchill together on the lorry ahead, squashed in between General Dwight D. Eisenhower and Field Marshall Bernard Law Montgomery of Alamein, as if protected from the adversary standing next to them – 'that bloody Frog' General Charles de Gaulle. She had been concerned about Mr Morell when they first arrived; his breath smelled distinctly of alcohol. So did Erika's, but that wasn't out of the ordinary. Rowena could have sworn he was teetotal … she distinctly remembered him refusing alcoholic drinks on every occasion, apart from that one time at Erika's when he had first claimed to be Hitler. He'd struggled to climb up onto the lorry, but once settled on a chair behind the easel with Erika next to him, all seemed well. He was generously padded out with a corset and several pullovers under the siren suit and as a result was sweating profusely, and none too fragrant. He wore his own homburg which was not dissimilar to one of Churchill's own preferred headwear: the bowker. He sat hunched forward, a paintbrush in his hand and an oversize unlit Cuban cigar clamped in the corner of his mouth; every now and again he took it out to spit away a flake of tobacco leaf, a look of disgust on his face. His brow was furrowed and his face pinched into a frown that could have been interpreted equally as deep concentration or intense irritation.

Once they were settled, Erika became aware that Lloyd George, in the far corner of the float, was leering at her and winking suggestively. She smiled back briefly out of politeness. His face was not unpleasant, and the eyes had an air of familiarity about them.

'Afternoon, Mrs von T,' he called. The voice was immediately recognisable.

'F for Freddie! I didn't recognise you with the wig, and behind that awful stick-on moustache.'

'It tickles,' he said, winking at her again.

She raised her eyebrows knowingly. 'I can imagine. 'Promise never to wear it when doing odd jobs for me.'

'I promise.' Lloyd George gestured towards Winston Churchill. 'Is that by any chance ...?'

'Bloody Maxwell? No, it bloody is not.'

'Just wondered. Let me know when you've got any more jobs need finishing off.'

'I will indeed,' said Erika, poker faced. 'You did splendidly last time.'

Mr Morell remarked: 'F for Freddie. That is an unusual way to address someone.'

'A private joke,' Erika explained.

'I met Lloyd George once ... the real one. He came to visit me at Berchtesgaden in the summer of thirty-six. I liked him. He was very impressed with me by all accounts and afterwards wrote an article describing me as a born leader with a dynamic personality. One of Britain's more perceptive statesman I think.'

Erika determined to change the subject. She watched as he wet his brush and applied watercolours to the blank paper on the easel. As there was no one else involved in their conversation, they began speaking German.

'What are you painting, Mr M?'

'The Berghof. Where Lloyd George came to see me. My home in Berchstesgaden.'

'You mean Hitler's home.'

'As you wish.'

'How funny, here you are, a man purporting to be Adolf Hitler now masquerading as his arch-enemy.'

'The irony of the situation is not lost on me, I assure you. However, Churchill was not the arch-enemy of the Reich. That was Stalin.'

Erika pointed at the easel. 'Do you think it wise to be painting Hitler's home, when you're dressed up as Winston Churchill? You ought to be painting his home – Chartwell.'

'I do not know what his home looks like.'

'It's beautiful, and not far from here, near Westerham.'

'I can only paint what I know. To be honest, painting anything when we are moving like this is proving difficult. Perhaps I should try something abstract.'

The other characters on the float were subdued, still smouldering after the earlier fracas. They appeared puzzled by the replacement Churchills, even more so when they began speaking German with each other. But they seemed to accept it and concentrated on the crowds, encouraging them to throw money into their buckets. They were passing through the centre of Redhill.

Erika waved at the crowds and smiled in all directions. 'Come on, Winston,' she said, 'show them your Victory sign.'

Randomly, Morell stuck two fingers up, then returned to his painting.

Erika took out a cigarette and lit it. 'I really fancy another gin,' she said, with genuine longing in her voice.

'I would like to join you.'

She rummaged in her handbag and pulled out a silver flask. 'Here, take a swig of this.'

Morell did as he was told, coughed and wiped his lips on his sleeve. 'Frau von Tirpitz, you are very resourceful.'

Erika drained what was left and grinned. 'I have my moments. I hope you're not too sloshed. We don't want you announcing to the word that you're Adolf Hitler again. Today you are Winston Churchill, and don't forget it.'

'I will try.'

Tell me, do you like modern art, Mr M?'

'I detest it. Some self-proclaimed artists appear to see things other than as they are and use it as an excuse to produce talentless, degenerate rubbish. There are men, it would seem, who feel they should paint meadows blue, the heavens green and the clouds sulphur-yellow. They are charlatans.'

'What about the Impressionists – Monet, Renoir, Pissarro – all wonderful painters?'

'Charlatans, as are *all* Impressionists, Expressionists, Surrealists. There isn't a talent amongst them.'

'What about Picasso – a genius surely.'

'The greatest charlatan of them all!'

'I disagree,' said Erika, sounding irritated. 'You know, I had a huge admiration for what the *Führer* did for Germany in the thirties – he achieved so much and lifted the country and its people out of the mire and put them back on track. But it was his excesses, his extreme opinions about many things that were his downfall. Everything was black and white. *Either agree with me or you are my enemy.* So counterproductive, so self-destructive. Your views about art remind me of that. Dogmatic, blinkered ... and more often wrong than right.'

'And you, I suppose, are not being dogmatic.'

'By his standards certainly not, I'm merely making an observation. I was a great admirer, not so much at first, when he became Chancellor in thirty-three – I hadn't really taken him seriously until then. I never imagined he would achieve power, like many others I knew. But over the ensuing years as he consolidated his position and turned Germany around, I was impressed. A man of cast iron commitment and belief. A truly impassioned leader. Karl and I disagreed about much at that time. He saw what was going on behind the scenes as evil – the violence, the corruption, the anti-Semitism – whereas I felt they were sacrifices worth making for the common good. Germany was really going somewhere.'

'We are in agreement in that respect.'

'He had such charisma. Meeting him briefly at that dinner in Berlin had a profound effect upon me. Extraordinary really. He was not a physically attractive man, far from his own Aryan model of perfection. His voice was coarse, and his grammar often poor, yet he was an inspirational orator. He gave a speech after dinner that was extraordinary. I was mesmerised. He won people's hearts and was adored by men and women alike. I read somewhere that women used to write to him offering to get pregnant by him.'

'They did, frequently. But that idea did not appeal.' Morell dabbed at his picture. 'And yet you abandoned the Fatherland and came to England.'

'It was Karl's wish,' said Erika wistfully. 'If the choice had been mine, I would have stayed.'

'But you left despite the charisma of your *Führer*.'

'Ah yes, his charisma was extraordinary. And you know, Mr Morell, without any disrespect intended, that's why, despite everything you say and all this pretence, I don't believe you could be him. You don't have his charisma.'

'Perhaps I did once but have since lost it.'

'I don't think that is possible.'

'Things change. *The bad jokes of fortune. Village pierrots yesterday, arbiters of life and death today, tomorrow cleaners of the public latrines.*'

'Who said that?'

'I can't remember, but there is truth in those words.'

They had reached the war memorial at Shaw's Corner. Mr Morell thought he recognised it; in fact, throughout his conversation with Erika about art the surroundings they passed had seemed familiar. Then he remembered. Not so long ago he'd ridden a stolen police bike along the same route, and stopped at the war memorial for breath.

The procession forked left and made its way along Blackborough Road, a long, fairly straight approach into Reigate. They hadn't progressed far when Erika suddenly became tense and grabbed Morell's shoulder, squeezing it hard. 'Oh, fucking hell!'

'What is the matter?'

'Down there. Look, you see that man on the pavement ahead of us, the one with the moustache and who looks as if he's standing to attention with a ramrod up his arse.'

Morell looked. 'Maxwell?'

'Colonel Peregrine bloody Maxwell.'

'Perhaps he will not recognise you.'

'I don't care if he does. I'm sick to death of him. It's no coincidence. How the hell did he know I'd be in the procession. Do me a favour, Winston, would you kindly give him the V sign?'

As the float drew level, Mr Morell leaned forward and pointedly stuck two fingers up at the man on the pavement. It was not the Victory sign. The man stared back at him, his face reddening. Then he looked across towards Mrs Churchill and his face brightened.

'I say, Erika, is that you?'

'My name is Clementine Churchill,' she called. 'Friends and family call me Clemmie.'

'It is you! What the blazes are you doing up there? I didn't know you had connections with the British Legion.'

'I don't. I'm up here to be with the man I love … the man who saved this country from the tyranny of the Nazi hoards.' She gave Winston's shoulder another squeeze, with affection this time.

'You deceitful, treacherous woman,' hissed Morell.

'I say, who's that with you? Looks nothing like Churchill. He certainly doesn't know how to do the Victory sign.'

'I know exactly how,' said Mr Morell.

'Erika, was he speaking German to you just then?'

'That's right, Winston is bilingual, didn't you know?'

'No, he bloody well is not. He can't speak a word of Kraut. He can't even say Nazi properly. He says "Narzee".'

Morell nodded in agreement. 'Even I knew that.'

Maxwell was walking along the pavement, keeping pace with the float. 'Listen Erika, I need to talk to you.'

'Not now, some other time, can't you see I'm busy?'

'It can't wait. Will you come down off that lorry?'

'No, I will not.'

'In that case I'm coming up.'

'Don't be ridiculous!'

Colonel Maxwell marched towards the back of the lorry and grabbed hold of the tailgate, which had been left down and stuck out horizontally to allow extra space. He pulled himself

150

up until he was lying flat on the wooden floor, then twisted sideways and hoisted his legs on board. Squeezing through the cream of twentieth century wartime leaders proved a struggle. He first bumped up against Lloyd George, who brushed him aside and turned to Mrs Churchill with a questioning look.

'Yes,' said Erika. 'This time it is.'

Maxwell then barrelled into General de Gaulle.

'What yer doin', yer bleedin' tosser!' exclaimed de Gaulle who, surprisingly, had a strong South London accent. 'Clear art of it.'

He next backed into General Eisenhower who, equally surprisingly, was Scottish. 'Watch yer step there, wee laddie.'

And so into Field Marshal Montgomery of Alamein, who sounded just like Monty. 'I say, do mind where you're stepping, will you, there's a good fellow?'

He found his way to the Churchills. Erika was very angry.

'For God's sake, Maxwell, what *are* you playing at? Get off this float at once.'

'Yeh, 'op it,' called out de Gaulle. 'There's no room up 'ere for no more and you ain't welcome.'

Maxwell glared at him. 'What rank were you when you were in the forces?'

'Sergeant.'

'Well I'm a colonel. I outrank you.'

'Not today you don't. Today I'm a general. Now scarper.'

Maxwell ignored him and turned his attention to Erika. 'Can we please get off this contraption and go somewhere and talk? I want you to reconsider my offer.'

'There's nothing to talk about, I've told you how I feel, and no I can't just walk away and abandon everyone here.'

'Of course you can. This dressing up is all nonsense – stupid amateurish undignified tomfoolery.'

151

'Oi!' piped in Eisenhower. 'You haired the lassie, on yer bike.'

'Do the honourable thing, there's a good fellow, would you?' added Monty.

Winston Churchill felt duty bound to comment, to Erika, in German. 'Your would-be spouse is not endearing himself with the others, Frau von Tirpitz. He is an idiot.'

Maxwell bristled with indignation. 'Did he just say *Dummkopf*? That means idiot. Are you talking about me?'

'Yes, we're talking about you, Maxwell,' said Erika. 'Now get off this float before someone pushes you off.'

'I'll do it gladly,' said Eisenhower.

'If not I bleedin' will,' said de Gaulle.

'Include me, if there's going to be fisticuffs,' said Monty.

'Idiot,' said Churchill in German.

'He called me *Dummkopf* again!' whined Maxwell.

Afterwards, when explaining themselves to the police, no one would admit to throwing the first punch: Colonel Maxwell said it was de Gaulle; Eisenhower thought it was Churchill; Churchill swore it was Monty. Lloyd George, who appeared to back away from the fray but had in fact landed a couple of effective rabbit punches, said nothing. There was an uncorroborated report from a spectator that at one stage Winston Churchill had shouted out that he was the *Führer*.

On the Women's Institute lorry behind, Rowena stared in horror as the brawl developed.

'Oh my Lord,' she sighed. 'They're at it again.'

Chapter 17

As chance would have it, the fight kicked off just as the procession was reaching its designated resting point at the junction with Crakell Road. The organisers managed to prise the great leaders apart and the police were called. PCs Bent and Tobin arrived soon afterwards and Inspector Thorne a while later. There were cuts and bruises but no bones broken; Inspector Thorpe cautioned them all and gave an assurance that if there was any recurrence of this unacceptable behaviour in public, arrests would be made. Breach of the peace.

PC Bent took down the names and addresses of those involved. He hesitated in front of Winston Churchill.

'Do I know you?' he asked.

'I should certainly hope so, young man. I was your prime minister during the war. I led the nation in its fight against Narzee oppression.'

Bent consulted his notebook. 'I mean you, err, Mr Morell, not the character you are portraying in the carnival procession. Haven't I seen you somewhere before?'

'That is possible as I live in Reigate.'

'Hmm, thank you, sir. I'm sure I recognise you from somewhere. It'll come to me.'

The organisers discussed whether or not to exclude the British Legion float but agreed to let it stay in the procession, which it did, minus General de Gaulle and Colonel Maxwell – the former nursing a badly dented sense of pride and the latter clutching a painful groin. No one owned up to the below-the-belt assault on Maxwell; however, as she stood by her husband's side, Mrs Churchill wore an enigmatic expression that may have implied inner contentment at a job well done.

The atmosphere on the float was subdued again as they turned into Bell Street and round into the High Street.

'Blimey, cheer up, Winston, the war's over!' yelled a boy of about twelve wearing a pair of ill-fitting trousers and a shabby pullover. ''Ere mum, he don't look nothing like Churchill.'

Mr Morell gave him the V sign.

'Same to you with brass knobs on!' yelled the boy.

Ahead of them in the crowd, Erika noticed Ruth Kitchen standing with her husband and son. They were waving enthusiastically at the floats as they passed by. As the British Legion lorry drew level with them, Ruth recognised Erika.

'Splendid!' she called. 'You look just like Mrs Churchill, Erika. Who's that as Winston?'

'It's the real thing,' she called back, grinning impishly.

Mr Morell recognised the woman on the pavement. '*Gott im Himmel*,' he groaned. 'It's that Kitchen woman!' He started to raise his arm in her direction, two fingers at the ready, but Erika pushed it firmly down again.

'Tempting I'm sure, Mr M,' she said. 'But we'll resist this one I think, for all our sakes.' She saw another woman with a young child, little more than two years old, smiling and waving at her. 'There's Pamela Day … and young Jennifer.' She waved back enthusiastically.

'Who?'

'Friends of mine.'

'Shall I salute them?'

154

'Absolutely not. A lovely family … I know her uncle, Arthur. He lives in Margery Lane and keeps goats.'

'In which case, they are exempt.'

At Reigate Heath, the floats pulled onto the grass adjacent to the funfair stalls where the mayor wandered from one to the other, inspecting them with a critical eye and making comments to a young girl who trotted in his wake, scribbling notes on a clipboard. After much deliberation, arms folded and a thumb and forefinger rubbing his chin, he strode up to the St Philip's Youth Club float and handed them a Second Prize rosette, then across to the Women's Institute and presented First Class to Rowena who blushed profusely at the ensuing round of applause. She came over to join the others.

'Well done, Row, and justly deserved,' said Erika, removing her hat and headscarf. 'What now? I've had enough of being Mrs Churchill and I'm sure the appeal of being Winston will have worn off by now. Mr M, you must be baking hot inside that siren suit.'

Mr Morell nodded. 'The appeal was never there. I only did this to please Frau Furse … and yourself.' He peeled down the top of the siren suit, pulled off the corset and jumpers and threw them onto the back of the lorry. Rowena and Erika took a pace back as a wave of body odour hit them.

'Well,' said Rowena, 'Howie will be here soon to drive you back to Earlswood, so you can collect your car. While we're waiting shall we have a look around the fair?'

'All right,' said Erika grumpily. 'But I detest the bloody things so I hope he won't be long.'

They meandered around the attractions, stopping to watch at the coconut shy, the quoits, the rifle range, the helter skelter and a rather tame carousel. It was early evening. Although still light, the sun was way past its zenith and there was a hint of twilight in the air. In the corner of the heath was a colourful

155

gypsy caravan next to which stood a crudely-written sign resting on what appeared to be an artist's easel.

QUEEN ESMERELDA
GENUINE ROMANY FORTUNE TELLER
SPECIALIST IN PALMISTRY
YOUR FUTURE IS IN YOUR HAND'S
CROSS MY PALM WITH SILVER

Erika took Morell's arm. 'Do you fancy having your fortune told, Mr M? I'd be fascinated to know what lies ahead for you, and also what lurks in your mysterious past.'

'No thank you, I do not care for gypsies.'

Rowena was peering at the sign. 'They didn't fare any better than the Jews under the Third Reich I believe.'

'With good reason,' said Morell. 'They are an inferior breed of human being.'

'Be that as it may,' said Erika, 'Queen Esmerelda is no doubt a complete fraud without a drop of Romany blood. Probably born in Peckham or some such place.'

As if on cue, a figure appeared in the entrance to the caravan, a stout woman wearing a flowing patterned skirt, a white blouse and dark lace head scarf. She beckoned towards them, grinning broadly to reveal rotten teeth, nodding her head encouragingly for them to come inside.

'Come on, Mr M, look here's half a crown, cross her palm with that and I'll accompany you.'

'I really do not want to do this. It is unwise.'

Erika leaned forwards and kissed him firmly on the cheek, leaving a bright red lipstick stain behind. 'For me?'

Morell visibly melted. 'I am a weak old man at the mercy of irresistible younger women,' he muttered and climbed gingerly up the few steps into the caravan, Erika close behind him. As she closed the door, she turned and winked mischievously.

Rowena found herself alone. To kill time, she wandered along the edge of the heath which was skirted on different sides by the road towards Dorking, a row of cottages and some dense woodland. The caravan backed on to the woodland and she soon noticed a path leading through some low bushes into the trees. She headed down it with no real purpose or intent. Presently the path narrowed and the trees became thicker and were enveloped by bushes and shrubs. It was darker, too, which was a little unsettling, so she turned around to retrace her steps.

As she did, she heard a rustling noise somewhere to her left. At first she thought it might be an animal, a rabbit perhaps, or even a fox. She stood still and listened. To her surprise, instead of further evidence of natural wildlife, she heard the gentle gasping of a young female voice.

'Oh Bishop!'

The expression on Rowena's face, had anyone been present to see, was one of wide-eyed astonishment. To her knowledge there was only one 'Bishop' in the Reigate area, and he was not ordained; nor did she approve of the notion of fake clergy enticing sweet, innocent young girls into woodland, which she assumed was the case.

'Good evening, Jane,' she called, addressing the bushes in a firm and commanding tone.

The rustling stopped. There was absolute silence for a few moments.

'Evening, ma'am,' came a serene, unflustered reply.

'Everything all right in there?'

'Yes thanks … never been better.'

Rowena felt a pang of disappointment, anguish even, and a hint of disgust. She had rather hoped she might be about to save a young thing from what she had been brought up to regard as

157

a fate worse than death. She couldn't think of anything to say under the circumstances and so tramped her way back along the path.

In the bushes, there was another silence until the sound of footsteps had died away.

'Who was that?' whispered the Bishop.

'Dunno,' whispered Jane in reply. 'Sounded a bit like Mrs Furse, from church, but I couldn't be certain. Anyway, she's gone now … you can carry on.'

'Are you sure?'

'Oh yes, I'm sure.'

'I like it when you call me Bishop. Especially when we're, you know …'

'Oh Bishop!'

Back on the heath, almost the first person Rowena saw amongst the crowds was her husband. He hurried across to her. 'Hello Flossie old girl, how's it all going?'

'Swimmingly well, Howie, our float was awarded first prize and everything has been wonderful – apart from some fisticuffs on the float next to us. I'll explain while we wait for our mysterious neighbour to have his fortune told. He's in there right now with Erika for moral support.'

'You mean Morell support?'

'Ha ha, very good!'

Rowena began narrating her tale of anguish on the British Legion float and had just reached the point where Colonel Maxwell climbed on board and tempers frayed for the second time that afternoon when she was interrupted by a shrill voice from inside the gipsy caravan. The door burst open and Queen Esmerelda could be heard screeching loudly.

'Get out, get out! You're evil – pure evil! Never darken my doorstep again!'

Erika appeared first, skipping nimbly down the steps, then turned to lend Mr Morell a hand. She was grinning from ear to ear, whereas he was frowning deeply. As they reached the ground, Queen Esmerelda hurled the half-crown piece after them and slammed the door shut.

'What on earth was that all about?' asked Rowena.

Erika picked up the coin. 'Madame Arcati in there seemed to take an instant dislike to Mr M. After the preliminaries and the crossing of her palm with silver – which seemed to take forever – she went silent for a while then took Mr M's palm and studied it. Her face clouded over and all of a sudden she erupted, shouted he was evil and told us to get out.'

'We heard that part. What does it mean?'

'It means,' said Mr Morell, 'I do not like gypsies and they do not like me. I told you it was a bad idea.'

'It also means,' added Erika, 'that if you are who you say you are, her powers are genuine. I wonder if she was looking into your past or your future.'

'We shall never know.'

'Come along, Erika, I think it's time Howie drove you back to your Alvis in Earlswood. Mr Morell, you haven't met my husband yet.'

'Indeed not. Herr Furse.'

'Mr Morell.'

They exchanged pleasantries and shook hands.

'What are you plans for this evening?'

'I'm taking Mr M here for dinner,' said Erika. 'Might drive out into the country and find a nice pub … Leigh perhaps, or Godstone. Somewhere Colonel bloody Maxwell isn't likely to pop up out of the blue.'

As they wandered across the heath towards Howard's car, a man approached them from between two stalls and stood purposefully in Mr Morell's path. He was short and stockily built with heavy, powerful shoulders. 'Morell,' he said.

'Yardley.'

'I will take you home.'

'Thank you but I am going out for dinner.'

'I would like to talk with you.'

Mr Morell turned to the others. 'Please excuse me, I shall be along shortly.'

The two walked away out of earshot and as they did so the others noticed two men moving with them, positioning themselves on either side as the men talked, keeping at a discreet distance.

'What *is* going on?' said Erika.

'I'm not sure,' replied Rowena. 'But I know that's the man Mr Morell is staying with, Peter Yardley, our reclusive neighbour. I've seen him once before, when I dropped Mr Morell off outside the house.'

'He doesn't seem too pleased about something.'

'I don't think he approves of Mr Morell having friends.'

'It's none of his business, surely.'

'You'd imagine so.'

'Not a very handsome specimen.'

'Did you notice the scarring on his face?'

'Yes. War wounds perhaps?'

'They look more recent. Plastic surgery perhaps.'

'Erika, what do you make of Mr Morell now … do you think the fortune teller's reaction to him tells us anything?'

'I don't know what to think any more. It's just too crazy to imagine Mr M as Adolf Hitler. Besides, we've been through it all – he's the wrong age, he bears no physical resemblance, he died in a bunker in Berlin years ago and his death is thoroughly documented. He can't be. A senior Nazi perhaps, one that slipped through the net and is on the run still?'

160

'That's possible, although why pretend to be Hitler – what is the point of doing that? It doesn't make sense.'

'He might have cracked at some point and be plain bonkers,' said Erika. 'I've suggested it before. Perhaps he has some sort of fixation that he's his dead *Führer*. A way of helping to convince himself he's still alive.'

'Howie and I have been reading up about it some more,' said Rowena. 'Apparently, Hitler aged rapidly from about 1943 onwards, for a number of reasons, mainly nervous tension. Mr Morell told me as much himself. Germany was losing the war and the tide was turning against him. Then he was nearly blown up by a bomb at his Wolf's Lair. He had a miraculous escape but it must have shaken him badly. All these things affected his health which wasn't helped by his doctor prescribing all sorts of quack remedies that almost certainly did him more harm than good. I'm talking about Theodor Morell of course – the real one. So, if that's the case he could conceivably appear ten years older than his true age. Look over at him now, in the half light, the way he is talking to Peter Yardley. It's not out of the question that it could be the same man. We've been focusing on obvious characteristics – the moustache and the jet black hair swept across his forehead – the classic image we all have of him. Take them away and would anyone recognise him in a crowd?'

'Maybe not,' said Erika. 'And the charisma, or rather lack of any? That's the one thing that convinces me he is lying. I experienced it personally and will never forget the impact it had on me. Mr M over there has none whatsoever.'

Howard Furse had been listening to their conversation.

'It can come and go, depending on circumstance, and particularly change of status. I've seen it before. Corporal Hitler, for example, had very little status in the Great War – none whatsoever in actually. His best friend in the trenches was a stray dog. Yet ten years later he was being hailed as a motivational orator with nigh on mystical powers. If he is still alive, his fortunes will have turned full circle and he'll be nothing again – an abject failure in fact.'

'He said as much himself this afternoon when we were talking,' said Erika. 'He mentioned something about the bad jokes of fortune.'

Howard recognised the reference. 'Village pierrots yesterday, arbiters of life and death today, tomorrow cleaners of the public latrines …'

'That's it.'

'Juvenal – one of his Satires. I learnt it at prep school. Well if that applies to your friend Morell over there then he's most certainly in the latrine cleaning stage of his life and I can well imagine he and his charisma parted company long ago, even before the war was over.'

'The fortune teller sensed something sinister about him,' said Rowena, 'that's for certain. She didn't even want to keep his money.'

'My money actually,' corrected Erika. 'Mind you, Mr M didn't exactly endear himself to Madame Arcati by farting in the close confines of her caravan.'

'Erika!'

'All right, breaking wind. But whatever you like to call it he let one off while she was at her most mystic and intense. That's why I was giggling when I came out.'

'He does seem to have a problem in that department.'

'Did Hitler?'

Rowena shrugged. 'There's no mention of it in anything I've read. He was vegetarian, that can quite often …'

'Yes, quite.'

'They're coming back.'

'Frau Furse, Frau von Tirpitz, Herr Furse,' said Mr Morell, 'I would like to introduce you all to my friend, Peter Yardley, whose guest I am. He is anxious to meet you.'

Peter Yardley bowed his head slightly. Close up they could see that he had a well-rounded belly, and a chin that stuck out pugnaciously. He was wearing jodhpurs and brown riding boots and looked as if he had just climbed down off a horse. Most of all they noticed the scars on his face, around his eyes and forehead, and out almost to his ears.

'Mr Yardley,' said Rowena, 'how nice to meet you at last. Howard and I have been neighbours for some years yet our paths have never crossed. How strange.'

'Yes, strange. I am pleased to meet you, also. Theodor has told me much about you, and your days out together. It is good to know he is in safe hands.'

'Quite safe. And you like to keep a tight rein on him as your guest, too, I understand.'

'We have known each other for many years, so I could hardly do otherwise.'

'I gather you are helping to make arrangements for him to settle somewhere new?'

'That is correct. Frau Furse, I believe you are a keen gardener. So am I – passionate in fact. Perhaps we can talk about flowers and shrubs. I have done little in Wray Park Road as I am only leasing the property. I would very much like to see your garden one day, if you would be kind enough to show it to me.'

'I'd be delighted. How about tomorrow?'

'That would suit me well. May I come through the gate in the hedge, like Theodor when he comes to tea?'

'You may. Come after lunch … at three.'

'Then I shall see you tomorrow. I was trying to persuade Theodor to come home with me, he has had a rather exciting time today I gather, with one thing and another. I heard what happened in the procession.'

'Very exciting,' said Erika.

'He is adamant he is having dinner with Frau von Tirpitz.'

Yardley looked towards Erika; his eyes ran up and down her in a way that made her feel distinctly uncomfortable.

'That's right, Mr Yardley, I'm taking him out to dinner. My treat for being my paladin today.'

'I would kindly ask you not to keep him out too late.'

'Goodness you sound like his father!'

'I am merely concerned for his wellbeing. Now if you will excuse me, I must be getting along … as you British say.'

'Until tomorrow.'

'Until tomorrow.'

They walked off the heath together, Peter Yardley chatting first with Rowena and then Erika until they came to Howard's car. As the Furses drove off with Erika and Mr Morell in the back, they could see Yardley standing at the side of the road. The two men who had been hanging around in the shadows were with him and all three stood together, watching them.

'Thoughts on Peter Yardley?' said Howard, turning towards his passengers for their opinions. Erika replied first.

'The kind of man who makes your flesh cringe. He gives me the creeps.'

'That's not all he gave me,' said Rowena. 'He squeezed my behind when we were walking to the car.'

Morell's voice floated from the corner of the back seat. 'Do not be upset or annoyed, please, that is just his way.'

'He squeezed mine, too,' added Erika.

'He squeezes everyone's if they are female and under the age of sixty. Over sometimes.'

Chapter 18

Terry Angel wasn't feeling well. His stomach had been making rumbling noises all afternoon and he had made several trips to the toilet, newspaper under arm, expecting the worst. But each trip had been a false alarm. Whatever was brewing inside his intestines was waiting its moment to explode upon the world. He blamed the steak and kidney pudding Beth had served up for dinner. It had tasted off.

By mid-evening he had still not managed to shift it, and work called, so he set off on his bike as planned.

He'd done his homework well; hours of what the Yanks would call 'casing the joint' had paid off. He'd had his eye on the large detached house in Somers Road for weeks, and tonight, as on most weekend evenings at this time, it appeared unlit and empty. Tonight was better than most for thieving, with many people out enjoying the carnival festivities.

He strolled past at a reasonable pace, as nonchalantly as he could manage, then cut down a side alley and behind the high fencing that provided the back gardens some privacy from the small patch of woodland they overlooked. He found the back gate to the property. It was bolted on the inside, but Terry soon had it open courtesy of a coat hanger fed over the top and looped into the handle of the bolt. He crept inside and pushed the gate shut, leaving it unlocked in case a hasty retreat was in order.

He stood still and surveyed the back garden. To his right was a privet hedge that separated the garden from next door, to his left a flowerbed, and ahead of him about sixty feet of neatly mown lawn. Embedded in the lawn were stepping stones, and he made his way forward along them, to avoid leaving boot prints in the grass. Terry Angel was no fool.

He was halfway across when suddenly a shaft of light shot out from the rear of the house. The back door opened and he heard a woman's voice saying: 'Off you go, Cassie, do it for mummy ... good girl.'

Terry plunged sideways across the lawn and dived into the privet hedge, curling up into a foetal position, his face pressed into his canvas swag bag. The crowbar in his inside pocket rattled conspicuously against the other tools of his trade for a second.

'Is anyone there?' called the voice.

Terry lay absolutely still. Cassie sniffed her way down the hedge until she reached him, poked her nose around his curled-up body and licked his face playfully. Then she turned around, squatted and peed over him.

'Come on, Cassie, I've got what I came back for now, so off we go.'

Cassie did as she was bid and scampered back to the house. The back door closed and the light was turned off. Moments later Terry heard the sound of a car starting and driving off along the road at the front.

He climbed out of the hedge, stood up and shook his trousers. He could smell the urine on him. He winced in disgust and wondered whether to carry on or not. At least he knew now there was no one at home. He decided to carry on.

At the back door, he pulled out a torch and set to work with a set of skeleton keys. He had the lock open in seconds with practised ease. The door led to a utility room then onto a hallway with rooms off to the right and a staircase to the left. He climbed the stairs, crept into the master bedroom and began rifling through drawers and trinket boxes, stuffing anything of interest into his bag. Then on to a second bedroom that had been converted into a study. In a desk drawer, he found a wad of banknotes that brought a grin to his face.

He was almost at the bottom of the stairs again when he felt his stomach rumble ominously. A sharp pain darted through his abdomen. He stopped dead and felt the tell-tale clenching of the muscles in his rectum.

This was it, he realised. The moment had come.

He started back up the stairs again. Each step was an ordeal as it meant lifting one leg above the other and risking some leakage. He tightened his muscles as much as he dared, but it was agony. By the time he reached the top of the stairs he was convinced he wouldn't make it. He gritted his teeth and shone his torch round to identify which door was the toilet. It was the furthest away, at the far end of the landing.

He looked like a penguin as he waddled along, his feet shuffling forward with as little movement above the knees as he could possibly manage. When he reached the toilet door, he knew that the last couple of feet would be the worst. Mentally you want to let go because you're so very nearly there. But physically you're *not* there and the movement from standing up to sitting down in those last seconds before relief is at hand can be disastrous.

Terry Angel turned around, unbuttoned his trousers, pulled down his underpants and leaned back to slump onto the toilet. He let loose his straining muscles and heard and felt a minor avalanche being unleashed beneath him. Unfortunately, in the dark he'd failed to notice that the toilet seat cover was down.

There was shit everywhere.

****

Sunday 8th July

'Good morning. It's Benjamin, isn't it?'

Ben looked up from his book, irritated at being interrupted, and smiled politely. 'Mr Wells, and Mrs Wells ... Barbara ... Barb. What a surprise.'

He was sitting on a bench next to the lake in Priory Park, reading. He was close to finishing *The High Window* and was keen to see how all the strands of the story fitted together. He had become intoxicated by the characters with their beguiling names – Linda Conquest, Lois Magic, Mr Morningstar – and he empathised with Philip Marlowe who was turning out to be something more than just a hard-boiled detective, by rescuing a damsel in distress. Raymond Chandler described him as '*a shop-soiled Sir Galahad*'. Perfect.

The Wells were standing next to the bench, one on either side. Barb Wells smiled down at him affectionately, whilst her husband stared absentmindedly across the lake. Not a couple in tune with each other, Ben concluded.

'Not such a surprise really,' said Barb. 'A Sunday morning stroll here is a regular of ours.'

'I like to feed the ducks,' added Mr Wells, tossing some bread into the water.

Ben's mind had been absorbed with Merle Davis, the vulnerable young secretary Philip Marlowe was intent on saving, and the interruption had come between them. On the other hand, being confronted by the enticing Barb Wells was more than welcome.

'What about you, do you come into the park often?' she asked. 'I haven't seen you here before.'

'Not especially. I just happened to find my way here and fancied a bit of a read. That's all.'

168

'What's the book?' Ben showed her the cover. 'Hmm not my cup of tea. Give me a good romance any day. Did you see the carnival procession yesterday?'

Yes, I watched it as it came through Redhill. You?'

'I saw some of the floats as they passed the shop. But it was near to closing time, so I was busy tidying up.'

Mr Wells had wandered off along the edge of the lake. Barb sat down next to Ben, close enough so that her knee just brushed against his.

'We went to the fair on the heath in the evening. Did you?'

'Yes, I was there.'

'How funny, we were both there but didn't see each other. Pity.' She indicated towards Mr Wells. 'I lost him for a while so was wandering about on my own. You could have saved a damsel in distress.'

'Like Merle.'

'Who's she – your girlfriend?'

Ben held up his book. 'A character in this book. She, too, is a damsel in distress in need of rescuing.'

'Do you think I need rescuing?'

'You said … at the fair …'

'Do you have a girlfriend?'

'No, I don't.'

'Would you like one?'

Ben ran his fingers through the pages of his book as he considered this forthright question. He wondered, as he often did, what Storm would do in this situation. It occurred to him that his big brother would almost certainly match bluntness with bluntness. Ben glanced along the lakeside to check that Mr Wells was not within hearing distance, then said: 'Yes, I would like you.'

Barb Wells did not move a muscle. She sat in silence looking him in the eyes for what seemed to Ben to be forever.

He soon wished he hadn't come out with it and his mouth opened several times to begin a retraction; an apology. He must have looked like a goldfish, he thought. When she eventually spoke, Barb sounded perfectly calm, as if she was giving an answer to the most banal of questions.

'All right, you shall. Are you doing anything on Wednesday evening?'

'No, nothing.'

'Do you know Hardwicke Road?'

'Off London Road?'

'That's it. There are some redbrick Victorian semi-detached houses towards the Yorke Road end, on the right.'

'I know. What number?'

'Just look for the bright red door – there is only one. Come round at seven o' clock. There's a gate at the side into the back garden. I'll let you in by the kitchen door.'

'Wh … what about your husband?'

'Wednesday night is Bridge night. It's early closing at the store, so we eat early and he's off out by six. Never comes home before midnight and usually well and truly in his cups.'

'I'll be there.'

'You'd better be, my lad.'

'What are we going to do?'

Barb cocked her head to one side as if to imply it was a rhetorical question. 'Let's play it by ear, shall we? I'm open to suggestions, so long as it is doesn't involve playing bloody Bridge.'

'Bit difficult with just two,' said Ben in a vain attempt to appear nonchalant.

Barb stood up to set off and catch up with her husband. 'There are other card games,' she said. 'How about a few hands of strip poker?'

Ben nodded his approval at the idea.

'But I have to warn you,' she called. 'I'm hopeless. I will almost certainly lose every round.'

****

Ben's hands were shaking as he stood outside the phone box, smoking. He couldn't believe his luck. It was like a dream come true; every young man's fantasy, to be seduced by an older woman. He was so excited that he simply had to tell someone, and there was only one person he could confide in, which he intended doing as soon as the old fossil in the box finished her call and gave him the chance.

He was still shaking when he lifted the handset off its cradle. Slotting coins into the phone was no easier, nor dialling the number, nor pressing button A when he heard his brother's voice answering.'

'Storm, it's me.'

'Uh … Ben … what are you doing calling at this time in the morning. Bugger off.'

'Storm, it's midday. Noon.'

'Bugger off anyway.'

'How's things in Fleet Street?'

'I'm not there at this precise moment in time. I'm in bed – and a little the worse for wear.'

'Listen, I think I've cracked it. I think I'm going to do it at last.'

'Do what?'

'You know … it. The deed.'

'Oh, that. About time. What are you, twenty and still a virgin? That's not right. Not normal.'

'I suppose you were an experienced veteran by my age.'

'By comparison, yes. So, you've found yourself a girlfriend I assume?'

171

'Sort of. She works in Knight's in Reigate. Not exactly a girlfriend. She's … well she's married.'

'Do I know her?'

'She's the manager's wife.'

'Wells?'

'That's him.'

'I remember. Met him a couple of times. A bit odd. His wife's called Barbara – works there too as I recall.'

'That's right. They've had some shoplifting and I went to report on it. That's how I met her.'

'Married eh? You know my advice on the subject.'

'I do. Be careful and don't get caught.'

'With an emphasis on not getting caught.' Ben heard a cigarette being lit and the sound of smoke being inhaled then exhaled. 'Well, you've woken me up now, so what's she like?'

Ben told Storm all about Barb Wells; how he had been to Knight's, twice, to investigate the shoplifting incidents, and how she had flirted with him and made suggestive comments, and run her finger over the spout of the teapot in the window.

'And now she's told me to come around to her house on Wednesday night, for a game of strip poker.'

'What about her old man?' asked Storm cautiously.

'Card night with his mates – won't be home until midnight.'

'Well a tip from me, little brother. Make sure you've got your trousers back on and you're out of there by eleven at the absolute latest, to be on the safe side.'

'I will, Storm, don't you worry.'

'I'm impressed. Sounds like you'll be dipping your wick and no mistake.'

'I can't wait.'

'What else is news? I'll be down in a few weekends. See the old place, catch up with a few old faces.'

'Make it soon. News … oh yes, I do have some news. Nearly forgot. A story of my own I'm working on. I told the boss about it and he thinks it's a load of bollocks. But I'm on to something, I'm certain.'

'Tell me.'

'You'll never believe it, I've discovered Nazis here in Reigate. And not just any old Nazis … only Hitler himself!'

Ben heard more smoke being inhaled.

'What do you say to that, Storm – a scoop or what?' Silence. 'Storm …?'

'He's right.'

'Who's right?'

'The boss. It's a load of bollocks.'

'No it's not. Listen, I overheard these people talking in The Dinner Gong. They were speaking German, then they changed into English and I heard them …'

'The Dinner Gong? How's Suki?'

'She's well, sends her love. Look Storm, don't change the subject, this is important to me okay? One of them was an old bloke, a German, and I think, not absolutely sure, just think, he might be …'

Ben heard a growling noise from the phone. He stopped and listened. Storm was pretending to snore. Ben slammed the handset down angrily.

'Not bollocks,' he snarled. 'I'll show you.'

Chapter 19

'My God, what happened to you last night?' said Beth Angel. 'You stank when you came to bed.'

'Sorry,' replied her husband grumpily as he sipped a cup of tea and smoked his first of the day. 'Had a bit of an accident. I washed and everything.'

'To no purpose. You smelled like a cesspit. And your clothes! I'll have to boil them. What kind of an accident?'

'Don't ask.'

'I'm asking.'

'The kind your steak and kidney pud causes.'

'Oh. Yes, well I have to admit my stomach wasn't how it should have been after dinner either. But at least I managed to get to a toilet and sort it out decently.'

'I wasn't so lucky. Didn't quite make it.'

'Where were you?'

'Out – seeing a man about a dog.'

'Up to no good, I'll be bound.'

'If you're out of work like me you do what you can to make ends meet.' He sniffed haughtily. 'Ask no questions and you'll be told no lies. You know that.'

'Well be careful, that's all I ask. If anyone found out what you get up to, I'd be booted out of the Women's Institute.' Then as an afterthought: 'And take some newspaper with you next time.'

****

Shortly before three that afternoon, Rowena was hovering expectantly around the garden gate, waiting for Mr Morell and Peter Yardley to appear, which they did a few minutes later. She proudly showed them around the garden while Howard sat on the terrace ensconced in The Times.

Peter Yardley was very complimentary and clearly knew his subject as, to Rowena's delight and surprise, he identified nearly everything planted in the herbaceous borders. After her experience the night before, she tried not to stand too close to him and when she felt his hand brush against her thigh at one point, she positioned herself on the other side of Mr Morell, who was shadowing them, listening to their conversation with interest, though not contributing.

After half an hour or so of pottering around the garden, they made their way to the terrace and Rowena brought out tea and some cakes. Howard put away his newspaper.

'Please help yourself, Mr Yardley.'

'Thank you. Call me Peter, I would prefer that.'

He chose a large slice of Dundee cake and proceeded to cram most of it into his mouth. Rowena stared in amazement.

'I should have forewarned you about Yardley's eating habits,' said Morell quietly. Yardley appeared oblivious and washed the cake down with a large gulp of tea.

'Peter,' said Rowena. 'I am curious. How do you come to be in this country?'

'I came here after the war because it was a very difficult time in Germany. The British authorities were sympathetic towards me as I was able to help them in certain ways. In exchange, they arranged for me to stay.'

'Do you like it here?'

'Yes, I like it very much.'

'And why Reigate?'

'Apart from a brief visit as a child I had never been to England before and didn't know the country. They arranged temporary accommodation for me here in Reigate when I first arrived. When the time came for me to find a place of my own I thought, I do not know anywhere else, Reigate is a nice town and as good a place as any. So I stayed.'

'Do you have family with you?'

'Not here. I have children, in Germany. My wife died, so I am a … is the word widow?'

'Widower, for a man. I am sorry to hear that. Recently?'

'Six years ago. Cancer.'

'And do you intend staying here?'

'I have no plans to do otherwise.'

Peter Yardley stuffed another piece of cake in his mouth and Rowena paused to allow him time to finish.

'I'm also curious how you know Mr Morell.'

'We worked together for many years.'

'Yardley worked for me,' corrected Morell.

'We took different paths when the war ended, but I managed to track him down.'

'I tracked you down,' Morell corrected again.

'We tracked each other down.'

'That's nice,' said Rowena. 'What is your line of work?'

'I am fortunate enough to have private means. Additionally, I own a farm which is profitable. I breed pigs and horses and grow vegetables, also some fruit. Apples mainly. In Germany, amongst other things, I used to manage a farm and I have returned to my roots, so to speak. I ride, and travel often. I keep

176

busy. So, tell me about yourselves – my turn to be curious about my neighbours who have taken Theodor under their wing.'

Rowena reciprocated and told him about their lives whilst Howard nodded in agreement every now and again. When she reached the point where she had befriended Mr Morell, Yardley interrupted.

'Ah yes, this occurred when I was away. I did not know about it until I returned and saw you driving him home.'

'All perfectly innocent. Isn't that right, Howard?'

'Oh certainly,' replied her husband. 'All above board, I have no doubt.'

'We've struck up a friendship and had some rather fun outings together. No harm done.'

Morell said: 'I don't have to tell you everything, Yardley.'

Yardley replied in German. 'Perhaps not, but it is important for me to know of your whereabouts – you know that. You are taking too many unnecessary risks.'

'Beware,' warned Morell, responding in German. 'Our hostess understands.'

Yardley bowed slightly. 'Excuse me, that was rude.'

Rowena smiled. 'That's quite all right. Do you live alone … apart from Mr Morell of course?'

'I have two men who live in the house, a valet and a chauffeur, so not entirely alone. I also have a housekeeper who comes in most days who is also an excellent cook.'

'I am surprised Mr Morell is in the summer house. There must be plenty of room in such a large house.'

'It was his choice to stay there.'

Morell nodded. 'That is the truth, Frau Furse, I like the feeling of being alone in there. In a small way, there is a feeling of being in the Alps also, living in a wooden home. Foolish I know.'

'And do we know how much longer we have the pleasure of Mr Morell's company? How are your arrangements coming along … whatever you're planning?'

Peter Yardley finished his tea. Rowena topped up his cup.

'Thank you. Theodor's circumstances have changed recently in a number of ways and I am helping him to find a new home. There are financial matters to resolve, some unfinished business to attend to, travel arrangements to be made. We are getting there. I hope to have everything finalised for him shortly.'

'We'd better make the most of you while we can then, Mr Morell,' said Rowena. 'Shall we fit in another trip to London? The Festival of Britain is still on, or how about another opera. We talked about that before.'

'I don't think that is advisable,' said Peter Yardley. 'I would prefer it if you entertained Theodor locally if you must. And please, no more dressing him up as Winston Churchill and getting him into fights in public places.'

Morell stirred in his chair. 'I will do as I please, Yardley. As you know, I have never held back from taking risks.'

Peter Yardley changed the subject rather pointedly. 'I am disappointed that Frau von Tirpitz is not here. She is a most attractive woman.'

'She is indeed,' agreed Rowena. 'She had made other arrangements for this afternoon.'

'I would very much like to meet her again.'

'I'm sure you would, Peter, she is very popular, in particular with the men.'

'Please pass on my respects and tell her I would like to invite her to have dinner with me one evening at my house. Mid-week perhaps. Wednesday evening at eight?'

'Well, I don't know. I shall pass on the message, naturally, but I cannot be certain she will accept.'

Yardley stood up. 'I am sure you can influence her. Now we will take our leave and thank you for your hospitality. Especially for showing me your garden. It is most beautiful.'

Both men said their goodbyes to Rowena, then Howard.

'Thank you once again, Frau Furse,' said Mr Morell. 'Let us talk soon about that trip to London.'

Rowena escorted the two men to the gate and returned to the terrace. She sat down heavily and breathed a huge sigh. 'Phew, that was awkward at times, don't you agree?'

Howard, who had barely spoken during tea, nodded in agreement. 'Revealing though, Flossie. We learnt a fair bit about our neighbour.'

'Not least of all that he eats like a pig. Disgusting. He said they worked together for many years, but wasn't any more specific. Then Mr Morell corrected him and said Peter had worked for *him*. In what capacity, I wonder? He clearly tries to control Mr Morell who doesn't like it and rebels at every opportunity. I wonder what their relationship was.'

'Hmm, and if we are to surmise that your Mr Morell is in fact Adolf Hitler?'

'Goodness me, I don't know. That would be something to consider … his adjutant, chief of staff perhaps? Trevor-Roper mentions some of them being in the bunker with him, but I can't remember names.'

'If so, he's clearly not one of the key players. If they didn't commit suicide, they were either hanged or imprisoned at Nuremberg – Göring, Hess, Speer, von Ribbentrop et al.' Howard became pensive for a moment and his voice tailed off into a whisper. 'With one major exception …'

'And that is?'

He started, surprised he'd been heard. 'Oh nothing, Floss.'

'You said with one major exception. Who was that?'

'No one. Ignore what I said. All the top Nazis have been accounted for one way or another.'

'Are you certain about that? There are often stories in the newspapers about sightings in different countries.'

'Lower ranking Nazis … not the top dogs. They've all been bagged now.'

Rowena eyed him suspiciously. 'Hmm, I'm not so sure.'

Howard rustled his newspaper dismissively and focused on an article that quite suddenly demanded his undivided attention. 'Is that the garden I hear calling for your attention, Floss?'

Rowena followed his suggestion and headed towards part of the border she had noticed needed tidying up when she'd been showing Peter Yardley around. As she worked she pondered over her conversation, firstly with Yardley then with Howard. Yardley's relationship with Mr Morell was puzzling her and she was confused. She felt instinctively that Morell was superior in some way – the boss as it were – and that Yardley's attempts to control him were out of place, certainly in Mr Morell's view. And Howard had confused her further. Why hint at an idea who Yardley might be then close down the conversation. Odd. She needed to do some digging of her own … and not the gardening kind.

After a while she took off her gloves and made her way back down the garden towards the house. Howard had vanished from the patio. She wondered into the lounge and headed for the bookshelf, glancing along the shelves. There was a space where Trevor-Roper's book had been. She looked around the lounge but it was nowhere to be seen.

'Howard?' she called. 'Where are you?'

'Here, Floss,' came a distant reply. She heard his footsteps on the stairs.

'Have you seen Trevor-Roper?'

'Never met him.'

180

'His book, I mean.'

'On the bookshelf in the lounge, last time I saw it.'

'Well it's not there now.'

'Curious. Have you looked elsewhere?'

'All over.'

He strolled past her, took out his tobacco pouch and began to fill his pipe. 'No doubt it will turn up.'

'Yes,' said his wife vaguely. 'No doubt it will.'

****

PC Bent was tucked up in bed, cuddling his pillow and having a happy dream.

He was in the Redhill Odeon, canoodling with Meg in the back row of the stalls. They were sitting holding hands, and allowing their legs to touch. Every now and again they turned to each other and kissed.

He was barely aware of what was going on, on the screen – a comedy of some sort, about a Cockney window cleaner called Sid who got into one scrape after another, usually involving seeing more than he should on his rounds. Between kisses, one scene did grab Bent's attention, in which Sid fled on his bike from an irate husband who had caught him peering in their bedroom window. The husband chased him up the road, almost caught up, then tripped and fell flat on his face.

Several kisses later, the *Pathé News* came on. Mr Winston Churchill was arriving outside the Houses of Parliament to take his seat for a debate as Leader of the Opposition.

Bent pushed Meg away, stood up and glared at the screen. Then he was back at home, sitting up in bed, glaring at his bedroom wall, shouting: 'Winston Churchill stole my bike!'

Seconds later he was asleep again, cuddling his pillow, imagining it was Meg.

181

The next morning he'd forgotten all about it.

Chapter 20

Monday 9th July

There were several libraries in Reigate – Boots, Paynes, Ancient House, the Castle – but the main one was upstairs in the Old Town Hall, at the top of an impressive winding mahogany staircase. The doors opened at ten sharp and Rowena was outside ready and waiting. She knew the chief librarian, Rose Bryant, quite well and approached her at the counter with an urgency reminiscent of someone with a weak bladder desperately seeking the whereabouts of the nearest public convenience.

In no time at all she was seated at a reading desk holding a copy of Trevor-Roper's *The Last Days of Hitler*. She flicked through it for a while, then looked again at the title and frowned. There was a good deal about the last days but little in there to explain what had happened *after* the events in Hitler's bunker and his apparent suicide. She flicked some more then went back to the librarian, explained her need as best she could, and, after a bit of a wait, returned to her seat clutching more books and several newspaper clippings. She began ploughing her way through them.

In a dog-eared, earth-stained notebook that contained mostly names of plants and shrubs, she started to make a list. Each entry consisted of a first name and a surname, plus their position within the Nazi hierarchy, and a comment as to their status. At the top was:

Adolf Hitler – Führer. Dead or alive?

Gradually the list grew, more or less in order of seniority, as she identified them.

Hermann Göring – Reichsmarshall. Suicide.
Heinrich Himmler – Head of the SS. Suicide.
Joseph Goebbels – Minister of Propaganda. Suicide.
Albert Speer – Minister of War Production. In prison.
Joachim von Ribbentrop – Foreign Minister. Hanged.
Ernst Kaltenbrunner – Chief of Reich Security. Hanged.

Using newspaper sources, she then cross-referred to the main defendants in the dock at Nuremberg. Some she had already identified, others were disregarded as not feasible or not actually Nazis. More were added, including some senior military leaders.

Rudolf Hess – Formerly Deputy Führer. In prison.
Wilhelm Keitel – Field Marshal. Hanged.
Hans Frank – Reich Commissioner for Justice. Hanged.
Wilhelm Frick – Nazi Minister of the Interior. Hanged.
Alfried Jodl – General. Hanged.
Karl Doenitz – Admiral. In prison.
Erich Raeder – Admiral. In prison.

By midday, Rowena was bleary eyed and could feel her concentration waning. But she was done. She closed her books, folded the newspaper clippings back into shape and returned them to the librarian.

'Thank you, Rose, you've been most helpful.'

'Only too happy to be of assistance,' replied Rose. 'I must say it was a surprise to hear you asking for books about the war, especially the Germans. Rather a change from gardening and horticulture.'

'Yes indeed, however I had my reasons.'

'And were you successful in your research … whatever it was about?'

'Very successful, thank you.'

Rowena stepped outside onto the High Street and looked around with a sense of satisfaction. Successful indeed, she thought. Howard was wrong. Not all the top Nazis were accounted for. Most were dead, or in prison serving long sentences; but there was one exception. A man who seemingly vanished when the war ended and at Nuremberg had been sentenced to death *in absentia*, should he be alive and ever brought to justice. The Head of the Nazi Party Chancellery and Hitler's private secretary.

'I think it's him,' she said aloud. 'I think Peter Yardley is Martin Bormann.'

****

That evening, Erika von Tirpitz telephoned to find out how the afternoon with Peter Yardley had gone the day before.

'He loved the garden,' said Rowena. 'He was highly complimentary. And he's extremely knowledgeable – I was impressed. Apparently, he owns a farm.'

'Come on, Row, I don't want to hear all that. What did you make of him?'

'Pleasant enough, but still gives me the creeps.'

'Did he try to touch you? You know, did he grope you?'

'He tried once, but after that I kept my distance.'

'There's no doubt he's a dirty old man.'

Rowena heard the sound of smoke being inhaled.

'Not so old. Early fifties I would say. And he's taken a fancy to you. He's invited you to have dinner with him, on Wednesday evening at eight, at his home in Wray Park Road.'

'Oh Lord, that's the last thing I want, to have dinner with a lecherous creep with wandering hands. You can imagine what his idea of dessert will be.'

'Ha ha, yes I think I can!'

'Tell him thank you, but no thanks. I've just managed to get rid of one unwanted suitor and I'm in no hurry to take on board another. What else did you manage to glean?'

'Well quite a bit actually,' said Rowena, 'He's a widower with children in Germany, though he didn't elaborate as to how many and where. He said he came here after the war as he was of help to the government.'

'What on earth does that mean?'

Rowena shrugged. 'Haven't a clue. Apparently, he has a private income and doesn't need to work, and he owns a farm. He and Mr Morell have known each other for a long time, but in what capacity exactly we didn't find out. He's very protective towards Mr Morell, who doesn't like it a bit. They broke into German at one point. Peter Yardley didn't know I speak it and before Mr Morell warned him, he made a comment about it being important to know his whereabouts. He told Mr Morell that he takes unnecessary risks.'

'So, either they are both ex-Nazis of some description, not big enough fish to be caught in the net after the war, or we have as our guests Adolf Hitler and …?'

'Still not convinced about that. But if Mr Morell were in fact Adolf, I've now got a good idea who Peter Yardley is. I've worked it out by a process of elimination.' She explained about her trip to the library and how she had been through a list and come up with the only top Nazi still not accounted for.

'Are you going to tell me?' said Erika impatiently.

'I think he is Martin Bormann.'

The phone went silent. Rowena waited for Erika to say something but nothing came.

'Are you still there, Erika …?'

The voice when it did come was half its usual volume. 'Yes, I'm here.'

'Are you all right?'

'Fine.'

'No, you're not. What is it … something to do with Martin Bormann?'

'Yes.'

'Tell me, what about him?'

No response.

'Erika?'

This time the voice was barely audible, it was so quiet. The words were spoken slowly and mechanically, almost robotically. 'Martin Bormann raped my sister.'

It was Rowena's turn to fall silent.

Chapter 21

Tuesday 10th July

Erika sat on her sofa, a glass of gin and tonic in one hand and the other stroking Mr Chips who was curled up next to her. Rowena sat opposite, a wine glass in her hand and a look on her face that combined sympathy with eager curiosity to hear the tale her friend was about to tell.

'It happened in 1940,' Erika began. 'What I am about to tell you I know because Maxine, my sister, wrote it down in detail in a long letter to me. We sent mail to each other via Lisbon where a friend of Karl's worked as a diplomat. It was slow – letters often took weeks, sometimes months to arrive. But it kept us in touch, with my parents also. I have the letter still, in a drawer by my bedside. I know the content almost by heart I have read it so many times.'

'You have another sister too – Maria?' said Rowena. 'You have mentioned her, but not Maxine.'

Erika nodded. 'Maria is my elder sister. She's two years older than me, and lives in my home town, Freiberg, not far from our parents. Maxi was my younger sister, by four years. She lived at home and worked in a music store. She was stunningly pretty and with talent to match – she could play the piano and the guitar well, dance and had the most beautiful singing voice. Our family name, my maiden name, was Vogel and it couldn't have been more appropriate for her. She sang like a bird. Her job was to do the books and keep the paperwork in order, though she spent most of the time on the shop floor talking to customers and singing for them. The owners didn't mind – she was an attraction and drew people into the store. Good for business. But she was ambitious and after four years in the shop she became restless and wanted to make something of her life. So, in spring of that year, just before things really kicked off in France and Belgium, she gave up her job and, against the wishes of our parents, set off for Berlin. I don't think she had much of a plan beyond finding somewhere to live, a job to pay the rent and hopefully making some contacts in the entertainment business.

'She found an apartment which wasn't bad, in a fairly decent part of Berlin, and soon got a job as a waitress in a restaurant on the *Kurfürstendamm*. With her looks and figure, she was very employable. It was only meant to be a stopgap until she broke into … I'm not really sure she knew what. She was rather naive about life. It wasn't long before she found herself a boyfriend, a young soldier called Horst. He was a customer in the restaurant. I believe he'd gone there with his family to celebrate his birthday. Maxi served them. Horst was smitten at once and kept coming back all week to eat or drink coffee, just to see her. She was lonely and although gaining a good deal of attention from men hadn't been asked out properly by anyone. She had had boyfriends at home, but no one special. Then along came Horst. Quite soon she was as smitten with him as he was with her.

'He lived with his parents in Berlin, I don't know where exactly, but quite central I believe. Horst took Maxi to meet them and they approved of her. Who wouldn't! He wasn't a combat soldier. Maxi used to write to me often and I'm sure she said he was involved in logistics and supplies and spent most of

189

his time sitting at a desk, so they were able to spend a lot of time together.

'Nothing much happened to further her career. She had a few auditions for cabaret shows but they were more interested in her body than her voice, and wanted her to wear next to nothing on cramped stages just to give their clients something to ogle at. As I said, Maxi was naive, and shy, too. So, she didn't take up any offers and stayed at the restaurant on the *Ku'damm*.'

Erika stopped to light a cigarette.

'This is all background of course. I knew about her move to Berlin, and Horst, from previous letters … but nothing of what followed until that long letter came.'

'I understand,' said Rowena. 'Do carry on.'

'One lunchtime, a group of senior Nazis came into the restaurant. This would have been mid-June. The war in the west was going fantastically well – Holland, Belgium and France all crushed and the British pushed into the sea at Dunkirk. Everyone was on a high. Germany, and Germans, couldn't put a foot wrong. They were well on their way to ruling the whole of Europe. The lunch party was boisterous and loud. They downed a lot of wine and schnapps and got very drunk. She didn't know who they were by name but could tell they were important men.

'One in particular paid her a great deal of attention. He seemed entranced by her. She soon discovered his name was Martin Bormann. When they left, he insisted on leaving his contact details – his private telephone number no less – and told her that if ever she wanted a better job than being a waitress he always had opportunities on his staff for bright young women. She told him she really wanted to work in films or on the stage. He said he could help her with that, too, have a word with Joseph Goebbels on her behalf, the man who knew everyone worth knowing in the film world.

190

'Maxi had mixed feelings. Here was the opportunity she had been hoping for, but from a decidedly unappealing source. She told Horst. He saw only the positive – a break, a chance to move into the world she had come to Berlin to seek. She should embrace it. He'd never heard of Martin Bormann but made a few enquiries and soon discovered he was none other than Chief of Staff to the Deputy *Führer*, Rudolf Hess. An important man. Too good an opportunity to ignore if he could pull strings for her.

'A few evenings later, feeling excited but at the same time reluctant, she called the number. Bormann himself answered. He sounded bored and disinterested at first, but his tone changed instantly when he realised who she was. He invited her for dinner a few days later, to talk about her future and how he might help her to further her career. Again, she consulted Horst who was full of encouragement. She should definitely go.

'By all accounts he was charming at dinner, captivated by her good looks. He treated her like a lady and apart from a fumbled attempt at a kiss when he dropped her off at her apartment, he behaved like a gentleman. He told her he'd had a word with Goebbels and arranged a screen test for her at the Babelsberg film studios, in the suburbs of Berlin. She would almost certainly be offered some 'extra' work in one of the films currently in production. And, he assured her, once her name was on the list she would be guaranteed regular work. He promised to take her to the studios himself as soon as he could find the time.

'A week went by and she didn't hear from him. Then out of the blue he phoned her at the restaurant and told her to be ready at three the next afternoon. She was supposed to be working but pleaded with the restaurant manager to change her shift. When she explained why, he readily agreed; he'd been a dancer in his younger days and was keen to encourage others to realise their dreams.

'At the allotted time, Maxi was waiting outside her apartment block and the car pulled up. On the journey to the studios, Martin Bormann was mostly silent, preoccupied with something, she knew not what. He had a briefcase with him and pulled out some papers, ignoring her, focusing on what he was reading. When they arrived at the studio gates, he nodded sternly at the guard who let them through without hesitation.

'They stopped outside an administration building where a sharply dressed man greeted them and escorted them up to a large, airy office on the first floor. There they met the director who, with much arm waving and vocal dexterity, began to explain in detail the plot of the film he was embroiled in, quoting dialogue from both male and female parts. Bormann cut him short, said he didn't have time for all that and could they get on with the screen test. Crest fallen, the director nodded his head and asked them to follow him.

'It was a period drama, set at the time of the Franco-Prussian war. Maxi was whisked away to the costume department and came back wearing the flowing skirt and simple blouse of a peasant girl. For an hour, she stood in front of a camera and powerful studio lights and was photographed from every angle, told to smile, to look distraught, to laugh, to cry, to be angry. After a short break, during which a woman taught her a line of dialogue by rote, she spoke it several times into the camera as directed, one time as if pleading with it, another as if in love with it, and finally as if scared by it. All this time, Bormann sat at the back of the set, reading and making notes, with an air of absolute disinterest. At one point, he disappeared for twenty minutes to make some phone calls.

'The director announced he was pleased with the test and would let her know if he could use her when the film had been processed – hopefully in a few days. Maxi changed back into her own clothes and met up with Bormann who was keen to get back to Berlin. He dropped her at her apartment and said he would come and collect her in two hours for dinner. There were a few important matters he had to attend to first.

'When he returned, he was more attentive towards her and seemed more relaxed. Again, he was charming over dinner and ordered champagne to celebrate Maxi's break into the world of films. After dinner, she was driven home. Bormann told his driver to wait and insisted on walking her to her apartment door. He asked if he could look inside, to see where she lived. As soon as the door was closed, he made his move. He pushed her against the wall, kissed her roughly, pulled at her clothes and grabbed her breasts. She made it clear she did not want this and resisted in every way. But she was not physically strong, and he easily overpowered her. The more she struggled the more excited and aroused he became. His persona had changed, he was now the ruthless bully who got anything he wanted. One good turn deserved another, he told her – he had introduced her to the world of film, now she must show her gratitude. He bundled her into her bedroom, tore off her clothes … and raped her. Brutally. He took his time, threw her around the bed like a rag doll, forced her to do things that disgusted her. Then, when he had finished, he got dressed and left without saying a word.

'The next day she was due to meet Horst for lunch, but she was too distraught and put him off. She managed to struggle in to work in the afternoon and got through her shift like an automaton, then rushed home and collapsed in a sea of tears. Horst turned up at her door and knocked and called her name. She didn't respond but he could hear her sobbing and refused to go away. Eventually she let him in and in the comfort of his arms told him what had happened. He stayed with her until she had calmed down, put her to bed and then quietly let himself out.

'Early the following morning, Horst was outside the main entrance of the New Reich Chancellery in *Voss Strasse*, staring up at the four enormous pillars and the Reich eagle that took pride of place above them. Somewhere inside the building was Martin Bormann's office. He had no idea where, he didn't even know what Bormann looked like, and he had no real plan in his head. All he knew was the feeling of rage inside him, the red hot anger towards the man who had violated the girl he adored. He was intent on punishing him somehow. It might be a public shouting match to embarrass the Chief of Staff to the Deputy *Führer*, or a punch in the face, or … he had his gun inside his jacket, if he had the courage to use it.

'He walked up and down *Voss Strasse*, looking across at the building, wondering what to do. Time passed and people came and went, some in uniform, some in civilian clothes. For a while he wandered away into the *Tiergarten*, then came back with no clearer idea in his head. Eventually he crossed the road, marched purposefully up the steps into the Chancellery and asked at the reception desk to see Martin Bormann. He was in uniform and said he had an urgent message for him that had to be delivered in person. After a brief phone call, the man at the reception desk gave him directions to the suite of offices belonging to the Deputy *Führer* and his staff. A prim, smiling secretary told him to wait while she went into the office next door. She came out and indicated that he could go in. There, at a desk amply covered with papers and files, sat a man he had never seen before. Horst opened his mouth to speak, but nothing came out. He stood there confronted by a complete stranger, finding it hard to reconcile the outrage he knew had been committed with the figure in front of him. He blurted out something accusatory, called him a rapist, an abuser of women, a monster. With hand shaking he fumbled for his gun, but Bormann had seen what was coming and was round the desk before Horst could aim properly. One hand thrust out towards the gun arm, pushing it upwards towards the ceiling. With the other he punched Horst hard on the cheek, jerking his head sideways. Horst lost his balance as the gun went off, the bullet embedding itself in the wall behind the desk. He fell to the floor and Bormann was on top of him, pummelling both fists into his face time and again. By the time two SS guards separated them, Horst was almost unconscious and his face a bloody mess.

'He was dragged away and thrown into a cell-like room. Someone rummaged through his pockets and found his identity papers, then demanded the name of the woman he claimed Bormann had violated, which he gave. A doctor came and tended to his face, no bones broken, but there was heavy bruising. A voice told him to go home and forget about the whole thing, to tell his family and colleagues that he'd been knocked down by a car.

'He went to see Maxi and they stayed in her apartment for the rest of the day, both hurting and not knowing what to do next. She told him it was foolish to confront Bormann like that, a powerful and dangerous man. He was lucky to come away with just some bruises. It was Maxi who eventually suggested the simplest course of action of all – report the rape to the police. It was, after all, a crime. Horst agreed but didn't think they would believe her story. The next morning, they went together to the nearest police headquarters, where they were interviewed by the *Kripo* – the *Kriminalpolizei*.' Erika paused in her narrative. 'I think the equivalent in this country would be the CID, plain clothes detectives who investigate serious crimes.'

'I think that's right,' agreed Rowena.

'The difference of course was that all police activity in Nazi Germany was linked to the SS in one way or another and they were rarely able to investigate domestic crime impartially, without interference.

'At first the *Kripo* were sympathetic and keen to help as best they could, until Maxi told them the identity of the man who had raped her. She wrote in her letter that as soon as she came out with the name Martin Bormann, it was as if a door had been slammed shut. Suddenly they weren't interested. They said they'd make enquiries and would be in touch, but it was very apparent they could hardly wait to see them out of the door.

'Two days later, Horst disappeared. Maxi had gone back to work at the restaurant and Horst to his desk. That morning he left home for work, on foot, but never arrived. He simply vanished. His parents reported him missing, and the *Kripo* supposedly investigated, as did the military police. But they came up with nothing. A week later, Martin Bormann telephoned Maxi at the restaurant as if nothing had happened and invited her for dinner. She put the phone down on him, finished her shift and went home to her apartment.

'That night she wrote her long letter to me. Her last. She told me how guilty she felt about Horst, that she was responsible for his disappearance. She was convinced by now he was dead, and who was behind it. She thought her ambition was to blame, and if she hadn't had that burning desire to go places she would never have had anything to do with Martin Bormann. And Horst would still be alive. She felt worthless, that she had let all her family down, myself included, which of course was nonsense. If I could have spoken to her I might have put her mind at rest, but that was not possible.'

Erika's voice faltered. 'And she felt something else, too.' She struggled to continue.

'What was it that she felt, my dear?' asked Rowena sympathetically.

'Dirty. She felt incredibly dirty. Inside more than out. She used the word *schmutzig* … in English I would say stained.'

Erika picked up her glass and drained it. 'The letter ended with words of love and apology. I assume the next morning she went out to post it. It was probably the last thing she did, apart perhaps from visiting a drug store. The following day, when she had failed to turn up for work for the second day running, her landlady let herself into Maxi's room and found her dead in bed. She was only twenty-two.'

'Erika, I am so sorry. I had no idea.'

'How could you, I never told you. I have never told anyone.' She smiled at her friend. 'Rowena, please inform that man living in Wray Park Road I will have dinner with him on Wednesday.'

Rowena was astonished. 'Are you sure?'

'Yes, I'm sure. I need to know one way or the other – whether he's Martin Bormann or not. And if I find out for certain he is, I shan't think twice about tearing his balls off with my bare hands.'

Rowena sat in a daze, numbed by the shocking details of the story she had been told. With sincerity, she said: 'If you need any help …'

Chapter 22

Wednesday 11th July

Benjamin stood at the end of Hardwicke Road, frowning impatiently and looking at his wristwatch for the fifth time in as many minutes. Only six fifty-five … how could time go so slowly! He walked down the London Road to the corner of West Street, legs trembling, then back again. Not far, but enough to kill a couple more minutes.

He'd propped his bike up against the wall where Hardwicke Road met the London Road and, as he drew level with it, he saw a familiar figure walking towards him. Toffee Thompson. An old schoolmate.

'Grimshaw! Hello, mate – long time no see.'

'Toffee,' he replied, trying not to sound too dismayed. Just what he didn't want; the distraction of bumping into someone he knew.

'Still working for the Mirror?'

'I am. You still at Frith's in Raglan Road?'

'I am. Dull as ditch water … just a load of boring old photographs.'

'A lot of people would find that really interesting.'

'Not me. What you up to?'

'Oh, nothing much – just hanging around.'

'Come for a drink then. Some of us are meeting at the Black Horse on the heath.'

'Thanks, but I can't.'

'Come on, you just said you're not doing anything.'

'I'm meeting someone.'

Toffee Thompson raised his eyebrows and smirked. 'A bit of skirt, eh? I bet it is, you sly old dog. Just like your brother. Anyone I know?'

'I'm on an assignment. Work.'

'Ooh an assignment! Sounds like you're a spy.'

'Nothing exciting. Anyway, must go. Good to see you, Toffee. Say hello to the others.'

'Come and say hello yourself.'

'I can't … really.'

Toffee shrugged. 'Suit yourself.'

To Ben's relief, Toffee strolled off down the road. He watched until the figure had disappeared out of sight, then breathed a huge sigh of relief. He looked at his watch. Five minutes past seven. Now he was late – bollocks!

He hurried down Hardwicke Road. Oddly, the distraction had relaxed him rather than added to his nervous state, and his legs had stopped shaking. He knew precisely where the house with the red door was located; he'd cycled past it that morning, when he knew Mr and Mrs Wells would be at work. He reached it in no time and without slowing down turned onto the path that led alongside the front garden and down the side of the house. As he entered the back garden via a waist-height gate, he heard Barb's voice.

'Benjamin … hurry!'

She was standing in the kitchen doorway, beckoning him in. Once inside, the door was closed firmly. She backed against it and looked him up and down.

'Well, well, here we are at last. I thought for a moment you were going to let me down.'

'I'm only a few minutes late. Sorry, I bumped into someone I know at the end of the road. An old school friend.'

'Did you tell him what you were doing and who you were going to see … and why?'

'Of course not.'

'Well that's all right then. Care for a drink?'

'Yes please.'

'Ale or brandy?'

'Ale please.'

As she brushed past him, she pecked him on the cheek. He caught a whiff of her perfume. 'Do you make a habit of this, young Benjamin – being seduced by older women?'

'Is that what this is then … seduction?'

'Frankly, yes.'

'No, I don't. Do you?'

'You have to take your pleasures in life when you can. If you're not having much fun, then you have to do things to make it happen.'

'I'll take that as a yes then.'

Barb handed him a half-pint glass of beer. 'Sit down, Benjamin boy.'

He sat down on one of the Windsor chairs around a stout mahogany table that filled the centre of the kitchen. Barb stood next to him, leaning back against the table, arms folded, brandy glass in hand. She was barefoot and wearing a light summer skirt and blouse. Her hair was down, cascading onto her shoulders, the auburn colour more apparent with more to see. He caught her perfume again.

'You smell nice,' he said.

She leaned forward and brushed her cheek against his so that her nose was close to his ear. She breathed out, sending a slow stream of warm air floating its way inside his ear canal. It sent a shiver down him. She breathed in deeply. 'So do you.'

'Blimey, you don't hang around!'

She looked at him curiously. 'We both know why you're here, so what's the point of wasting time?'

'I suppose so.' He took a sip of beer. 'Why me?'

She ruffled his ginger hair and slid her palm around his face, allowing her forefinger to trace itself around his lips. 'Why not?'

'I think you should know … I'm not exactly …' He dried up. Words wouldn't come to express what he wanted to say.

'Experienced? Do you mean you've never done this before – been with a woman?'

'That's right.'

She smiled. 'Good, just how I like it. A clean slate. Now, to business. Did you bring the cards?'

'Cards?'

'Playing cards. I thought we were going to play poker.'

'I thought you were joking. Don't you have any?'

'Not to worry, we can manage without. Let's just strip.'

'Do you think we should talk a little first?'

'We just have.' She unfolded her arms and undid the top button of her blouse with one hand. Then the next button, and the next. Ben could see the pale skin of her neck and chest gradually being revealed, then the mounds of the top of her breasts. They weren't large but they were shapely. More buttons came undone. She wasn't wearing a brassiere, just a sort of underslip, and he could see the dark circles of her nipples though the fabric. He was transfixed.

'Would you like to touch them?'

He said nothing, just leaned forward and placed a hand gently on each breast. They were beautifully soft and warm. He could feel himself stiffening inside his pants. As if she knew,

201

Barb stretched out her arm, touched him between the legs and pressed slightly.

'Now then,' she said. 'The trick when you're new to all this is … any idea?'

'Tell me.'

'To relax and take your time. Don't rush. Otherwise it'll all be over in seconds, if you know what I mean.'

Ben thought he knew. Yes, he was fairly certain he knew what she meant.

She moved away from him slightly and finished undoing the buttons on her blouse. It fell to the floor. Then she lifted her arms in the air and the slip came over her head and landed next to the blouse. She shook her head so that her hair spun round in waves, and her breasts bobbed up and down. 'Another trick,' she said, 'is to get naked quickly. All that build up can get you over excited – make you come to the boil too soon.' She undid the claps on her skirt and it, too, fell to the ground. She wasn't wearing any knickers and was now completely naked. 'Your turn, Benjamin.'

He did as he was told, starting with his jacket, then shoes and socks, then shirt and trousers. All the time he stared at Barb's body; he couldn't take his eyes off her breasts, apart from to glance down at the mound of reddish-brown hair between her thighs. He'd never seen a woman naked before.

He stood facing her with just his underpants on, too embarrassed to take them off, and very self-conscious about what was protruding at the front. Barb smiled, stepped forward and slipped the pants down so he could step out of them. She threw them on top of her skirt.

'Now what,' asked Ben. 'To the bedroom?'

Barb shook her head. 'That's my least favourite place for having fun.' She tapped the kitchen table. 'This will do nicely.' She pressed her buttocks against the edge, took Ben's hands and pulled him towards her until their bodies were touching. His erection was in the way, so she raised it so it was pointing upwards and pressing flat against her stomach. Then she moved her hands round his sides and placed them on his buttocks, squeezing them a little. Gently, she touched his lips with hers, and they melted into their first kiss.

To Ben's surprise, her tongue licked playfully around his mouth and suddenly darted inside. He started. He'd kissed girls before, but never like this. French kissing. The idea seemed disgusting and it had never occurred to him to try it. Now it was being done to him … and it wasn't disgusting all. It felt really good.

The kiss seemed to last forever. Their lips didn't want to part. Ben had never experienced anything like it. Why, oh why had it never happened before! He was twenty, and most of his mates had got there long before … or so they claimed. Storm had for certain, but then he was different; Storm had the Midas touch with women, and just about everything else. Ben let his hands wander down Barb's back, following the ridge of her spine to the top of her thighs, and back again. He felt her follow suit, her hands tracing their way up to his shoulders and down again.

Eventually she took her lips away, put her hands on his shoulders and pressed down on them so that he had to squat a little. When his head was level with her breasts, she felt his mouth envelope a nipple and begin to suck.

She winced. 'Gently.'

'Sorry,' he mumbled.

'Don't talk with your mouth full, bad boy. Hmm…' She purred appreciatively. 'A quick learner. You have no idea what that is doing to me.'

'What is it doing?'

'Making me wet.'

'Wet?'

She took his hand and guided it to the base of the mound of hair between her legs. 'Wet. So it's easier for you to get inside.' Ben had no knowledge that this happened to a woman and was fascinated. He really was very naive. He had much to learn and realised that here was someone who was only too willing to be his teacher.

Barb hoisted herself onto the table, and spread her legs outwards, one on either side of Ben's thighs. He moved towards her, then hesitated, not knowing how to progress, where precisely to go from here. Barb came to his rescue. She steered him gently towards the core of her wetness.

Ben let out a moan of pleasure as he felt himself being enveloped by the moistness. Like the kiss, it was a totally new experience, and even more exciting.

Barb moaned. 'Gently now,' she whispered.

'Am I hurting you?'

'Not at all – I just want this to last, not all be over in a flash. Take your time, Benjamin boy.'

'I will. This is heaven.' He leaned forward and kissed her, this time pushing his tongue into her mouth. She wrapped her legs tight round him.

'Goodness,' she gasped. 'You do pick things up quickly.'

'I have a good teacher.'

'I knew the moment I saw you, in the shop, that I wanted you. There's something about you.'

'Same,' said Ben, which wasn't quite true. He'd found her attractive but never for a moment imagined this would happen.

'Oh God, this is fun. This is fun, Benjamin!' She wriggled her hips and swayed to left and right so that her breasts wobbled again. 'Life is all about having fun, or it should be.'

'Why did you marry him if you don't like him?'

'Security. My parents were poor, I had a lousy childhood. Along came Tunbridge and swept a young girl off her feet. His family has money. Look at this house – he inherited it. We couldn't afford this on shop wages. And we have plenty of money in the bank.'

'So why this?' Ben thrust into her a little harder to make his point.

'He likes to grope young girls, that's what excites him, but when it comes to the act he's hopeless. Can't stay the pace.' She looked at him appreciatively. 'Which is something you appear to have no problem doing. I think you're a natural.'

Ben was not going to let her into another piece of advice from big brother. *Have a practice run on your own before leaving home … you'll have more staying power second time round.* Even with this precaution under his belt, he still felt a familiar tingle building up already. Barb sensed it.

'I spoke too soon,' she cried. But it had excited her, the thought that he might climax at any moment, and she felt her body respond. She slipped a finger down and began to rub. No way was she going to miss out.

Suddenly she went still. She froze.

'What's wrong?'

'Shhhh!'

From the end of the hallway they heard the rattle of a key in a lock, followed by the sound of a door opening. 'Shit!' exclaimed Barb.

'Barb it's me – I'm back. Barb?'

Quick as lightening, she pushed Ben away and scrambled about for her clothing.

'Tunbridge?' she called out. 'You're early.' Then in a whisper to Ben: 'Take your clothes and go out the back. I'll distract him. Go!' Then louder: 'I'm in the kitchen – hang on I'm coming out. Is anything wrong?'

With blouse and skirt on, she disappeared into the hallway where her husband was removing his shoes, looking confused and dazed.

'Not feeling too grand. I think I'm coming down with something. Wasn't enjoying the game so bailed out.' He looked at Barb. 'You look flushed. What've you been up to?'

'Not feeling great either,' she said. 'Might be coming down with the same thing.' She took his arm and led him into the living room, on the opposite side of the house from the path leading to the back garden. 'Sit yourself down on the settee and I'll make you a hot toddy. Would you like that?'

'Sounds just the ticket.' He slumped down, flipped some slippers on and closed his eyes.

'You rest yourself,' said Barb. 'I'll boil the kettle ... won't be long.'

She made her way back into the kitchen. It was empty. She looked out of the window in time to see Benjamin disappearing up the path, pushing his bike, tucking his shirt in and trying to flatten down his hair. As he did so, he barrelled straight onto the dustbin and sent it crashing.

'What was that?' called out Mr Wells.

'Bloody cats after the rubbish again. I'll sort it.'

She went outside, picked up the bin and placed the lid back on. She caught a glimpse of Ben cycling off up the road as calm and as cool as you like.

'That was close,' she said to herself. 'But worth it. I think you and I have some unfinished business, Benjamin boy.'

****

As it was windowless and below ground level, the room was, unsurprisingly, dark, dank and cold, even in July. The walls, ceiling and floor were all concrete and in appearance it bore a strong resemblance to a prison cell, though larger. Terry Angel knew because he'd been in a few.

When he first came across it a couple of years ago, the room had obviously been abandoned and unused for a long while. The steel door had not been locked but it was ill-fitting and took an effort to pull open. There had been no lighting, so he fed a cable from the much larger, much damper, room outside and rigged up a lamp that shed a soft white light from a corner. It cast long shadows that gave an eerie feel to the place. Terry didn't care. He loved it up here. His sanctuary.

Along one wall stood a row of wooden packing cases, all resting on pallets a good foot away from the concrete behind to avoid any moisture. Some had lids, others were open, revealing an array of contents ranging from household goods to engine parts to bottles of beer and spirits. Stretching along the adjoining wall, at right angles, were several more pallets upon which lay sheets of lead and some piping. In the far corner, on the floor, stood a medium-sized green safe.

Terry had pinched an armchair from next door. It was musty but comfortable. There were a couple of sofas in there, too – he had no idea why – but he'd chosen the armchair as he had absolutely no intention of ever inviting anyone else into this, his private haven-cum-store room. He'd also brought up a nice paraffin lamp he'd stolen from a house in Lesbourne Road. He lit it whenever he visited, to take the edge off the cold and the damp.

Sitting in the armchair with a bottle of stout in one hand and a Woodbine in the other, it felt like home from home. Only more peaceful – much more peaceful – with no Beth ceaselessly exercising her lungs. He found himself coming here more and more recently. At first, he only came when he needed to stash away some loot, or collect something if he had a buyer for it. Nowadays he sometimes came simply to get away from it all and to daydream about the life he would like to lead in a perfect world.

The room wasn't ideal, located as it was at the top of Reigate Hill. The cycle ride was a real struggle sometimes, especially if he had a heavy bag with him. Coming down was easier. Sometimes he borrowed a mate's truck if he had a lot to shift one way or the other – lead for example, bloody heavy stuff – and getting the safe up there, which had nearly given him a hernia. But the place was secure. No one ever seemed to come up here, or if they did Terry had never seen anyone, apart from a young couple a while back who had been leaving the fort as he arrived, looking dishevelled. He thought he recognised the girl. He'd seen her somewhere before, serving in Knight's perhaps, or was it in The Old Wheel ... or both? The lad had probably just got his leg over, lucky beggar. Terry would dearly love to get his leg over, but Beth had lost interest a long time ago. He'd forgotten how it felt, it had been so long.

He surveyed the packing cases in front of him as he drank and smoked. He'd just added a few bits and pieces to his collection of ill-gotten gains and there was another nice big white five-pound note tucked away in the safe now. But he had nothing going out this visit, nothing he had a taker for that would bring in cash over the next few days. At least the ride down the hill wouldn't be the precarious balancing act it sometimes turned out to be.

Terry sat back, closed his eyes, and his mind wandered into dreamland. He was on a beach of white sand, with palm trees leaning over obligingly to give shade from the hot sun beating down from a cloudless sky. The sea was calm and greeny-blue in colour; turquoise, he thought the word was. He had no notion where such a perfect place might be. He'd never been aboard before. The South Seas? Jamaica? Not Brighton, for sure, the only beach he'd ever seen, and which looked nothing like this one, imagined from pictures in magazines.

He was wearing shorts and lying on a deckchair with slats rather than fabric; more luxurious than the ones in his garden shed in Woodhatch. In his hand, he held a large cocktail glass with all manner of fruit and an elaborate straw sticking out. He took a sip. He'd tasted a cocktail once and hated it, so as this was a dream, where anything was possible, it tasted miraculously of his favourite stout. His face wore an enormous grin that reached from ear to ear.

Next to him, wearing one of those bikinis he'd seen in the *News of the World*'s coverage of the build-up to the new Miss World Competition, lay Diana Dors; young, blonde, big-breasted, nubile and utterly desirable. Best of all, she wasn't talking. The fact that she came to mind because he'd recently seen her photograph in the same newspaper on her wedding day mattered not one bit.

Behind them, in amongst the palm trees stood a wooden hut. Through the open door Terry could see a huge double bed. Diana blew a kiss to him from her ruby red lips, inclined her head towards the hut and winked suggestively. Terry stared down at her magnificent breasts. He needed no more encouragement and stood up ... too hurriedly. He spilled his cocktail down his front. The sun seemed to fade away and was replaced by a harsh white light. He looked around him. To his dismay he found himself sitting in a grubby armchair in a damp concrete cell in the old fort on top of Reigate Hill.

Time to make a move, he decided reluctantly. Back to the harsh reality of his prosaic, humdrum existence. He checked that the combination wheel on the safe was well and truly spun, closed down the paraffin lamp and switched off the light. He'd fitted a new lock to the door, and it was a good one. He knew about locks. Then he climbed up the steps to the ground level

209

of the fort where he'd left his bike and headed along the footpath towards Reigate Hill for the freewheeling trip back into town.

It didn't take long to build up speed and when he was fair flying, he lifted his feet well off the pedals, allowing them to spin round freely.

He shouted: 'Diana Dors, you married the wrong man! It should have been meeeeeeeeee!'

****

Too restless to go straight home, Ben found himself in the castle grounds, bike resting against a tree and a rasper between his lips; the same lips that had been kissing Barb Wells only a few minutes earlier.

My God that had been good. So now, at last, he knew what it felt like to do it. Not to the very end, granted, but close. He'd found himself a real woman, and this was the start of something regular, he was certain. The close shave with Mr Wells hadn't scared him in the least. Next time they would meet somewhere neutral. Somewhere safe.

It worried him that she seemed to have done this before. Who with, and how often, he wondered. Was he just one of many? The latest in a long line?

When would the next time be? Soon, he hoped. Very soon, please. He closed his eyes and imagined himself back in her kitchen, writhing about with Barb Wells. On the kitchen table of all places!

What to do now. It half crossed his mind to cycle over to the Black Horse and meet up with Toffee Thompson and the others, whoever they were. But he really wasn't in the mood for socialising. What to do …

An idea dropped into his mind. It had been floating around in there towards the back for some time but had been swamped of late by other thoughts, most recently the highly erotic kind.

Of course, that was it. A bit of sleuthing. Time to meld into his hero, Philip Marlowe, and follow up on a lead just a few streets away. He'd need to kill some time, though, until it was dark. Easily done.

Yes, that's what he would do.

Chapter 23

Erika's stomach was in knots as she approached Peter Yardley's house. She stopped at the end of his road and smoked a cigarette to calm her nerves before continuing and parking her Alvis in the driveway, reversing in to accommodate a quick getaway if it came to that. She wore an unseductive trouser suite, and a blouse with a high neckline, the items in her wardrobe she felt were most likely to discourage wandering hands and lusty intentions.

The front door was opened by a man who said nothing and bowed as she walked past him into a large hallway. She recognised him as one of the two men who'd been with Peter Yardley at the fair on Reigate Heath. Yardley was standing close behind.

'Frau von Tirpitz, how good to see you. I am most flattered that you accepted my invitation.'

'It was good of you to invite me. I'm not sure why as we do not know each other.'

'An attractive woman with German roots … why would I not want to dine with you!'

'That is kind.'

'Please come through to the lounge and have an aperatif.'

'Thank you – a G and T would go down nicely.'

As he directed her towards a door off the hallway, Yardley's hand slipped round her waist and, predictably, down and around the curve of her bottom. Erika cringed at his touch. This was going to be a difficult evening, she realised; very difficult. Handling unwanted advances wasn't usually a problem – she'd had plenty of practice – but tonight was different; she knew she may have to be prepared to compromise in some ways, or at least exercise inordinate tolerance, if it helped to achieve her objective. On the positive side, this was England in 1951, not Nazi Germany, and if her host was indeed Martin Bormann he no longer held a position of power, nor would he be above the law in a way he had become accustomed to in a previous corrupt life. Nevertheless, she knew only too well that she could be dealing with a man who didn't take no for an answer lightly, if at all. She could be playing a dangerous game.

The lounge was spacious and inviting with a sofa and armchairs surrounding a large open fireplace. In a corner stood a drinks cabinet. She sat down, choosing an armchair rather than the sofa, and Peter Yardley handed her a large glass which one sip revealed to contain a great deal more G than T.

Yardley sat on the sofa and patted the empty space next to him. 'Come and sit here,' he said. 'So that we can become better acquainted.'

'I'm quite comfortable where I am, thank you. You have a lovely home, how long have you been here?'

'Thank you, about five years. I like it.'

'Rowena tells me you're alone apart from some servants.'

'Correct, I have a valet and a chauffeur who live with me – also a housekeeper, Mrs Dory, who is an excellent cook as you are about to discover. She is Irish but has perfected a number of German dishes for me. A treasure.'

'And you are a widower?'

213

Yardley nodded. 'Frau Furse has briefed you well.'

'She was the bearer of your surprise invitation. It was natural I should want to find out more about the man who was so keen to dine with me.'

'And here we are, two Germans, speaking to each other in English. Shall we revert to our mother tongue?'

'As you wish. Then we can try and guess where from.'

'We could simply tell each other, it would be simpler that way. I was born and brought up in Prussia.'

'And I am from Freiberg.'

'The Black Forest.'

'Indeed.' Erika drank some gin. It was going down too well; she was still nervous. 'Peter Yardley is not a very German name.'

'I changed my name when I settled here. Wilhelm Korngold was too Teutonic for someone living in the land of the victors immediately after the war.'

'Korngold – sounds Jewish.'

'A Jew I am most definitely not,' stated Yardley. 'You have kept your name?'

'I have indeed. Erika von Tirpitz continues to stand me in good stead.'

'With no recriminations?'

'Occasionally it generates an unfortunate response, socially, though nothing I cannot deal with. Most English people are fair-minded people in my experience. The Germans they come across in this country have suffered greatly – more so than themselves more often than not – and receive a sympathetic hearing. Have you not found so?'

'I cannot complain.'

'I am one of the fortunate ones who has suffered very little, although my family did not come off as lightly. They have been through a great deal.'

'In Germany?'

'Yes. Freiberg was heavily bombed towards the end of the war. My parents survived but they lost their home and all their possessions. Life was very hard for them from then onwards, worse in many ways after the surrender, with little food and so few amenities. Only in the last few years have things really returned to something resembling normality. It has been a long hard road for them.'

'Have you been back to see them?'

'Frequently. I tried to persuade them to come to England, but they wouldn't hear of it. Germany is their home and always will be.'

'But not yours?'

'No longer. I have lived here now for thirteen years. I am settled. And you, Mr Yardley …?'

'Peter.'

'Peter. Do you intend staying here?'

'I have no plans to the contrary at present, but things might change in the future. Who knows.'

'Would you go back to Germany?'

'I think not.'

'What about your children?'

'They are all well catered for.'

'Surely you miss them?'

'Life must go on. War has a habit of fragmenting human relationships and moving people in new directions, and not always together and in the same direction.'

'That sounds over pragmatic to me, if not lacking in any sense of parental duty.'

Yardley stiffened. 'Do you have children?'

'Sadly not.'

'Perhaps you are not in a position then to pass judgment. In life, the pragmatic are more likely to survive and flourish. Have you read *A Farewell to Arms*?'

'A long time ago. Why do you ask?'

'In that book Hemingway wrote … *The world breaks everyone and afterward many are strong at the broken places.* I think there is a lot of truth in that. I have grown strong in the broken places. So too will my children, and their children too.'

The door opened and the housekeeper appeared, smiling encouragingly.

Yardley stood up. 'Ah, dinner is served. Come through, Erika. May I call you by your first name?'

'You may.'

'I hope you are not vegetarian. If so there will be nothing but disappointment tonight. If not then you will dine well.'

'I am not. That is an unusual question to ask.'

'You have to be mindful of these things sometimes. Our mutual friend Mr Morell, for example, is a vegetarian.'

'As was the *Führer*.'

'So I believe,' said Yardley blandly.

The dinner was excellent. The main course was *Schweinshaxe* – pork knuckle – served with sauerkraut and potatoes, accompanied by a bottle of *Spätlese*, from the Mosel; a little sweet for Erika's taste but pleasant enough. They chatted about a range of topics ranging from life in Germany before the war to life in Surrey in 1951. She found his conversation interesting on some topics but dull on others; the arts, or anything cultural, were of no interest to him and he knew very little. The Hemingway quote, she discovered, was something he had come across in a magazine and memorised. He'd never read *A Farewell to Arms*, or any other book of substance so it appeared. Nevertheless, he was amiable and not without charm, though rough around the edges. She made him laugh several

216

times and when he did it was loud and raucous. His table manners were crude; at times, she could hardly swallow her food for the sound of grunts coming from across the table.

Dessert was a choice of either *Prinzregententorte* or *Apfelstrudel* with fresh cream. Erika chose the latter. As she ate, and Yardley was in the middle of a long and tedious explanation of something to do with farm management, her attention was drawn to the French windows behind him which were in her line of vision as she looked towards him. It was approaching ten o'clock and virtually dark outside, but she had noticed earlier that the window led onto a lawn at the back of the house. Low down in the corner, illuminated yellowish-orange by the light from the room, was a face. The face of a young man, peering into the room.

She was fascinated and curious, but said nothing and tried not to stare too obviously. The face remained there for a good few minutes, staring first around the room, then at Yardley's back, then directly at her. She made no direct eye contact, so he, whoever he was, had no idea he had been seen.

'Well, do you, or don't you?' said Peter Yardley.

'I'm sorry, what did you ask me?'

'I don't think you are interested in farms or farming, Erika, but I merely asked if you ride.'

'Oh, I see. Yes, I do, though only occasionally. And you?'

'I have just been telling you that I breed horses, so yes I ride. You seem distracted.'

'Not at all, I am enjoying this delicious *Strudel*.'

'Made with apples from my farm. More wine?'

'Thank you. Where is your farm?'

'In Kent – not far from Sevenoaks, in a village …'

Yardley broke off, distracted by noises from behind where he sat; a thump followed by the shattering of glass and a cry of pain. Erika's attention was already on the source. The face she'd

217

seen had been pressed forward against the window, with such force that the pane had broken. She saw the expression on the distorted face change from shock to pain and fear. The first cry was followed by more muffled cries and indistinct voices as those involved moved away.

Peter Yardley jumped out of his chair. 'Excuse me, I must see what is happening. I won't be a moment.'

As he reached the dining room door, it opened and a man half appeared before Yardley pushed him out and closed the door behind him. Erika stood up and walked across to the French windows. She knelt down. There were shards of glass on the carpet and others still in the lower frame of the window; the latter were covered in fresh blood. Whoever had been peering into the room would have nasty cuts to the face. She stood up, turned the key in the lock, opened the windows and looked out. She could neither hear anything nor see anyone. When Yardley returned, she was seated at the table again.

'We had an intruder in the garden. A trespasser.'

'Who was it?'

'Oh no one, a local boy I believe. He has been given a talking to and sent on his way.'

'Was he injured?'

'Not at all.'

'There is blood on the window, surely he will need medical attention.'

'He was fine.'

'But surely …'

'Shall we take coffee in the lounge? I have an excellent selection of liqueurs to tempt you with.'

Yardley's tone had hardened, indicating this was more an order than a suggestion. As they left the room, Erika glanced once more towards the bloodstained glass in the French windows, unconvinced that the trespasser had walked away unscathed. In the lounge, a tray with coffee was awaiting them. Again, she chose the armchair.

'Now, dear Erika, this time I must insist that you sit next to me here on the sofa. I have enjoyed this evening and would like to feel we are on less formal terms now. We won't be disturbed again and so we have the opportunity to be a little more intimate with each other.' Erika said nothing but, hesitantly and unwillingly, moved across to the sofa next to him. 'That's better. Now, here is coffee, and also, I have managed to acquire some of my favourite liqueurs from home – *Ratzeputz*, *Jägermeister*, *Killepitsch*, *Kuemmerling*. Which do you choose?'

'None for me thank you. I still have wine.'

'Well later then. I also have *Steinhäger*, not unlike the gin you had earlier.'

'Perhaps.'

Yardley stood up and walked over to a table covered in bottles and glasses and poured himself a drink. 'I think I shall have *Killepitsch*, from Düsseldorf. Not so well known as some others, but excellent.'

He took a sip, set the glass next to his coffee and instead of sitting down again moved to the back of the sofa and stood behind Erika. He placed his hands on her shoulders, squeezed them gently as if to begin massaging them, then in a sudden crude movement slid them down to cup her breasts.

Erika was startled and spilt some wine. Her first reaction was to turn around and slap his face. Instead she edged forwards so his hands were out of reach and said calmly: 'Now, Peter, that is no way to treat a lady.'

'I'm sorry, Erika, but I have been admiring your body all evening and I simply could not resist the temptation to touch.'

'I'm flattered but would prefer it if you did not.'

She stood up. He moved round the sofa and stood in front of her, his face close to hers.

'May I kiss you?'

'No, you may not.'

'That is no way to show appreciation to your host.'

'Am I expected to offer you sexual favours in exchange for dinner?'

'I would like that very much.'

He leaned forward and pressed his lips against hers. His hands went around her waist. Despite her better judgment, she allowed it to happen. His body moved close to hers and she could feel him grinding his groin into hers. His hands were on her buttocks, squeezing them hard. She pushed her head back to free herself from the kiss.

'You are not exactly very subtle in your intentions, Peter. Shall we sit down and talk?'

'I don't want to talk. You are a very attractive woman and I want you.'

'Well I'd prefer to talk, and just because you find me attractive doesn't mean you can have me. The attraction needs to be mutual.'

'I assure you, Erika, you won't be disappointed, you will find me very satisfying.'

'I don't wish to find out either way.'

They stood looking at each other for an awkward few seconds, then she sat down again on the sofa. 'Tell me about your wife, what was her name?'

'Gerda.'

'Was she pretty?'

'Very, but you are prettier. Let us not talk about her at this precise moment.'

He bent down and kissed her again, at the same time using both hands to spin her round and push her backwards so she was forced to lie across the sofa. He was half on top of her and his body weight meant she could struggle but not get up. One hand kept her pressed down, the other roamed across her breasts, squeezing them roughly.

'This is what you want, I know.'

'I know I do not.'

'I like women of spirit, and you have a great deal.'

He groaned as the groping hand slid down from her breasts, across her stomach and plunged between her legs. She winced and in response managed to ease a hand down his body and onto the bulge in his trousers. He took this for encouragement and groaned again.

'See, I knew you'd come around to my way of thinking.'

Erika's hand lingered there, her teeth clenched with disgust. 'So, you find me attractive.'

'Very.'

'You should have seen my sister – she was even more so. Stunning looks, and a magnificent body.'

'I can believe it if she was your sister.'

'You'd have loved Maxine,' said Erika. 'Talented, too. She was a singer, an instrumentalist, and a budding film actress in the making.'

'Was?'

'She died.'

'I'm sorry.' His head had buried itself into the space between her breasts. He nuzzled against them like a baby.

'Maxine Vogel. Does the name ring any bells?'

Yardley paused for a moment then replied: 'No.'

'She died in Berlin in 1940. Suicide. She killed herself after she was raped by a high-ranking Nazi official who then had her boyfriend murdered for seeking justice.'

'A sad tale.'

'Sad indeed.' He mumbled something else which sounded like 'Shit happens'. Her hand meandered its way beyond his erection and surrounded the soft scrotum beneath.

'Hmm,' moaned Yardley appreciatively. 'I like that.'

'Some would say a tragic tale.'

'Indeed.'

'Criminal even.'

'Oh God that is good,' moaned Yardley. 'That is so good.'

'How is this?' Erika suddenly tightened her fingers round his balls, clenching them with a grip of steel.

'AAHH!' screamed Yardley.

'Did you rape my sister?'

'AAAAAAAHHH!'

Erika yelled at him. 'Did you?'

'I … I don't know what you are talking about!' Yardley was having trouble thinking, let alone constructing an intelligent reply.

Erika yelled again. 'My sister, Maxine Vogel. Did you rape her?'

'I can't …'

'Can't what? You can't what?'

'I can't …'

By pulling himself sideways Yardley managed to free himself from Erika's grip, but not before Erika had clenched her fist even tighter for a moment and twisted his balls savagely round. He slumped to the floor, both hands between his legs, his face contorted with pain. Erika sat upright and adjusted her clothing.

'You did or you didn't, you bastard, and if you did you have me to contend with. If I ever find out for certain, you will suffer more than bruised balls. Now, how about that *Steinhäger* you promised me? I'd much prefer that to sexual interference.' Then as a barely audible addition: 'From you at any rate.'

Yardley groaned once more from the floor.

That pause when she had mentioned her sister's name. Was it the precursor to a lie? She couldn't be sure; she wanted to know badly, but she couldn't be certain. Whichever he was, vicious rapist or a mere priapic nobody, he deserved what she had just meted out.

Erika looked down at him with disgust, and decided enough was enough.

'On second thoughts, forget the *Steinhäger*. I've had enough of your hospitality for one evening. Don't worry, I'll see myself out.'

****

The car that had followed Erika's from her house in Smoke Lane to Peter Yardley's was parked opposite and a little along Wray Park Road. At that point, the road was lined with trees which in midsummer were densely populated with leaves. One such tree overhung the car and left the man in the driver's seat shrouded in deep shadow. When darkness fell, the street lighting was poor and, sitting in the driver's seat, he was almost invisible.

He sat there all evening, from the moment she arrived to the moment she came out of the house and drove away again several hours later, with one brief exception to relieve himself up against the tree outside. It had been a difficult vigil, his head spinning as he imagined what might be going on inside. Dinner obviously. But then what? A romp on the sofa, or upstairs in the bedroom? He felt his face redden and his heart race at the thought. Erika was his, and no other man was allowed anywhere near her, in his mind. Who was this other man? He hadn't caught a glimpse of him when the door had opened to let her in, but he'd seen him with her in Reigate; a shrivelled up specimen of a man with hunched shoulders, far too old for her. He even needed a stick to walk properly. And a German to boot ... outrageous! What on earth did she see in the man.

There were few people about. At one stage, he saw a young lad cycle past on a bicycle and dismount on the pavement somewhere near the German's house. It was too dark to see where he went, but he didn't come back and there had been no further sign of him, so he assumed he'd continued on up Wray Park Road. Later a car had emerged from the driveway and headed off in the direction of Reigate, one man driving and another in the passenger seat. They were mere silhouettes, but even in a split second as they passed him he could see they were younger, more upright; not the man he was gunning for.

When Erika drove away, he was able to relax a little. Whatever had gone on in the house, at least she wasn't staying the night, which for him would have been unbearable. He started the engine and drove off. He lived no more than a few minutes away, across the road that led up towards the top of Reigate Hill; very close to the house that had been commandeered as the headquarters of 21st Army Group, where he had proudly served towards the end of the war, having escaped the tediousness of the Home Guard back into the real world.

Tonight, he had achieved a good deal. He had kept a watchful eye on his woman, and he now knew where the Kraut lived. Next objective?

Pay him a visit and explain to him, in plain simple English, some home truths.

****

The phone rang and rang. Eventually there was a click as the handset at the other end was picked up.

'Freddie … I thought you'd never answer.'

'Mrs von T?'

'It is.'

'Same as before?'

'Not quite the same. However, your services are most certainly required nevertheless, to help restore my faith in the male of the species.'

'Give me half an hour.'

'Fifteen minutes.'

'Twenty.'

'Fifteen!'

The phone went dead.

Chapter 24

Thursday 12th July

On days like these, mused Bob Weaver as he cycled along a leafy path from Reigate Heath up towards Colley Hill, his line of work was pretty good. It was a bright, warm, sunny summer morning and here he was heading out into the countryside, into the open air, instead of a drab factory or office. He'd done his time in factories before the war – bottling mineral water and before that at the Mellersh & Neale brewery – and he'd hated every minute. He'd been glad when they laid him off both times. Working at the mine suited him very well; and Mr Naylor was a fair guvnor.

When he told people he was a miner, they sympathised at first, as if it was a curse, automatically assuming he spent his days deep in the bowels of the earth, never seeing daylight and living the life of a mole. But it wasn't like that at the Hearthstone Mine, not for him at least. These days he worked as much on the surface as underground, since the guvnor had made him foreman.

They mined a chalky white stone, found commonly in the Surrey Downs, which was dried, crushed and sieved into a fine powder. Then it was pressed into artificial blocks before being shipped off by train to London for packaging. All that to provide the housewives of Britain with Panda, Osowhite and Snowdrift, products that kept their hearths and doorsteps bright and clean. Managing the whole process was Bob's responsibility.

It was early – not yet seven. He was always first to arrive and enjoyed that half hour of peace and quiet before the others put in an appearance, three miners and Mr Naylor if it was his day to visit, as it was today. He managed three other mines in the vicinity and divided his time between them. Bob cycled towards the metal gates at the foot of the Downs as usual and, even from a distance, he could see something wasn't right. The gates weren't shut or padlocked, the way he had left them the afternoon before. They were gaping open, and when he got nearer he saw the padlock lying discarded on the ground. He dismounted, walked his bike up to the entrance and leaned it against the fence. Still hanging down from one of the gates was the chain that had been attached to the padlock. It had been cut clean through.

Bob looked through the gates into the site, which was rather like a small quarry. He could see no one. He entered the yard cautiously, looking around from side to side. Directly ahead of him was the entrance to the mine; to his left the main building, to his right the stacking shed. Dotted around were a few barrows, some planks on the ground and not much else. He walked across to the main building, which was never locked, and looked inside. Nothing appeared to be missing, not that there was anything worth stealing, and nothing had been moved in any way. He crossed over to the stacking shed; all was in order there, too.

There had at one time been a good many more buildings – until the day in 1944 when a stray doodlebug fell to earth near the drying shed and destroyed them all. Luckily the miners had finished for the day and the place was empty. Bob had heard the explosion at home in his terraced cottage on the edge of the heath, but hadn't known it was the mine that had been hit until the next morning when he turned up for work. The yard had been a mess. All the buildings had been flattened; they found sheets of corrugated iron wrapped around the branches of nearby trees. The main building was rebuilt, only smaller than the original, and so was one of the stacking sheds, but that was all. The heyday of Hearthstone, in the twenties, was over and they weren't needed any more. Despite this, the mine had kept open throughout the war and Bob remained there for the duration. He'd been forty when it all kicked off and knocking on forty-five by the time of D-Day; too old for the call up. So, he'd had a cushy war compared with others. Mr Naylor had even managed to wangle the miners extra rations in exchange for allowing local residents to use the mine as an air raid shelter when the bombing was at its worst.

He approached the mine entrance, following the rails that brought the trucks full of stone out direct to the stacking shed. It had a sturdy wooden door, but rarely did anyone shut it, especially not in the summer months. The dark gaping hole in the hillside seemed ominous and he could feel himself tensing up as he drew nearer. Someone had broken in for a reason and if there was nothing untoward in the yard it made the chances of discovering something in the mine greater. There might even be someone in there.

He saw a broken pickaxe handle lying on the ground nearby and felt better when he'd picked it up and had it firmly in his grip. He edged his way forward.

'Who's there?' he called out, his voice feebler than intended and with a slight shake to it.

No response.

'Come on, show yourself!'

Nothing. He reached the entrance. Bob had walked in and out of that mine a thousand times and knew he was at a disadvantage compared to someone inside. They would be

228

looking out towards daylight and be able to see him clearly, whereas looking in, all he could see was pitch black. He needed a light. He hurried over to the main building and was back in less than a minute with a powerful torch. He flicked the switch and shone the strong beam into the tunnel. Feeling more confident, he stepped inside. He saw nothing amiss, just the rail tracks and the tunnel walls and ceiling stretching ahead of him. It wasn't spacious; Bob was five feet seven inches tall and his head almost touched the roof. Fifty yards in, the tunnel doglegged to the left and the rails ran onto a small turntable so trucks could make the bend. There were also several side tunnels. If someone was hiding in there, they had plenty of choice and it was potentially dangerous to go any further. Perhaps he should hold back and wait for the others, or even call the police and report the break-in. Let them take the risk. That would be the wise thing to do.

Just a bit further.

'Anyone there?'

Nothing.

'Show yourself!'

Then Bob noticed something unusual. He stopped. He could see an object on the ground, sticking out from one of the side tunnels ahead and to the left. It looked like a boot, or a shoe. He edged forward, shining the torch beam in that direction. Definitely a shoe.

Not just a shoe; he could see a leg now.

'Who's there?'

No reply.

Before long he had reached the dogleg and could see around the corner. His torch illuminated a body; the lifeless body of what appeared to be a young man. His legs and arms were tied and he was lying face down in a very unnatural position, like a broken shop manikin. The face, turned sideways and clearly visible, was badly bruised and swollen and there were cuts to his mouth, nose and forehead. The back of his skull was missing and the brains inside were exposed. What was left of his ginger hair was matted with blood.

Shortly afterwards, Mr Naylor arrived at the mine. He, too, saw the padlock which was still lying on the ground, and the broken chain hanging limply from the gate. He headed towards the main building, but his attention was drawn to a figure at the side of the mine entrance, leaning forward, hands on knees. It was Bob Weaver, retching up his breakfast.

'Bob!' he called. 'You all right … what's the matter?'

Bob looked up, his face bleached as white as the stone they mined.

Guv,' he croaked. 'You need to call the police. Now.'

Part Two

Chapter 25

Monday 16th July

It was quiet in The Old Wheel. The lunchtime rush was over
and two-thirty was too early for afternoon tea. Consequently,
Rowena and Erika had the place virtually to themselves. The
only other customers were what appeared to be an elderly
gentleman at a table in the corner hidden behind a broadsheet
newspaper, and a couple of men a few tables away who were
deep in conversation.

'Well,' said Rowena. 'Now you've had some time to mull
it over, what do you think?'

'What do I think about what?'

'You know exactly what. About Peter Yardley. Is he, or
isn't he?'

'Is he or isn't he Martin Bormann?'

'Who else?'

'I don't know.' Erika shook her head slowly from side to
side then stared out of the window. 'I just don't know. I made a
mess of things the other night. If only I could have held onto his
crown jewels a few moments longer, I might have squeezed the
truth out of him.'

'On the contrary, I think you did remarkably well, and you
were very brave taking such a risk. Just imagine what might

have happened if he'd overpowered you. He might have, you know …'

'Oh, I can look after myself. The frustrating thing is, no result. I'm not certain that I got a positive recognition when I told him about my sister. There might have been, but I just cannot be sure. I still don't know. He started a sentence. He said *I can't* … but never finished.'

'*I can't remember*, perhaps?'

'*I can't stand the pain*, more like.'

'So,' said Rowena calmly. 'We are no further forward than we were before. We have on our hands two men who are either Adolf Hitler and Martin Bormann – probably the most wanted men on the planet, the evil remnants of the Nazi regime – or we have Mr Peter Yardley and Mr Theodor Morell, two perfectly innocent human beings, refugees, unfortunates and victims as much as any others.'

'Ah but it's not quite that black and white, is it. Even if they aren't Hitler and Bormann they are not entirely innocent. For a start, one of them claims he *is* Adolf Hitler – and if he isn't then why is he doing that?'

'You said it yourself, my dear,' said Rowena. 'He could be bonkers. Howard is firmly of that opinion.'

'Howard could well be right. But tell me, Row, what do you think? You've spent more time with Mr Morell than I have. Does he strike you as crazy?'

'No.'

'I agree.'

'And yet he is maintaining this charade. Why? What's it all about?'

Erika drew on her cigarette then took a sip of tea. She pulled a face, pulled out her silver flask and emptied some liquid into her cup.

'Tea and gin? Ugh!' Rowena pulled a face.

'Try it. The gin hides the taste of the tea nicely.'

'No thank you. So, if we don't think Mr Morell is crazy, we are saying the opposite, that he is sane – a rational, normal person. The problem is, this rational, sane man tells us he is Adolf Hitler. So, what is there to stop us believing him?'

'The main reason is that we know Hitler is dead.'

'He says he escaped from the bunker by trickery … sleight of hand he called it. That's not impossible I suppose. If he did escape then why else shouldn't we believe him?'

Erika rolled her eyes. 'We've been through all this before. There are a dozen reasons. He doesn't look like him, he's the wrong age, he has no charisma. Let's face it, Row, it's just a plain bloody stupid idea altogether.'

'So, he isn't Hitler – in which case he has to be someone else, a different man altogether, and he is deliberately lying to us. Why? Who is he? A man of some standing, otherwise he wouldn't have been at that dinner in Berlin where he remembers meeting you. That's one of the few facts we have actually. Curiously he is using a false name which makes a direct connection with Hitler, that of his personal physician, who we know for certain is dead. Again, why?'

'Surely, if Morell is someone else, that should lead us to accept that Peter Yardley is also someone else, and not Martin Bormann. Do we believe that?'

'I don't know. But whoever we have, they know each other. There is history between them.'

The two sat in silence, pondering the situation. Rowena was the first to speak.

'They may not be a pair.'

'What do you mean?'

'Well, it occurs to me that we may have one but not the other. We may have an Adolf Hitler and a Peter Yardley, or we may have a Martin Bormann and a Mr Morell, or whatever his

235

real name is. But … we may not necessarily have a Hitler *and* a Bormann.'

'This is hopeless!'

Their attention was drawn to the two men at the other table. One of them had spilled his tea and they were both giggling, rather like schoolgirls.

'Sorry, Mickey, bloody clumsy of me,' said one. 'Can't take me anywhere.'

'Makes me wonder how you manage any business at all on stage,' said the other.

'With difficulty sometimes. Lots of careful planning.'

'Ned, you have nothing but my pure admiration.'

The tea spiller, Ned, had stood up and was mopping the front of his trousers with a serviette. The man called Mickey noticed that the two women on the nearby table had stopped chatting and were looking across at them.

'Sorry for the disturbance, ladies,' he called. His voice was high and reedy in tone, squeaky almost. 'My friend is a liability in public sometimes. Typical thespian – always seeking the limelight.'

'That's quite all right,' replied Erika. 'My friend here has trodden the boards in her time, so we can sympathise.'

'Erika,' whispered Rowena. 'Be quiet for heaven's sake – that was years ago, and opera, not acting.'

'You have to act in opera as well as sing, surely?'

'Yes but …'

Mickey stood up and walked across to their table. 'An actress – really?'

'Ha ha, not at all!' said Rowena bashfully. 'I studied opera at music college but have never sung professionally.'

The man was smartly dressed; tall, slim, almost bald and with a pencil-thin moustache. 'Ah but I know very well about the need to be able to both sing and act well in opera. You'll like my latest film then – *The Tales of Hoffman* – when it eventually sees the light of day.'

'Offenbach?'

'That's right. We finished filming a year ago but it hasn't been released yet – should be in cinemas soon, at last, I hope.'

'When you say *my* latest film …'

'Allow me introduce myself.' He held out his hand. 'Michael Powell – director.'

'Delighted to meet you. I'm Erika von Tirpitz and this is Rowena Furse.'

The man called Ned walked over and joined them. He was shorter than Powell with dark hair and an appealing face. 'You've deserted me for these charming young ladies, Mickey – who are they please?'

'And this is Esmond Knight, a fine actor whom I've had the pleasure of directing on many occasions. May we sit down for a moment?'

'By all means, said Erika. The men sat on either side of the women. 'We have a department store called Knight's here in Reigate.'

'What an extraordinary coincidence,' said Esmond Knight. 'No relation that I'm aware of. My family originates from Kent.'

'Weren't you in *The Red Shoes*?' said Rowena.

'Amongst others, that is correct.'

'And *Black Narcissus*. You played the old general. *Let them eat sowsages*!'

'Goodness, you do know your films,' laughed Esmond Knight. 'I enjoyed playing that character – pity I was bumped off so early in the story.'

'Blame Emeric, not me, dear Ned,' said Michael Powell. 'He wrote the screenplay. Or Rumer Godden for writing it that way in her novel.'

237

Rowena said: 'My husband's cousin was in one of yours – *A Canterbury Tale*.'

'Did you say your name is Furse? Ah Judith, of course. And her brother Roger is a wonderful costume designer and art director.'

'I was in *A Canterbury Tale*, too,' cut in Esmond Knight. 'Thrice in fact – as a pipe smoking soldier, the village idiot and I also spoke the introductory narrative. I know Roger. He's working on the production I'm in at the moment.'

'And what is that?' ask Erika.

'A double production I should say – *Caesar and Cleopatra* and *Antony and Cleopatra* – with Larry Olivier and Vivien Leigh.'

'I read the reviews,' said Rowena. 'Alternating one play with the other each night. Have I got that right?'

'You have indeed. One's by Shakespeare of course, and the other is George Bernard Shaw. I play Menas in the Shakespeare and Belzanor in the Shaw … or is it the other way around, I can never remember.'

Michael Powell grinned. 'We'll have to take your word for it, Ned.'

'In fact, curiously enough, Larry told me it was Roger's idea to put on both plays.'

'Must be a huge challenge – remembering the lines alone must be a huge task.'

'That's Larry for you, always up for a challenge. He wanted a mighty one for the Festival of Britain. You should come along. It's on at the St James's Theatre.'

'I think that's a definite,' said Rowena. 'And what, may I ask, are you doing spilling your tea here in Reigate's finest teashop, ha ha?'

'A delicate matter,' explained Powell. 'We've driven down on a mission to see the man behind the gong, Mr Rank. Ned

238

here has an idea for a film, which I'm very keen on, too, and we want to put the scenario to him. We thought we'd try the informal approach.'

'He lives over by the heath, I believe.'

'That's right. We're just going to happen to be passing, pop in, and just happen to mention the storyline – see what he thinks. Stopped in here first for some un-Dutch courage, the pubs being shut. Besides, mustn't turn up with alcohol on our breath. J. Arthur wouldn't like that. Methodist.'

'Why is it a delicate matter?'

'I won't bore you with film industry politics,' said Michael Powell. 'But we had a parting of the ways with Rank a few years ago. By "we" I mean myself and Emeric Pressburger, my writer and creative partner, or The Archers if you prefer, which is the name of our production company. We jumped ship in favour of Alex Korda … and for good reason. So, keen as I am to help Ned here, I rather think it might be more appropriate if I wait in the car.'

'Nonsense!' declared Esmond Knight. 'Might help do some bridge building.'

'What's your idea, Mr Knight?' asked Erika.

'Good heavens, well now, to answer that I'd have to insist that you both assure me of absolute confidentiality. Do either of you have connections with the film industry, other than being related by marriage to Roger and Judith?'

'Absolutely none.'

'All right, well I'll take a chance. In brief – and in the strictest of confidence – I have an idea to tell the story of the Battle of Agincourt. Not very original, I can hear you thinking. Surely Larry has already done that and better than anyone could ever imagine in *Henry V*, which I was also in, by the way, I'm proud to say … look you! And what a scriptwriter, William Shakespeare no less. Ah but my idea is to see the whole thing

239

from a very different perspective, not from the point of view of the king, but from that of one of the archers. They pretty much won the day at Agincourt with their incredibly powerful longbows. You know, five thousand archers could fire off fifty-thousand thousand arrows in one minute. Deadly! I want to tell his story from the day this ordinary man is enlisted into Henry's army to the day he returns home safe and sound to his family … and all stops in between.'

'The unsung hero.'

'Precisely.'

'Well, I wish you luck, it sounds very exciting.'

'Thank you. I hope J. Arthur Rank feels the same way.'

'And will you direct, Mr Powell?'

'That remains to be seen, and how the land lies with Rank. Haven't mentioned it to Emeric yet – but I'm sure he'll be keen to work up the script based on Ned's storyline.'

'We too have the beginnings of a wonderful film story,' said Rowena proudly. 'Playing out at this very moment.'

'Really,' said Powell, an air of caution in his voice. 'And what might that be?'

'Perhaps I shouldn't say anything, but well … this might interest you.'

'Try us.'

'In the strictest of confidence, we have discovered that Adolf Hitler and Martin Bormann didn't die at the end of the war after all. They both escaped. Hitler went to live in the Canary Islands, Bormann came to England and helped the British government with something or another, and they are both alive and well … and living here in Reigate. They're my next-door neighbours in fact.'

Mickey looked across at Ned and after a few moments they shook their heads and said in unison: 'Too far-fetched.'

Erika seemed taken aback. 'But it's a true story.'

'Sorry, no one would believe it. Good stories have to have at least a semblance of reality about them. Emeric would tell you so.'

Rowena was peeved and crossed her arms defensively. 'For example,' she retorted. 'A pilot jumps out of a plane without a parachute, survives an impossible fall without so much as a sprained ankle, cheats death, then is judged in a court case held in Heaven with God in charge of the proceedings. That's one of yours, isn't it?'

Mickey Powell laughed. 'Hoisted with my own petard!' he exclaimed. 'If I had time I would argue the difference, but Ned and I really must be making tracks.' He stood up. 'It has been a pleasure meeting you both. Good luck with the story – I look forward to seeing the film. How about approaching David Lean, he might like the idea? Or Michael Balcon at Ealing.'

'Cheerio, ladies,' said Esmond Knight, also getting up. 'Charming company, albeit brief. Not a word about my idea, now, and you must come and see us doing Caesar and Cleo. Vivien is wonderful! The St James's Theatre. Don't forget. Phone them and mention my name ... I'll arrange for you to have some House Seats.'

'Why thank you. We won't forget.'

'Come on, Ned, let's be off. I suppose I'm paying?'

When the two men had settled the bill and disappeared down the rickety stairs, Rowena turned to Erika and let out a huge sigh.

'Well, what did you make of that!'

'Rather exciting.'

'I'll say. Can't wait to tell Howie I've been hobnobbing with film people. Especially ones who know his cousins.'

'You seem to know all about them. I've seen *The Red Shoes* of course, but none of the others you mentioned. Is Ned, or whatever his name is, a good actor?'

241

'Esmond Knight – oh yes, he's wonderful. Such a shame he can't take bigger roles. Did you notice anything unusual about him?'

'He seemed a bit unsteady on his feet. If someone had been spiking their tea, I wouldn't be at all surprised.'

'Ha ha, no that's not it. Believe it or not he's almost completely blind.'

'You are joking!'

'Not at all. Injured during the war – he was in the navy and wounded in the battle to sink the Bismarck. Lost one eye and badly damaged the other.'

'Surely not. But he's on stage with Laurence Olivier and Vivien Leigh. How on earth does he get by?'

'I think the only way to find out is to go and see. Are you game? If Howard wants to come, we could make a threesome. If not then perhaps Mr Morell.'

'Would love to – let me know when. You said something about a pilot falling out of a plane and cheating death, then a court case in Heaven. That rings a bell.'

'*A Matter of Life and Death* – a remarkable film. David Niven is the pilot, Peter Carter. He jumps out of a burning plane without a parachute. He was supposed to die, but survives by landing in soft sand on a beach, and they were waiting for him in Heaven …'

'So, they send someone down to collect him, and he refuses to go because he's met a girl and fallen in love with her in the meantime?'

'That's the one. The court case takes place in his imagination during an operation on his brain. Such an original idea. But my point to Mr Powell was that there is more reality in our story than there ever was in his.'

'I don't know, Row, perhaps there isn't. Perhaps we've been imagining things when there is nothing there and a fantasy based in Heaven and on Earth is more credible than Hitler and Bormann popping up in Surrey in 1951.'

'I think you're probably absolutely right. And I think Mr Morell has been guilty of leading us up a long and winding garden path. Let's forget the whole thing.'

'I'll drink to that.'

Erika took out her flask and poured again.

'I could get used this G and Tea.'

****

Colonel Maxwell peered over his newspaper and stared across the empty room, catching a glimpse of Erika as she made her way downstairs. His mouth was agape as he sat back in his chair trying to make sense of what he had overheard. Not the banal nonsense with the two men about films and plays, rather the conversation before that between Erika and her friend; he'd seen them about together but had never been introduced. He hadn't heard everything they said, but enough to get the gist. Hitler and Bormann here in Reigate – and one of them the man he'd seen with Erika and who might just be sharing her affections. What nonsense.

Total and utter balderdash in fact. Hitler was long dead, so what on earth were they talking about! Had they spotted him in the corner of the tearooms and decided to wind him up? Bormann he knew had vanished after the war, and been condemned to death at Nuremberg in his absence as no one could be sure he wasn't still alive. Sightings were rife in the newspapers; Australia, Egypt, Italy, numerous South American countries … Chile, Argentina, Ecuador. None had been verified. But Reigate was not among them, of that he was quite certain. What fugitive Nazi in their right mind – or was that an

243

oxymoron – would pop up in the English Home Counties for heaven's sake!

Would that it were true. What he wouldn't give for ten minutes alone with one of them. Some kind of payback for so many comrades lost in both wars, not to mention brother Masons. Six million Jews, gypsies, homosexuals and mentally subnormal killed at Auschwitz and other camps, that was common knowledge. But rarely were the eighty thousand Freemasons who also perished given a mention.

Resentment was boiling up inside him. He was overdue now to pay this Yardley, or Bormann or whatever his name was, a visit.

He called over to the waitress, paid his bill and walked home up Reigate Hill. Some strategic planning was in order.

Chapter 26

Tuesday 17th July

Mr Morell glanced at Peter Yardley, peering over the top of his spectacles like a headmaster weighing up an errant schoolboy. They were sitting in Yardley's lounge, Morell with a cup of apple peel tea, Yardley a glass of schnapps.

'Are you all prepared?'

'I am. We set off first thing tomorrow. Ferry from Newhaven to Dieppe, then a long drive across land into Spain and finally a boat from Cadiz. Easier and faster by sea all the way, but safer to drive where possible. Once on board a ship there are no escape routes.'

'You know where to find them?'

Yardley nodded. 'As you know, we tracked them down on the last visit. I am having them watched. They are staying just outside La Oliva, on the north side of the island, well away from Villa Winter. Personally, I would have left for the mainland as soon as they knew their secret was out. Islands are like ships – nowhere to hide.'

'Perhaps not as easy as it sounds. And they probably think there is safety in their remoteness.'

'Well they are wrong. Too near the scene of the crime.'

'Make it quick and painless … for Eva at least.'

'I will see to it. And him?'

Morell shrugged. 'Do as you please. I don't care.'

'While I am away you will be moving into the house, as we agreed?'

'It really is not necessary.'

'I would prefer it if you did.' Yardley pointed towards the garden. 'The summer house is not safe and after the incident last week I would be more comfortable if you were inside a solid brick building and behind a securely locked door.'

'Nothing untoward will happen, but as you wish. To change the subject, have there been any repercussions following the *incident*, as you call it?'

'None. They did a good clean job. There is nothing to connect the body with us.'

'A foolish act. A few unequivocal words in his ear and a beating would have been sufficient.'

'He was from the press. Too great a risk to let him keep nosing around.'

'Too great a risk to commit murder when it is prudent to keep a low profile.'

'And yet I am off tomorrow to do just that … on your behalf.'

'On a remote island, hundreds of miles from home where the police force is virtually non-existent, and what they do have is a joke. For a few pesetas, they will turn a blind eye to most things. Very different from this country.'

Yardley stood up and stretched himself. 'I have a question for you. Would you regard it as keeping a low profile to inform the indigenous population around here that you are Adolf Hitler?'

Still peering over the top of his spectacles, Morell said: 'You think I am playing with fire? Perhaps I am. Perhaps we both are. Perhaps there is a part of us that embraces danger and risk, and would relish the notion of being recognised for who we really are and what we have achieved.'

'You perhaps, not me. You are a leader, a front man. I'm more comfortable behind the scenes. I am anonymous by comparison. I take few risks. Killing that young man was risk free. Nobody saw anything and there are no loose ends.'

'Didn't Frau von Tirpitz see or hear anything? It happened the evening she was having dinner with you, surely.'

'She saw and heard nothing.' Yardley lied comfortably and with experienced ease.

Morell removed his spectacles and played with the arms, as if checking they were in good order. 'I hope that is so … for both our sakes.'

****

Business was brisk at Knight's that morning. After a slow start – not unusual for midweek – the tills began to ring steadily from about ten-thirty onwards, and when he sat down in his office for a coffee break a little later, Mr Wells was pleased with the way the day was shaping. He should be able to report a good day's trade at the end of the day. And the takings were looking promising for the week as a whole.

He sat back at his desk with The Daily Telegraph folded neatly into a small rectangle to display the crossword alone and, pencil poised, began to read the first clue 'across'. He couldn't make anything of it so moved onto the second. He rarely completed the whole thing and was pleased with himself if he reached halfway. It was tricky today. He took a sip of coffee, adjusted his pince-nez, and took a look at the 'down' clues to see if they were any easier. Apparently not, it would seem.

His mind started to wander, to the new girl who had started on Monday. She was pretty, with a very trim figure, and an especially shapely behind. Callipygian in fact; a favourite word of his which he enjoyed using as few people knew what it meant, and its sound and spelling bore no resemble to its true meaning. A good word for a crossword clue. He'd called the lady mayor 'callipygian' once at a local function and she'd been delighted. She may have felt differently had she known he was telling her she had well-shaped buttocks. Mind you, if the new girl wasn't pretty he wouldn't have employed her. Good looks sold – and brightened his day at the same time. He'd let his hand brush momentarily against her blouse as he was showing her out of the office after the interview. She hadn't objected. Promising. She even smiled at him, with a tantalising hint of naivety and budding femininity.

A ditty by his favourite comedian, Max Miller, sprang to mind:

> *I like the girls who do,*
> *I like the girls who don't;*
> *I hate the girl who says she will*
> *And then she says she won't.*
> *But the girl I like the best of all,*
> *And I think you'll say I'm right,*
> *Is the girl who says she never does*
> *But she looks as though she might!*

He closed his eyes for a moment as he allowed himself to sink into an erotic daydream.

Suddenly the door burst open and Barb stood there, looking flushed. 'She's back!'

Mr Wells almost fell backwards off his chair with shock. 'What? Who?'

'The shoplifter.'

'Where?'

'In household goods – she's looking at cutlery.'

He had regained his composure and crossed the room to the doorway. 'Show me.'

They walked a few yards across the shop floor to a display of dinnerware where Barb stopped and put an arm out to hold her husband back.

'There, look!' she whispered, nodding towards a figure about ten feet away.

He saw a woman wearing a brown coat and matching hat with a shopping bag hooked over one arm. She was inspecting a canteen of cutlery in an elegant wooden box, picking out individual items and popping them back in again.

'Are you sure?'

'A hundred percent. I'd know her anywhere.'

'We need to catch her in the act. You stay here and watch her and I'll go out by the other door onto the pavement. When she leaves the store, I'll be ready.'

There were two entrances to Knight's, at different ends of the shop front, a legacy from when two shops had been knocked into one many years before. He doubled back, out of the door by linen and along the pavement to the other door.

Inside the store, Barb kept vigil from a discreet distance. She didn't have to wait long. The woman wandered around the display of cutlery in a full circle, glancing in every direction, saw no one, so closed the lid of the box and slotted it into her shopping bag. Without hesitation, she headed towards the nearest door. Barb hurried after her and could see her husband through the window. She waved wildly as the woman opened the door and stepped out into the street.

Mr Wells blocked her way. 'Excuse me, madam, may I see in your bag please?'

The woman kept her head down to avoid eye contact. 'No, you mayn't.'

'I believe you have an item of merchandise in there that has not been paid for.'

She tried to push past him. 'Leave me alone.'

'I'm sorry, madam, I'm afraid I must insist.' He tried to take her by the arm but she pulled away. He tugged at her shopping bag and reached inside. 'That looks like one of our finest canteens of cutlery – by Arthur Price. As used on the Titanic. Do you have a receipt?'

'No, she doesn't,' joined in Barb from the shop doorway. 'I saw her put it in her bag and walk out without paying.'

'That's a lie,' said the shoplifter. 'Leave me alone.' She pulled herself loose and tried to barge past Mr Wells. He stood his ground and shimmied sideways across the pavement to stop her from getting around. She darted the other way, so he shimmied back again. When she realised she couldn't get past, she drew back her shopping bag in a wide arch, the weighty canteen of cutlery still inside, and swung it with both hands directly at Mr Wells.

He saw what was coming and ducked instinctively. A small crowd had gathered in response to the noise and commotion, and the bag flew right over his head, striking the man behind him full in the chest.

'Oof!' gasped PC Bent as he toppled backwards, winded, landing flat on his back on the pavement.

'You're for it now, lady,' smirked Mr Wells.

The woman stared down at the policeman and realised that she was indeed 'for it'. Clutching the shopping bag to her body she tried again to sidestep Mr Wells. Realising what she was trying to do, Mr Wells stuck out his foot and tripped her up. She tumbled over, spinning as she fell, and landing next to PC Bent. The bag hit the floor and the canteen burst open, spilling knives, forks and spoons in all directions.

Barb Wells rushed forwards, picked up the canteen and began gathering up the cutlery. She looked across at the shoplifter sprawled in front of her on the pavement and whose skirt had ridden up over her knees during the fall. The poor woman was struggling to pull it back down again and regain some dignity.

But Barb had caught a glimpse of something and had other ideas. She grabbed the hem and indecorously tugged it back up, peering underneath. She looked up at her husband.

'Do you see what I see?'

Mr Wells peered down. 'I do indeed,' he replied triumphantly. 'French knickers. *Our* French knickers!'

Chapter 27

Thursday 19th July

The funeral cortège snaked its way at a suitably sedate pace across the outskirts of Redhill from the church of St John the Evangelist, where the funeral had taken place, to Redstone Cemetery in Philanthropic Road. There were four vehicles; the hearse carrying the coffin, the car transporting close family, then one for other relatives and another for work colleagues. Friends and neighbours walked the mile-long journey.

The church had been nearly full, the service solemn and pitted with sobs. The vicar had known the Grimshaw family for many years, and two decades earlier had christened the baby who had grown into the young man who now lay in the coffin before them. Enough time had passed since the end of the war for sudden death to become a shock again rather than an accepted part of everyday life, especially when involving the young. The phrase that the vicar repeated several times during the service stayed in the minds of those who were present: 'A bright young man, taken from us too soon.'

Ben's parents clung together, arm in arm, heads bowed, at the edge of the grave. Next to them was a man who, in most respects, looked like an older version of the deceased; the same features, slim build and shock of ginger hair. The only difference was in height; this man was a good head taller, well over six feet. As the coffin was lowered into the ground and prayers were said, Storm Grimshaw's head was not bowed; he was looking around him all the time, noticing faces, curious about the ones he didn't recognise. He was one of life's natural watchers.

When the coffin had reached the bottom of the open grave and trowels of earth spilled onto it, there was a moment when no one moved or spoke, a final, silent, instinctive mark of respect for Ben. Then the gathering started to disperse, mostly still in silence and any talk reduced to a mere whisper. Storm edged his way over to a face he knew well.

'Hello, boss, thank you for coming.'

'Storm, dear boy, good to see you again, though not under such circumstances. Deepest sympathy to you and your family. How are things faring in Fleet Street?'

'Well, thanks. You were a good teacher.'

'Glad to hear credit being given where credit is due. Mind you, you were an excellent pupil. Dreadful, this business with young Ben … a good lad, and with your potential, there was no doubt. There's a piece in today's edition about him. Only brief but we'll follow it up next week with something more substantial.'

'Thank you,' said Storm. 'Boss, I need to ask you something. Ben telephoned me a couple of weeks ago – very excited he was. Reckoned he was onto a bit of a scoop, something about Nazis living in Reigate. Did he say anything to you about it?'

'He did indeed. Some cock-and-bull story he overheard in The Dinner Gong, part of it in German, part in English. He showed me his notes. I told him it was a load of nonsense and to forget about it.'

'And did he?'

'He never mentioned it again.'

'And now he's dead.'

The boss sighed. 'Alas, he is indeed.'

'Not just dead – brutally murdered. Shot in the head.'

'Are you implying there might be a connection?'

'Would you blame me?' Storm offered him a cigarette and lit them both one. They started making their way towards the cemetery gates. 'You're an experienced news man and fought the Germans in the war, boss. What do you think?'

The boss shrugged. 'The war is over, there are no Nazis anymore, and there never were any in Surrey to the best of my knowledge. There are Germans, people of German extraction certainly, and German speakers. But that doesn't automatically make them Nazis, far from it. I think Ben simply overheard part of a conversation out of context and put two and two together and made five. Much ado *über nichts*.'

'Do you remember what he actually heard? What did his notes say?'

'A few odd snippets gleaned from lunchtime tittle tattle, nothing really. I can't remember it all precisely – Hitler, Bunker, Berlin. And some names as I recall. Germans talking about Germany.'

'Did he say anything about who the people were?'

'Two women and a man. No descriptions.'

'He told me the same. Do you have his notebook?'

The boss shook his head. 'Never saw it again.'

'Might it still be in his desk?'

'Possibly. I haven't had the heart to clear it out yet.'

'I'm surprised the police haven't asked. I assume they know about this *Nazis in Reigate* business?'

'They didn't mention it when I spoke to them, and I didn't offer. To be honest I'd pretty much forgotten about it. Now then, Storm, I hope you're not thinking of trying to sniff out a story when there's nothing there. Wouldn't put it past you, mind. Wouldn't be the first time.'

'Bollocks,' said Storm bluntly. 'You know my track record. I'm bloody good at sniffing out stories other people have missed. Look, boss, I just want to understand exactly what happened. He was my brother and now he's dead. I'm going to talk to the police but thought I'd start with you. Who covered the discovery of Ben's body for the rag?'

'Did it myself. I wrote the piece in today's edition.'

'I read it. Not much detail.'

'The police don't seem to have an idea who might have killed him, not when I spoke to them at any rate. I'll be following with an update next week, including a piece about the funeral. You'll get a mention naturally.'

'Is Inspector Thorne still the man over at Reigate nick?'

'Yes, and CID from Guildford are involved, as you'd expect in a case such as this. Thorne will be able to fill you in – that's if he's prepared to talk to you at all, bearing in mind you're not down here officially.'

'I might be,' said Storm.

'Ah, I see. Well that would make a difference. I wish you luck. If you dig up anything interesting, you will share … for old times' sake? National news is still local news too.'

'I'll think about it. Does Thorne still like to drink in the same place?'

'He does indeed.'

They had reached the gates and stood still for a moment.

'Was Ben working on anything else?'

The boss thought for a moment. 'Not really. The usual dross, nothing special. He covered a couple of shoplifting incidents over at Knight's for me recently. A woman pinching stockings and knickers, amongst other things. Hardly of interest to you, I would have thought. She tried it again the other day and was caught red-handed this time. Case comes up in the

255

magistrates' court soon. It's a pity Ben won't be around to see the result.'

'Anyone we know?'

'Do you remember Terry Angel?'

'Petty thief and layabout?'

'That's the one.'

'Not him wearing women's clothing surely!'

The boss chuckled. 'The next best thing … his wife.'

'Don't know her.'

'You wouldn't. No form. A fine upstanding member of the community – member of the Women's Institute. Not for much longer though, I shouldn't imagine. Can they blackball you from the W.I.? Interesting notion.'

Storm nodded half-heartedly, failing to disguise his indifference. His thoughts were elsewhere. 'This whole thing about Ben stinks to high heaven, boss,' he said. 'I'm going to do everything I can to find out what it's all about while I'm down here. No one goes around shooting young lads and dumping their bodies in mine shafts for no reason. There's nothing random about this. Can you think of a reason, or anyone who might have had it in for Ben?'

'None whatsoever … he was well liked by all.'

'In which case, unless Thorne has found out anything, this Nazi lead is all I have to go on. Would you mind taking a look for that notebook for me?'

'Of course.'

'In fact, if you're going back to the office now why don't I come along? No time like the present. I'll just tell mum and dad I'll see them later and I'll be right with you.'

'That's my boy, Storm. I'd forgotten just how much you live up to that name of yours.'

'Thank you, boss.' They shook hands. 'It's good to see you again.'

****

Storm sat in his car in Holmesdale Road, opposite Reigate station, staring at the notebook in his hands; the notebook the boss had found earlier in the day, tucked in a drawer of the desk that had until a week ago belonged to Ben. A perfectly ordinary notebook, a bit dog-eared, half full, each page with a date and a brief header, underlined. The page he was looking at was dated three and a half weeks ago:

25 Jun The D. Gong
Morell Rowena Yardly delicate position
Telling locals your Hitler
Yardly making arrangements somewhere safe
Eva Brown bunker Berlin
Trick slight of hand   Furteventerer???
Erica NAZIs?

He winced at the spelling – never Ben's strength. Not much to go on, not without some context. It could have been a conversation about a book, or a play. Eva Brown was presumably Eva Braun, Hitler's lover whom he married just before committing suicide together in a bunker in Berlin at the end of the war; he knew that much. That all tied together. He read the notes again. The other names meant nothing to him. Morell, Rowena, Yardly (Yardley probably) and Erica. More Nazis? If so he'd never heard of them. Furteventerer – odd name if it was a person. And living in Reigate? Not likely. The boss didn't seem to think there was anything to it, and he had good instincts, though he always erred on the side of caution too often in Storm's opinion. Perhaps he'd been right to brush it off as insignificant. A weird prank of some kind even. And yet, a few days after scribbling down these words, Ben had been beaten up and shot dead. Was there a connection? If not then it was mere coincidence. Too much of a coincidence? Very likely.

It was Thursday. He'd taken a couple of days off work and wasn't expected back until after the weekend. Three and a bit days to find out as much as he could about how his brother had died. There was a story in it; he could smell it. Kill two birds with one stone. A good story, and pin down the bastards who'd done that to his brother.

He got out of the car, crossed the road and walked into The Prince of Wales pub. Propping up the bar in a fog of smoke was a line of men of varying shapes and sizes, in casual conversation with each other. Amongst them he recognised the figure of the man he was looking for; out of uniform but with the unmistakable posture of a copper.

'Buy you a drink, Inspector?'

Thorne turned around and eyed up the speaker with natural caution. His eyebrows raised in recognition.

'Well well, here's a bad penny come back to haunt me. Teacup Grimshaw, as in *Storm in a* … you young bugger. Ah but I shouldn't jest. Down here for the funeral I assume. It was this morning, correct? Sorry for your loss. Met your brother a couple of times briefly but can't say I knew him. It's me who's buying. Pint?'

'Thanks, on both counts. Light ale for me.'

Thorne drained what was left of his drink and re-ordered. He gestured to some chairs in a corner of the bar and they went and sat down.

'I hope the funeral wasn't too painful.'

'More numbing than painful. It hasn't really sunk in yet. Mum and dad are living in a kind of dream. I still can't quite believe what's happened.'

'Sometimes funerals make a difference, bring things to a close. They might come down with a bit of a bump now, you too for that matter. Are you staying with them for a while?'

Storm sipped his beer. 'Until Sunday.'

'They're in Redhill as I recall, off the Brighton Road?'

'That's right. Garlands Road.'

'And how's the job going … are you being as big a pain in the arse to the Met as you were to us?'

'Worse. And not just them. It's a national, so we can hound the Old Bill anywhere in the country if we need to. The Met are harder work than you, much more difficult to screw information out of.'

'Hmm, not sure I like the sound of that,' said Thorne. 'Makes us sound a pushover.'

'You were hardly that. More cooperative than average with the press in keeping the public informed. Sound better?'

'A bit. And what are you going to do while you're back home … catch up with some old mates? Chase a bit of skirt around, I'll be bound.'

'Not really in the mood for that. I thought I'd track down the bastards who killed my brother.'

'Steady now, leave that to us professionals. Pah! Why am I wasting my words, you never did leave alone. I wish I had a fiver for every time I told you to stop poking your bloody nose into police business.'

'You had good cause to thank me, on more than one occasion I can think of.'

'Can't deny it. But this is different. A nasty killing.'

'Can you give some details? I've seen the piece in the local Mirror but it's very sketchy.'

Thorne looked at him askance. 'Not exactly a chance meeting then, you walking into my favourite boozer. Are you covering this for your rag?'

'Not at all. This is unofficial, me asking you how my brother was murdered. That's all, honest.'

'So, what do you know?'

Storm thought for a moment. 'From the Surrey Mirror, I know that Ben was found early last Thursday morning in the Hearthstone Mine at Colley Hill, near The Clears, by a foreman when he turned up for work. Name of Weaver. Ben's body had been dumped in the mine – he'd been shot in the head. I know from my mum that Ben had tea with them the evening before, he then set off on his bike at around six-thirty. He was excited about something, mum said, but no idea what. Didn't say where he was going, just went out and never came back. That was the last they saw of him.'

'All correct. CID from Guildford are running the show … Detective Chief Inspector Hastilow, remember him?'

'I do.'

'And Chief Inspector Crimond – new man, so not a name you'd be familiar with. They're leading and I'm following. Nothing I couldn't handle myself, but you know the protocol, anything murder and they send in the big guns. Then when they balls it up, in come Scotland Yard.'

'What else can you tell me?'

'Not a great deal. Ben was pretty badly beaten before he was shot. He also had cuts to the face, not from the beating. Our sawbones found some shards of glass around his nose and mouth. Not sure what that was all about. Yet.'

'Was he killed at the mine or elsewhere?'

'Not much blood where he was found, apart from skull fragments and hair and flesh from the head shot, and the ground in the mine wasn't disturbed much. No sign of a struggle. He was probably roughed up elsewhere then finished off with a bullet at the mine. He was almost certainly unconscious or dead when whoever it was pulled the trigger, which will be some solace to you.'

'Have you found his bike?'

Inspector Thorne shook his head. 'No sign. We've scoured the area but nothing so far. There's a lot of dense undergrowth and woodland around there, so it could be tucked away somewhere. Or it may be somewhere else entirely. We've made house to house enquiries and that's still ongoing. He was spotted near Reffel's Bridge cycling towards Reigate by a work colleague – that was about a quarter to seven – but after that his whereabouts is unknown, until the mine foreman found him the next morning.'

'Any leads on who pulled the trigger?'

Thorne shook his head again. 'It's not like anything our local scallywags would get up to, or are capable of for that matter. I've talked to a couple of my narks and they don't know anything. They were appalled, frankly, and that reaction often ends up with someone grassing on someone else in my experience. But not this time. That suggests to me the perpetrator – or perps in the plural as I can't imagine this being a lone job – aren't local. Or if they are, they're not part of the known criminal fraternity around here.'

'A gang-related crime, perhaps? One of the London firms operating off their normal patch for some reason.'

'Possibly. This has the smell of an execution about it. Whoever did it knows their business. Professionals for sure. It may be related in some way to his job – you know, got caught up in something he was working on as a story and found himself out of his depths. He might have unearthed some facts that someone wanted to avoid getting into the newspapers at all costs. This is stockbroker country. Lots of people live around here and work up in town and have connections in all manner

261

of places, some of them very high indeed. Ironically that's more your territory nowadays.'

'Now you're getting on to motive. That's a possibility. Have you spoken to my old boss at the Mirror?'

'Yes, and he wasn't aware of anything. He certainly hadn't tasked Ben with a story that might cause a reaction as violent as this. He has senior reporters who cover the juicier stuff. Ben was jumble sales, shoplifting and petty crime.'

'We all have to start somewhere,' said Storm. 'That's what I was doing a few years ago.'

'And look at you now, Sunny Jim.'

'Any other possible motives you're considering?'

'You know, Storm, there are all sorts of possibilities, but to be perfectly honest I don't think any of them are even remotely plausible. Jealousy, revenge, financial gain … can you imagine any of those applying to young Ben?'

'Frankly, no.'

'Nor me.'

'The boss had no suggestions … stories Ben might have been working up, maybe on his own to try and impress his elders? Something a bit more substantial than shoplifting or jumble sales?'

'Well now,' said Thorne. 'You'd have already spoken to him about that yourself, I'd bet money on it, so you'd know the answer's no. What are you getting at?'

'Nothing – just pondering.'

'Do you know something I don't? If so you'd better come out with it.'

'I don't know anything you don't,' lied Storm.

'Well if you're holding out on me and I find out, I'll throw the book at you when it's as serious a case as this … even if your own brother was the victim.'

'No weapon found?' said Storm, changing the subject.

'No, and I don't expect to find one either. This has the hallmarks of a professional job and professionals don't leave their guns lying around. They take them with them. If we find the killer, we may find the weapon.'

'I can make sense of it in one way or another. A revenge killing between firms maybe, an execution as you put it, with the body dumped in a remote mine. No loose ends, no weapon, a clinical shot to the head after a beating. It's nasty but not very different from what goes on. It could even happen in a sedate place like Reigate. The bit of the puzzle that doesn't fit for me is the victim. Ben. Why a harmless young lad who never hurt a fly?'

'Well, I wish you luck if you're going to snoop around,' said Inspector Thorne. 'Just let me know if you find out something before we do.'

'I will if you will.'

'It's a deal. Now, whose round is it?'

'Yours I believe.'

'In your own words, Storm Grimshaw – bollocks. Get up to that bar!'

Chapter 28

Friday 20th July

Rowena was on her way back down the garden from the compost heap with an empty wheelbarrow when she glanced across at the gate in the hedge and saw Mr Morell standing there. He raised his hand to wave at her – forearm vertical, palm inclined back – a gesture which, to most people who had in their head that Morell might be Adolf Hitler, could have been construed as not unlike a Nazi salute. To Rowena, it looked like a friendly wave.

'You must have smelled the apple cake,' she called to him. 'Ethel has been busy in the kitchen this morning. Come and have some tea.'

'Thank you, Rowena, I would like that. I have been writing all morning and would appreciate some company.'

'Your memoirs?'

'Yes, however I find writing difficult. I prefer to dictate but have no secretary, which means it is a struggle.'

'I wish I could help.'

'Thank you, however it is my struggle.'

Morell sat down on the terrace whilst Rowena fetched the tray and poured tea and served cake.

'Apple cake is a favourite of mine. At home, they used to make it specially for me, sprinkled with added nuts and raisins. We called it *Führer* cake.'

'Oh really.' Rowena sounded unimpressed.

'How is Frau von Tirpitz? I haven't seen her for a while.'

'I haven't seen much of her either. I think she's keeping herself to herself at present.'

'I gather from Yardley they had dinner together. I get the impression it was not a success.'

'I heard that, too,' said Rowena.

'Yardley can be, how shall I say, very forthright towards the opposite sex. I should imagine that may have been a contributing factor.'

'You've hit the nail on the head there, Mr Morell. I gather he seemed to think that something more than food was on the menu.'

'Yardley has gone away again for a while, by the way. I have moved into the house during his absence.'

'A nice change, I imagine. You know, on the subject of the *Führer* – the man, not the cake. Erika and I have a theory.'

'I would be interested to hear it.'

'We have been putting bits of an imaginary jigsaw together. Assuming for a moment that you really are indeed Adolf Hitler …'

'I am.'

'Well that will make proposing our theory easier. It's quite simple really. We know that you and Peter Yardley have known each other for many years, and that you worked together in Germany.'

'To be precise, Yardley worked for me.'

'In which case, we believe he too must have been a high-ranking Nazi.'

'Not necessarily. Many people worked for me who were not. Thousands.'

'Be that as it may, it seems to us there is more of a connection between you than the leader of a major European power and, say, his chauffeur or valet. You seem far more on an equal footing.'

'Go on.'

'So, we worked our way through the names of the top Nazis to see if any of them fit the bill. Most of them are either dead or in prison of course.'

'Or in South America,' added Morell.

'Is that so? I'll take your word for it. However, there is one who doesn't fit into either category and who in many respects, as far as I am aware, would match the man you call Peter Yardley.'

'And that is?'

'Martin Bormann.'

Morell shook his head dismissively. 'Bormann is dead. Killed trying to escape from the *Führerbunker* in forty-five.'

'You died there, too, apparently, and yet here I am talking to you. Bormann's body was never found.'

'Many people died during the war whose bodies were never found.'

'Well if he isn't Bormann, who is he?'

'I am not at liberty to say.'

'Oh, come now,' said Rowena. 'On the one hand, you are quite prepared to declare openly that you're Hitler and on the other you're being coy about Peter Yardley's identity. It doesn't make sense.'

'Frau Furse, we had a similar conversation not so long ago about myself and I said to you … ach, what does it matter! Yardley is an unassuming man living a quiet life, managing his farm, doing no one any harm. I don't understand why it matters to you.'

'And I seem to remember saying that it matters to me to be told the truth.'

'The truth is an overrated commodity in my opinion. It is also relative to time and circumstance.'

'I disagree. I also question that he is doing no harm. If he is Martin Bormann, he has done many people harm, thousands of people, millions. And to be frank, so have you if you're Hitler. You're probably responsible for bringing more misery to the world than any individual in the history of the world. You're both war criminals who should be brought to account … hanged even, like they were at Nuremberg.'

Rowena suddenly burst into tears. She pulled out a handkerchief and covered her face until the fit of sobbing died away. Mr Morell sat quietly, his head down.

'I am sorry, Frau Furse, that you are upset. You would of course see it that way. However, I do not. I turned my beloved country round from abject misery and utter degradation after the First War, and the betrayal of the November criminals who signed the Treaty of Versailles – Jews, every one – into a strong and stable nation as mighty as any in Europe. Self-confident, proud. Just look how I transformed Germany … I worked miracles! No other man in the entire German nation could have achieved what I achieved. No one.'

'But you were a warmonger! You didn't stop at that. You had to invade other countries and dominate them. And with such awful brutality.'

'Some would accuse Churchill of the same, and of brutality and of committing war crimes. Stalin too. He was worse than anyone. He still is.'

'Look at the state of your country when you supposedly killed yourself and abandoned it,' continued Rowena. 'It was right back in the misery and degradation from where you started, only ten times worse. You led your "beloved country" down a road of self-destruction, and dragged all of Europe along with you.'

Morell sat motionless. 'My one major regret is that I allowed that to happen. I am only human. I could not see it at the time. I brought the Fatherland greatness but allowed it to slip away. At the time, I was guilty of blaming everyone else but myself ... the generals, Göring, Himmler, even the German people. Now I see only I was responsible for that failure. I was their leader. In my defence, I was not well, and battling all the time against short-sighted men who were intent on keeping the true facts from me and plotting against me.'

Rowena had composed herself and put her handkerchief away. 'I want to ask you again – and I want a truthful answer from you. Is Peter Yardley really Martin Bormann?'

'Why is it so important to you?'

'Because I want to know for Erika's sake. She leaned forward and looked Morell full in the eyes. 'Martin Bormann raped her sister and was responsible for her suicide. If that was Yardley's doing, she has a right to know.'

Mr Morell slumped back in his seat. 'Oh ... I see.'

They did not speak for quite some time. Mr Morell ate cake and sipped his tea and eventually broke the silence.

'I did not know. She has never mentioned this to me, but then we have never talked about Bormann. You know, he was not a popular man. He was generally hated by most people. He was capable of such brutality, towards both men and women.'

'Well we think he is Martin Bormann, and I think you are lying to me to protect him. I'm sorry, Mr Morell, but that is how I feel. I think we should report him.'

'Report him where?'

'I don't know. To the police, the authorities ... someone.'

Mr Morell leaned forward. He raised his hand as if to touch her gently on the shoulder, but held back from actual contact. 'Dear Rowena, I am sorry about Erika's sister and I will apologise to her in person when I have the opportunity. However, I don't advise trying to connect that event with Yardley, if that is your intention. Some things are better left alone. If you try reporting your suspicions to the police, you will be wasting your time. Yardley told you he has helped the British government, greatly in fact, and in return they have let him settle here. In effect, they have wiped the slate clean for him. As for me, I am dead. It has been reported widely throughout the world. Nor would anyone relish my sudden reappearance. Adolf Hitler is dead – Trevor-Roper's book has made that abundantly clear. I have no doubt his brief was to document the fact conclusively, to bury the leader of the Nazi movement and, by association, the entire movement itself once and for all. Short of producing a body, he did just that. If you walk into the police station in Reigate and announce that Adolf Hitler is your next-door neighbour, they will laugh at you. If you say I am staying as a guest of Martin Bormann, they will laugh even louder. If they come to interview me, they will leave convinced I am a harmless eccentric, a mad man … I will see to that. *Bonkers* as Frau von Tirpitz would say. A crazy person with illusions of being the *Führer*.'

Rowena had stopped sniffling and for the want of anything else to say asked Mr Morell if he would like some more tea.

'No thank you, no more tea.'

'Perhaps you are right,' she said pensively.

'I know I am right, I could not drink another cup.'

Rowena managed a smile. 'I meant about reporting you to the authorities. But Erika will need a great deal of convincing otherwise. She tried to find out from Peter Yardley his real identity when she had dinner with him. She came away with her hair ruffled but still not knowing. Nevertheless, she has strong suspicions and won't leave it alone until she knows one way or the other. That's a certainty.'

'Perhaps I should have a word with her.'

'That might be an idea.'

'Will you ask her to come and see me?'

'That won't be necessary,' declared Rowena. I propose another jaunt to the theatre in London – the three of us this time. You can talk to her then.'

'And this jaunt is when?'

'Next Friday evening – a week today. I have tickets to see our greatest living actor, Sir Laurence Olivier. He is currently performing in *Caesar and Cleopatra* and *Antony and Cleopatra*, playing the lead in each on alternate nights.'

'I read about this in the newspaper,' said Morell. 'With Scarlett O'Hara as Cleopatra.'

'Ha ha! Vivien Leigh, that's correct. We shall be seeing *Caesar and Cleopatra*, the play by Bernard Shaw. By chance Erika and I bumped into an actor in The Old Wheel the other day who is also in the cast – Esmond Knight.'

'Never heard of him.'

'He's quite well known in this country. A splendid actor. He's kindly arranged for us to have House Seats.'

'That sounds delightful, I look forward to it, very much.'

'The icing on the cake is – thanks to Mr Knight – the seats are just a few rows from the front of the stalls.'

'Excellent. Will Herr Furse be joining us?'

'He has to attend a dinner somewhere in town that night, so it's just you, me and Erika.'

Mr Morell reached for his walking stick and made to stand up. 'Now I must let you get on with your gardening. Thank you for tea.'

'You are welcome. Yes, the compost heap is calling.'

'I am sorry again that I upset you.'

'I'm sorry too, but I'm all right now. I prefer to think of you as just my dear friend Mr Morell. Nothing more.'

Morell held out his hand. Instead of shaking it, Rowena moved closer and opened her arms as if to hug him. He backed away.

'I am not comfortable with physical contact, I'm afraid,' he said. 'I prefer just to shake hands.'

Rowena blushed awkwardly. 'As you wish.'

When he had gone and she was busy filling up the wheelbarrow ready for another trip to the compost heap, she felt rather rejected. 'You didn't mind Erika kissing you on the cheek at the fair,' she griped to herself.

****

The one-pot vegetable casserole Mrs Dory had prepared had been delicious and very filling. She had left for the evening and Mr Morell was alone in Peter Yardley's house. He could feel the half-digested meal sitting pleasantly on his stomach as he relaxed on the sofa in the lounge, reading and occasionally nodding off so that he had to keep revisiting the same paragraph. As there was no one around and he had the place to himself, he farted at will, loudly and often.

The grandfather clock in the hallway had just chimed ten when he heard the noise; a scraping sound coming from the direction of the kitchen, like a chair being pulled along the flagstones that covered the floor. He had been dozing at the time but on hearing the noise became immediately alert. The kitchen was off the hallway towards the side of the house. He looked towards the doorway which led in that direction; it was slightly ajar.

He sat in absolute silence, listening intently, not moving. Nothing. Perhaps he had been mistaken about the noise. No, it had been real, faint but distinctive; not the kind of creak or groan that old houses sometimes emitted. After a few minutes, he stood up and crept slowly towards the door, his slippered feet silent on the plush pile carpet. When he reached the door, he stood still and listened again. Nothing. He reached out, folded his fingers around the handle and pulled it towards him.

Immediately in front of him stood a man, dressed in all dark clothing and wearing a balaclava. He stood with legs slightly apart, and dead still. In his right hand was a revolver. It was pointing straight at Morell.

'Martin Bormann.'

'Is that a question or a statement of fact?' asked Morell.

'Are you Martin Bormann?'

'Ah, so a question.'

'Answer me!' hissed the man.

'No, I am not.'

'Who are you then?'

'My name is Theodor Morell. And who might you be?'

'I think you are Martin Bormann – Nazi war criminal.'

'Well you are mistaken.'

'Prove it.'

'I do not have to prove anything to you, whoever you are, my friend, barging into this house uninvited, making wild accusations.'

'I am no friend of yours.'

'Then get out.'

'Not until I know who you are.'

'I have just told you.'

'You're a German!'

'Did my accent give it away? You are most observant.'

'I hate Germans. Especially Nazis.'

'Has no one told you?' said Morell, his voice laden with sarcasm. 'The war is over. Germany has undergone a process of de-Nazification. There are no Nazis anymore.'

'Certain people around here would disagree with you.'

'And who might they be?'

'You know who.'

'I do not know what you are talking about. Now get out of here before I call for a policeman.'

'I am going nowhere.'

'Very well, I shall make a telephone call.'

'You'll do nothing of the sort, you revolting Kraut. Now sit down!'

Mr Morell walked over to the sofa and sat down. The gunman moved into the room and stood over him, the gun pointing continuously at the centre of his body.

Morell said: 'May I ask you a question?'

'What?'

'Have you ever seen a photograph of Martin Bormann?'

'Why?'

'Have you?'

'No.'

'Do you have a description of him?'

'No.'

'So, you do not actually know what he looks like. That would explain a great deal. Would you like me to describe him to you?'

'Go ahead.'

Morell spoke slowly and clearly. 'Short, stocky, with a thick neck, and a large stomach. Like a retired boxer who has gone to seed and is no longer fit. Age, around fifty. Does that resemble the man you are pointing a gun at?'

The man seemed fazed for a moment, then said: 'You're lying – making it up.'

'I assure you I am not.'

'How do you know what he looks like?'

'Because I knew him. I know what I am talking about, which is more than you do.'

'I don't believe you. I think you're Bormann.'

'If you do not believe me, there is nothing I can do about that. So, if you have come here to shoot me, go ahead and get it over with. There is nothing more to be said. Pull the trigger. Or is there some other purpose to your visit? What do you actually want from me?'

'If you're Bormann,' said the man, 'I want the great pleasure of putting a bullet into your vile head.'

'That would be cold-blooded murder – you would be caught and you would be hanged.'

'It'd be worth it to see you dispatched once and for all.'

'Why, what did Bormann ever do to you?'

'Not to me, but to the millions whose lives he ruined – the soldiers who died unnecessarily, the women and children, the Jews. The Freemasons.'

'Bormann was not responsible for those things. He was the *Führer*'s private secretary, and Head of the Party Chancellery. He took over from Rudolf Hess after he fled in forty-one on his ridiculous peace mission. Bormann was a mere administrator. He spent all his working life sitting behind a desk.'

'And in so doing helped to administer the most evil, criminal regime in history. Most of the bastards are dead now, thank God. But if you are Bormann and still with us, then you represent the whole rotten Nazi Party and deserve to be punished. Better late than never. You should have been hanged at Nuremberg.'

Mr Morell relaxed back into his chair. 'Well I am not Bormann, so you are a dog barking up the wrong tree trunk.'

'Oh, I wish you were not Bormann! I wish you were Adolf Hitler himself, sitting in front of me now. How I would love to have the opportunity to put a bullet through *his* moronic skull – the jumped-up, ill-educated, loudmouthed little runt who never rose above the rank of corporal. No wonder you lot lost the war with that walking disaster in charge of the show, telling his generals what to do. Any one of them could have done a better job. Did you know that military intelligence – ours not yours, otherwise it would be an oxymoron – plotted to assassinate your precious *Führer* early on in the war? But when it became apparent he'd taken charge of the Wehrmacht and was controlling military strategy, they called it off. Scrapped the idea. They realised that Hitler was Germany's greatest liability. With him at the helm, the good ship Fatherland was heading for an iceberg and it was only a matter of time. Turned out to be absolutely correct.'

'That is such nonsense!'

'Let's face it, Kraut, your own side took over where we left off and tried to get rid of him. Damned nearly succeeded one time with that bomb – blew the trousers right off him.'

'Today,' said Morell calmly.

'What was that?'

'Today. It happened seven years ago to this day.'

'Did it by Jove. Well a pity it didn't kill him outright. It would've shaved almost a year off the war and saved a few more million lives.'

'You are talking out of your arse.'

'Not at all. Ask Winston next time you're fooling around with him on the back of a lorry. He'll confirm it.'

'Ah!' exclaimed Morell. 'I thought I recognised the voice. Now I know who you are … Colonel Peregrine bloody Maxwell. Well, this is beginning to make sense.'

'Makes no difference who I am. You're going to die.'

'Have you listened to nothing I've said? I am not Martin Bormann, and if you shoot me now you will be killing an innocent man.'

'Not innocent. Guilty of interfering in my personal life and muscling in on my woman, whoever you are.'

'If you mean Frau von Tirpitz, I doubt she would agree with you there. Besides, you said a moment ago that you hate Germans. Not all Germans then.'

'Erika is exceptional – and more English than German these days.'

'You are full of shit.'

'And you'll be full of bullets in a short while.'

Morell was losing patience and it showed in his voice. He found a fluency in English he had not experienced before. 'Now listen to me, Colonel Blimp, for that is surely what you are. Before you start firing that weapon, you had better get your facts straight. Firstly, there is nothing between me and Erika von Tirpitz. She has been a good friend to me, and that is as far as it goes. I happen to know from speaking with her the reason she is no longer *your* woman is because she has had enough of your emotional immaturity, your possessiveness, your childish jealousy without any reason. She grew sick of it. And here is the proof … the fact that you are standing there threatening to kill me because you think I have stolen her from you! So, if you came here to shoot me for that reason, then you will surely hang because that will be murder in cold blood. Secondly, if you have come to shoot me because I am Martin Bormann, you are equally mistaken. And if you are seriously thinking of pulling the trigger for that reason, you need to be *one hundred percent* sure of my identity, because if I am not Bormann, you will be no hero. You will have shot the wrong person and you will hang for it. I know I am not Bormann, I keep telling you I am not.

But if you know better, go ahead and shoot. But *only* if you are certain.'

Maxwell's trigger finger trembled. Half of him wanted to fire instantly and have it done with, to be able to report proudly to his Lodge what he'd done in revenge for all the brother Masons who had been slaughtered by the evil regime Bormann represented. But the bastard was right, he couldn't do it without knowing beyond the shadow of a doubt he had the right man.

He moved closer until he was standing directly in front of Morell and brought the gun forward until the end of the barrel was touching the centre of his forehead. He stood there for a long time, a good five minutes, in silence, his expression changing as various emotions overwhelmed him in a steady chain; anger, frustration, bitterness, disgust. Then he said simply, 'Leave my woman alone', walked out of the room and was gone.

Morell heard the front door open and slam shut. He sat back on the sofa and sighed a sigh of relief, pondering over the bizarre confrontation. The gas that had been building up inside him released itself in a long, noisy and hugely gratifying fart.

'Jumped-up?' he said aloud to no one but himself. 'Ill-educated, loudmouthed runt who never rose above the rank of corporal? The cheeky shit.'

Chapter 29

Barb Wells sat at the kitchen table, the Surrey Mirror spread out in front of her – and wept.

She had not seen or heard from Benjamin for a week and had been angry with him. Had he just wanted a quick one-off and gone on his way? Surely not, he didn't seem the type. Besides, they hadn't finished and that ultimate pleasure was still to come. But to ignore her completely was thoughtless. Rude. Unless he was embarrassed about coming into the shop, or had been scared off by Mr Wells turning up like that and almost getting caught. She had half hoped he would turn up again on Wednesday. Her husband's illness had been nothing more than a head cold and he'd gone off to his Bridge evening as usual. Ben wouldn't have known that of course.

Now she knew why. He didn't know about anything anymore. The poor boy was dead. The Mirror had been delivered the day before but she hadn't had a chance to read it until now, sitting at the table with a cup of tea after a hectic day in Knight's. She had heard gossip about a body being found in a quarry, but only from overhearing customers talking and hadn't paid it much attention. Now she realised it was Benjamin … her Benjamin boy.

The article was brief but told of the body being found early last Thursday morning in the Hearthstone Mine at the bottom of

Colley Hill. She knew exactly where that was; she'd walked past it many times, not twenty minutes from where she was sitting. *The victim had been a junior reporter on this very newspaper*, she read. He'd been trussed up and died from a bullet wound to the head. Local police had stated that so far the motive for the murder remained unclear and there were no immediate suspects.

His body had been found last Thursday – the morning after he had been with her, making love to her here in this very kitchen, over this very table. Losing his virginity. Her crying turned into choking as the shock hit home. He must have been killed that same evening, within hours of leaving her. How? Why? Who would do such a thing to a lovely young boy like that?

Her sobbing subsided. She read the article again. Hard to imagine that the person in the story was the same one she'd kissed and been so intimate with – she rubbed her hand along the edge of the table-top – exactly where she was sitting now as she read about his death.

A thought occurred to her. What if the police found out about them and wanted to interview her … Would they know about her? Had Benjamin told anyone? She doubted it, but couldn't be sure. He may have bragged to a friend about her, if she was worth bragging about. Maybe she should go and talk to the police. Get in first. The last thing she wanted was them coming into the shop, or to the house.

The idea scared her. She couldn't. She wasn't brave enough. She would just leave it and hope for the best. She started to cry again.

Mr Wells wandered into the kitchen from the living room.

'What's wrong with you?' he asked.

Barb pointed at the newspaper. 'I'm just reading about the body they found in the mine under Colley Hill. Apparently, it was the young reporter who came and spoke to us about the shoplifting, remember?'

'Yes, I remember.'

'He was shot. In the head.'

'I know, I've read it.'

For the briefest of moments, it entered her head that her husband might have something to do with it. Perhaps he *had* known about her and Benjamin and arranged for him to be killed. But no, he didn't care enough to bother.

'So terribly sad,' said Barb, staring at the newspaper.

'Hmm,' grunted Mr Wells, stretching apathetically. 'What's for dinner?'

Chapter 30

Saturday 21st July

The door of The Dinner Gong opened just enough for the woman inside to peer out and identify who was knocking. Two big eyes beneath a head of curly fair hair locked onto the caller and a huge grin lit up her face.

'Storm, you lovely man! Come in here right now and give me a huge hug.'

Storm Grimshaw felt himself being pulled inside; the door was shut and locked behind him and arms enveloped him, a warm body pressing against his.

'Suki, how are you?'

'All the better for seeing you. Oh Storm, what a terrible thing – poor dear Ben, such a lovely boy. Wouldn't harm a fly. I wanted to come to the funeral but I had to work.'

'That's all right, and thank you. He was fond of you.'

'He popped in for lunch quite often. He was here not so long ago. Ooh I've missed you!'

Her lips found his and they kissed. He pulled himself away. 'Slow down there, haven't you forgotten something? You're a married woman now.'

'I know, but I never could resist you.'

'I don't want your old man coming after me.'

'He'll never know – and even if he did he doesn't seem to care much.'

'Oh dear, not going too well, the state of matrimony?'

Suki's voice suddenly fell flat. 'No.'

'How long has it been?'

'Too long.'

'Honeymoon period over?'

'It was a mistake. I should have married you.'

'It would never have worked, Suki,' said Storm. 'You know it wouldn't. We talked about it and it was on the cards for years. We had great times together but it wasn't meant to be forever. Now put me down before we fall down these stairs. I need to talk to you.'

'It would have worked if you'd wanted it to.'

'It wouldn't. If we'd married and set up house it wouldn't have lasted more than six months. Lots of physical attraction but we're like chalk and cheese underneath. It's always been like that, ever since school days.'

She tried to kiss him again.

'Take it easy!'

'You're better than him … in every way.'

'Stop it and let's go downstairs. Is anyone around?'

'Only the chefs in the kitchen, prepping. The others won't be here for another half an hour. We don't open until ten.'

They went downstairs into the dining area and sat at a table where Suki had been folding napkins. Storm offered her a cigarette and they smoked as they talked and Suki resumed her folding.

'How's life up in London then?'

'Good. I'm enjoying working in Fleet Street. Quite a challenge, and it's really frantic sometimes, far more than it ever was here.'

'I can imagine. So frantic you don't even have time to write me a letter.'

He leaned forward and touched the ring on her left hand. 'Not appropriate to correspond with married women.'

'I wasn't married when you left.'

'No, but it was all over between us, after your ultimatum.'

'I regret that now.'

'The job in London or you. That was so unfair.'

'I'm sorry, it was a mistake. I realise that looking back.'

'Besides, you didn't waste any time getting together with whatever his name.'

'Rupert.' Suki said no more but blew him a seductive kiss.

'I'm looking into Ben's death, Suki. The police aren't making much progress so I'm kind of giving them a helping hand, if you like.'

'Like Sherlock Holmes?'

'Something along those lines.'

'Well it's a delight to see you, but I don't see that I can help, if that's what you're after. I don't know anything apart from what was in the Mirror. It said they found him at the Hearthstone Mine. We've been up that way a few times after dark, you and me, remember?'

'I remember.'

'We could go and take a look together, if it would be of any use to you.'

'I don't think that would be advisable. Behave yourself, please, I'm being serious now.'

'Sorry.'

'I'm not sure if you can help or not, but what I do know is that you know a hell of a lot of people in Reigate. Most of the population come in here at one time or another for a meal, and you have a great memory for names.'

'And faces.'

'And faces. But it's names I'm interested in.'

He put his hand into his jacket and pulled out Ben's notebook, flicking through until he found the page he needed.

'Now, when he was murdered, Ben was working on a story and I've got some of his notes. Keep this to yourself, mind. I don't know if they have any bearing on his death. There may be no connection, but I need to look into it to be sure either way. You said he was in here recently. Well these notes were made while he was having lunch here, on June twenty-fifth, almost a month ago.'

'Seems more recent than that, but I'm sure you're right.'

'I am. The page is dated.'

'Unless he's been in since then.'

'That's possible. However, on June twenty-fifth he overheard some people talking in here and wrote down bits of their conversation. Just words.'

'Let me see?'

'I'd prefer not to show you the actual notes. I have my reasons, I promise. Some of the words are names of people. I don't know if they're the people Ben overheard, or others they were talking about. If I say the names will you tell me if you recognise them?'

'I'll give it a try.'

'All right, here goes. Ready? The first is a surname, or at least I assume it is. Morell.'

Suki thought for a moment then pulled a face.

'I can't say it rings any bells. Of course, I don't know the names of everyone who comes here, not even regulars. Show me a face and I'll remember it every time.'

'I understand. Unfortunately, I don't have any pictures, just names. Let's move on to the next one. This is a woman or a girl's name. Rowena.'

'I know a couple. Do you have a surname?'

'I'm afraid I don't.'

'Not much use on its own.'

'Who are the Rowenas you know?'

'Both regulars. Rowena Black, she's a retired schoolteacher, comes in once a week on a Friday like clockwork. Always has fish. Then there's Mrs Furse, she's a Rowena too. Not as regular but comes in occasionally, usually with one of her friends or another. Talks a lot and has a very loud, frumpy laugh. Both nice ladies. I can't imagine either of them being mixed up in anything to do with murder.'

'Like I said, it might be nothing at all, but I need to try and find out. Now, does this mean anything to you – Furteventerer?'

Suki looked blank. 'Nothing, is it a person?'

'I'm not sure. Okay we'll skip that one. Here's the final name, let's try this one. Erica.'

'I only know one of those. The German lady.'

Storm's ears pricked up. 'German?'

'I'm pretty certain she's an Erica. Can't think of anyone else of that name, not that come in here, or at least that I know of by name.'

'Do you know her surname?'

'Von something …'

'Can you remember the rest?'

'I'm trying. It's something very German.' Suki looked up to the ceiling as if to seek inspiration from above. 'I keep thinking ships.'

'German ships?'

'Yes.'

'Warships?'

Quite possibly.'

'Bismarck?'

'No.'

'Scharnhorst?'

Suki shook her head.

'Graf Spee?'

'Definitely not.'

'Tirpitz?'

'That's the one!'

'So,' said Storm, adding to Ben's notes, 'we have Erica – better use the German spelling – Erika von Tirpitz.'

'And here's something for you at no extra charge. She and Mrs Furse are friends. They come in here once in a while.'

'Is that so? Recently?'

'Fairly. They come in with other people too sometimes.'

'Can you ever remember seeing them in here with a man?'

'Yes, an old man. Walks with a stick and wears a silly hat. Seen him in here alone with Mrs von Tirpitz, too. Nothing romantic – he's too old for her. She's rather glamorous and he looks, well a bit on the shabby side. Smells too. Ooh and now I think about it, I remember them being here on carnival day, the Saturday before last. They were having lunch over there and Mrs Furse rushed in all of a fluster, spoke to them for a bit and then rushed out again. I remember clearly because then they called me over and asked for Gin and ITs, and I thought bloody hell what's that all about!'

Storm nodded. 'Then what happened?'

'They had a couple of gins each, paid the bill and left.'

'As you say, I wonder what that was all about. Is there anything else you can tell me?'

'About what?'

'About anything at all to do with these two women, or the old man maybe?'

'Did I say he's German, too?'

'No, you didn't.'

'He and Mrs von Tirpitz speak to each other in German. Mrs Furse also – she's English, but her German's pretty good.'

'Well I never. I don't suppose you know his name?'

'No idea.'

'Pity. I wonder if it's Morell. Now, Suki, do you by any chance know how I can contact either of these ladies? Do you know where they live?'

'Haven't a clue. We don't take addresses of customers when they come in to eat.'

'I know that, I just wondered if you might know.'

Suki stopped folding napkins and took a drag from her cigarette. 'Sorry Storm, I really have no idea. Try the telephone directory.'

'That's exactly what I'm going to do. There can't be many von Tirpitzes listed. And Furse isn't a very common name, so it's worth a try.'

'Would you like me to keep my eye open for them? If they come in I could give them your telephone number so they can contact you. Would that be any help?'

'It would – thank you, Suki. Here, I'll give you my business card. My home number's on the back, that's my digs in Stockwell.'

Suki leaned across the table and ran her fingers lightly across the top of his hand. 'So, you gorgeous man, what's it worth then?'

'Let's say this. If you put me in contact with either of them, I'll show my appreciation any way you choose.'

'Hmm that sounds like a bargain to me. Are you serious?'

'Absolutely. You see, I never could resist you either.'

'How about payment up front?'

Storm stood up and pecked her lightly on the cheek as he made for the stairs. 'Strictly cash on delivery.'

Suki blew him another kiss. 'I hope they come in again soon. Bloody hell I hope they do!'

****

Sunday 22nd July

It was a quiet shift for PC Bent. He was on an early, starting at six in the morning, and in midsummer Reigate, little happened that required much policing. He wandered around the mostly deserted streets, keeping an eye out for anything out of the ordinary, but there was nothing, not even a drunk asleep on a bench or struggling to find his way home. His rounds took him in circuits that brought him back to the police box at the Old Town Hall every so often, where he checked in by telephone with the station. Things busied up mid-morning as people made their way to church, though hardly the source of any criminal activity. In all respects it was a mundane, ordinary day.

A little before noon he found himself in the castle grounds. There was no one about, so he sat down on a bench for a smoke and pulled out his pocket diary. On today's page, there was a one-word entry. Meg. He liked early shifts at weekends as it meant he could see his girl in the afternoon or evening, depending on her rota at the Odeon. She was free this evening so they planned to go dancing. He couldn't wait.

He flicked back through the pages. The entries were mostly brief jottings as reminders to do things, both work-related and personal. He came to the page for 23rd June. Pencilled in bold capital letters were the words *BIKE STOLEN!* Almost a month and still no sign of it. He'd kept his eyes open ever since, monitoring cyclists at every opportunity to see if they were foolish enough to be riding stolen property in public. He looked at the bicycles and their riders in equal measure. He would recognise both. The face of the old man was like a still photograph ingrained in his memory. So, too, was what he'd been wearing. What kind of a man went around thieving in a dinner jacket! A wave of anger rose up in him. He knew he

288

would find the culprit eventually; he would bring the bastard to task. He'd been issued a replacement, but the loss of his original still rankled.

He finished his cigarette and set off back down towards the High Street. As he approached the Old Town Hall, his head full of thoughts of stolen bikes, he saw, riding towards him, a middle-aged man on a cycle, both of which looked not dissimilar from the images in his head. He stepped out onto the road, held up one hand and called out assertively: 'Stop in the name of the law!'

The cyclist, who was balancing a large bag over one shoulder, wobbled to a halt. 'What have I done now?' he said.

PC Bent scrutinised him for a few moments, then took a good look at the bike. 'Oh, it's you, Terry Angel. Sorry, a case of mistaken identity, thought you were someone else. You can be on your way now.'

Terry Angel wobbled off again. From over his shoulder Bent heard: 'Silly sod!' He didn't pursue it because he rather agreed. He should never have stopped him at all. Angel looked nothing like the bike thief.

****

Like all public telephone boxes, the one next to the Old Town Hall smelled vaguely of urine. It was there all year round to a greater or lesser extent, but in midsummer it was more apparent than usual; specific rather than vague, bordering on offensive. Storm turned up his nose as the door closed behind him and the full impact permeated his nostrils. He pulled out the local directory hurriedly, intent on making this piece of research as brief as possible.

With his thumb, he skimmed forward to the residential listings and slowed at the Fs. Was it Furse or Furze? There were

289

four of the former and two of the latter listed. No Rowenas, but according to Suki she was Mrs so the entry would be in her husband's name. One was a Miss, but a Eucalyptus not a Rowena. Eucalyptus! Did people really give their offspring such names? He eliminated her and jotted down details of all the others.

Unsurprisingly, there was only one von Tirpitz, first name Erika. Divorced, surmised Storm; or widowed. The address was Smoke Lane, which he knew. This too went into his notebook.

He stepped out into the relief of fresh air and lit a cigarette. How did a German woman end up in Reigate, he wondered. Ben had come across a story linking possible Nazis with the area. A coincidence? Maybe … maybe not.

Storm crossed the road and made his way casually down Bell Street, then left into Lesbourne Road, heading towards Smoke Lane.

Chapter 31

Wednesday 25th July

It was late afternoon. The sun was past its zenith and sliding imperceptibly towards the western horizon, and yet it was still baking hot on the island, especially inland amongst the parched lava fields and sparse palm groves, away from the yellow sandy shores and turquoise sea. Here the landscape on Fuerteventura was barren and devoid of life, apart from an occasional goat.

The couple walked hand in hand along the dusty lane away from La Oliva. She had a wicker bag over her shoulder, he a shotgun over his. They had been to the village for provisions and were heading back towards their small stone villa at the foot of a rocky outcrop that had aspirations to becoming a hill one day. Although not young, their body language implied they were, if not husband and wife, then certainly lovers; they were relaxed in each other's company and talked in an easy, intimate way, smiling often and occasionally breaking into laughter.

When they reached the villa, she went inside and emptied her bag, and he busied around outside for a while before sitting down on the porch, feet up on a low wall, with a tumbler of wine and a cigarette. Soon she joined him.

He was tall, at least six feet, in his early thirties, olive-skinned and slim with jet black hair. His clothes were simple; corduroy trousers and a white shirt with sleeves rolled up to above the elbows. He wore them well. He hadn't shaved for several days and the stubble darkened his complexion even more.

She was older, almost forty, shorter with wavy light brown hair and a round face. She had a good figure, kept trim through exercise and healthy living. She wore a skirt and blouse with sleeves cut short. Her complexion was lighter, less familiar with the sun.

An hour or so later she went inside to prepare their evening meal which they ate at the large rustic table in the kitchen area. Then they went back outside and smoked, drank wine and talked until the sun disappeared and darkness fell. It was cooler when they retired to the bedroom to make love, their naked bodies thrashing in all directions over the bed until they fell asleep, exhausted, in each other's arms.

Neither of them heard the breaking of glass, softened as it was by a cloth held between the butt of a Luger pistol and the shattered pane. A gloved hand leaned through the hole and unlocked the door, opening it very slowly. The two men edged their way inside, stepping sideways to avoid the shards of glass on the floor. Both carried a pistol and one also had a large torch which was switched off.

It was a cloudless night. Moonlight flooded in through the windows, illuminating the kitchen area which was separated from the bedroom beyond by a central archway with a bead curtain that hung dead still. The sound of gentle snoring, which might have been the man or the woman, or a combination of both, drifted their way.

Cautiously they approached the archway, instinctively moving to left and right, looking at each other for reassurance ahead of what was to come. They had rehearsed, based on the instructions they'd been given, to kill them both. Make the woman's death fast and painless; do what you like to the man so long as he dies, eventually.

The man on the left held up three fingers, then two, then one. Go!

They burst through the bead curtain in unison. The torch beam of brilliant white light suddenly pierced the darkness and for a split second captured an image of two naked bodies entwined, half covered by a blanket. The man's head turned and his eyes flickered open, wincing at the bright light. The woman barely had time to stir.

'Mateo …' she mumbled, struggling to lift herself up. But she spoke no further. The man without the torch leaned across the bed, grabbed her by the hair to steady his target, and shot her through the forehead. She slumped back, dead before her head hit the bed.

The man with the torch struck Mateo hard on the side of the head with his Luger; enough to stun him. With Eva dead, both men grabbed Mateo by the arms and dragged him off the bed, across the room and into the kitchen. They forced him up against the sink, with his head down and either arm spread outwards, pinned down by their body weight. The torchless man gave him a viscous kick between the legs and took pleasure in watching him wilt with the pain.

The tap was turned on full and the sink began to fill rapidly. Water clogged Mateo's mouth and nose. He spluttered and spat, struggling for breath. He cried out as another kick in the groin shot pain through his lower body. Something hard struck him across the back, then again on his buttocks. He nearly collapsed but managed to keep his footing. His head was turned to the right and he could see a man's hand pressing down on his upper arm, fingers slotted into the gap between the sink unit and the solid stone work surface next to it.

Mateo knew the sink unit was not secured to the floor. He shifted his weight sharply to his right with force, slamming the sink against the stone surface, enough to trap the man's fingers and crush them. The man yelled and eased his grip on Mateo's arm. Mateo took advantage of this moment of weakness, pushed the sink harder and at the same time pressed his shoulder against the hand, forcing the fingers backwards in a direction nature had not intended. He heard a volley of short sharp cracks as the fingers broke. The man screamed.

Distracted, the other man also loosened his grip. Mateo immediately pushed himself backwards which freed his arms. His left forearm came upwards into the other man's throat, followed by an elbow to his solar plexus. The man instinctively hunched his shoulders and staggered back. Mateo put both his hands on the man's lowered head for leverage and rammed his knee up into the groin.

'See how it feels, bastard!' he yelled.

Seconds later Mateo was gone, sprinting out into the darkness, still naked, protected by the night. He scrabbled his way up the rocky outcrop and found a vantage point, squatting down behind a boulder. They did not pursue him. Eventually he saw the outlines of the two men as they withdrew out of the villa, helping each other. Then he heard car doors slamming shut, an engine starting, and saw headlights cutting through the blackness, heading back along the lane towards La Oliva.

Only then did he see flames flickering at the windows of the villa. He ran back down the outcrop and into the kitchen. It was only a small fire, a pile of papers and rags set alight on the table. A parting gesture. He was able to douse it easily. Inside the bedroom he leaned over Eva's body. There was little blood. He kissed her on the lips, then rearranged her limbs into a foetal position and covered her with the blanket. He dressed, packed his few belongings into a rucksack and set off across country, heading towards Puerto del Rosario.

By mid-morning he had rented a room in the town under an assumed name. At midday, he sent several telegrams. In the afternoon he rented a scooter, a Lambretta, for a few days and made his way towards the south of the island. By sundown he was secreted on high ground half a mile from the Villa Winter, observing through powerful binoculars. He knew the layout thoroughly, having worked there for a year. The place where he had met Eva and fallen in love with her.

He watched and waited and smoked, keeping the lit end of the cigarettes low by his side to avoid it being seen. He was biding his time; waiting for his moment. He had plenty of time to spare.

****

Thursday 26th July

As was her custom after breakfast, Erika von Tirpitz strolled down from her house in Smoke Lane into Reigate with Mr Chips on his lead, then let him loose in Priory Park for a run and to do his business. On her way home, she called in at the newsagents and bought cigarettes and a newspaper, usually The Times. As today was Thursday she also bought the Surrey Mirror, hot off the press that morning. Back in Smoke Lane she settled down in the garden with a coffee and an ashtray and spent the morning reading firstly about what was going on in Great Britain, then closer to home in her adopted county.

It was another warm and sultry day and as she had no other commitments she read at a leisurely pace, absorbing every news story in detail, getting up only to make fresh coffee. Having read The Times from cover to cover, she started on the Surrey Mirror.

The front page was mainly public notices, auctioneers' announcements and classified advertisements. But in the bottom right hand corner was a header that read:

MURDERED MIRROR REPORTER LAID TO REST

She remembered reading about it the previous week – a young lad, shot and dumped in an old mine just outside Reigate. There was little further information apart from that the police investigation was ongoing, which presumably meant they hadn't found out anything so far. There was more about the funeral on page five, including photographs.

Erika was not one to flit from section to section; she liked to start at the beginning and read to the end, page by page. Page five would have to wait its turn. When she did reach it, she found a full spread about Ben Grimshaw's funeral. The main photograph was of the coffin being carried out of the church, and there was another of a group of mourners around the empty grave with the vicar prominent, prayer book open in his hands. Inset to one side was a portrait of the lad himself, a formal photograph of some sort in which he looked awkward and self-conscious.

Erika glanced at the face; a good looking young man, she mused, with an appealing smile. A tragedy, and such a waste of a life. She hoped they caught his killer soon and brought him to justice. She thought she recognised the face; perhaps she'd seen him around the town. She read the piece about the funeral, then moved on to page six.

Moments later it came to her and she was turning hurriedly back to page five.

She focused on the face, peering at it closely, then gasped. Of course! It was *that* face – the face pressed up against French windows, peering through the glass; the face with a quizzical expression turning for an instant into pain and fear as the glass smashed.

Erika turned back to the front page again and reread the piece about his murder. The body had been found in the mine exactly a fortnight ago, on the morning of Thursday 12th July. She reached for the diary in her handbag and flicked through it hurriedly. She had had dinner with Peter Yardley on Wednesday 11th July. The night before.

Her hands were shaking and the colour drained from her face. She felt a surge of nausea overwhelming her and rushed indoors. She got no further than the kitchen where she leaned over the sink and was violently sick.

****

Storm Grimshaw had been at the Central Criminal Court – more commonly known as the Old Bailey – covering a particularly nasty murder trial. Having been stuck in a cramped press gallery all day he took his time walking back to the Daily Mirror offices in Fleet Street and didn't get back to his desk until nigh on five o 'clock.

He slumped down into his chair. Tucked neatly under the keyboard of his typewriter were some slips of paper – memos and telephone messages that had accrued during the day. He flicked through them half-heartedly; he was tired and had no intention of dealing with any of them until the next day. He would type up the notes he'd been taking assiduously since ten that morning, then off to the pub for a pint or two before heading back to his digs.

That was the plan, until one message in particular caught his eye. No details, just to call a familiar name on a familiar number. He immediately dialled the number and a familiar voice answered.

'Hello boss.'

'Storm, dear boy, thank you for getting back to me. Listen, I've got a lead that will interest you.'

'I'm all ears.'

'I had an unexpected visitor today. A rather imposing female actually. She's German and goes by the very splendid name of Frau Erika von Tirpitz. Can you believe it! And there was I thinking it was a semi-submerged wreck rusting in a Norwegian fjord.'

'Did you say Erika?'

'Indeed, I did. Does that mean something to you?'

'It might do. Go on.'

'Well, Frau von Tirpitz is by all accounts a resident of Reigate, and a regular reader of our esteemed periodical. She buys it every week and, wait for it, reads every word … every word! Time on her hands clearly, nothing better to do. Anyway, what inspired her to come and see me was my piece about young Benjamin's funeral. You see, Storm, as well as pictures of the funeral itself, we also published a full face portrait of Ben.'

'And she recognised him?'

'Indeed she did.'

'Where from?'

'Listen to this …'

Storm listened. When the boss had finished, he said: 'And she said this was on the 11th July – the night before Ben was found dead?'

'That's correct.'

'Is she absolutely certain?'

'It would appear so.'

'And she's absolutely sure it was Ben she saw at the French windows?'

'One hundred percent.'

'Has she been to the police with this?'

'No, I told her to leave it with me for the time being, until I'd made some enquiries. But she may well do. Dear boy, I think we should come clean with the boys in blue. This is heady stuff.'

'Not yet,' said Storm firmly.

'I'm not at all proud of the fact that I failed to mention Ben's notebook to them. Withholding evidence, albeit unintentionally, doesn't bode well.'

'Give me some time, boss, please. This is really interesting and I'd like to talk to this Tirpitz woman. It's Friday tomorrow. I'll come down for the weekend. Can you give me until, say, Monday?'

'On one condition.'

'Let me guess … that I share the lowdown with you?'

'Ugh, I wish you'd keep away from those vulgar Americanisms. But yes, equal dibs, please.'

'All right, boss, it's a deal. Now, details. Address, phone number, vital statistics …'

'The first two I can give you. The third you'll find out for yourself soon enough, no doubt. And I think you'll like what you see. As you know, I'm somewhat indifferent to the female form, but even I was impressed.'

Chapter 32

Friday 27th July

'Erika, darling, are you all right? You're very quiet. Cat got your tongue?'

They were sitting in the Palm Court salon at The Ritz having afternoon tea ahead of their trip to the theatre. Their table was towards one corner of the room and afforded a clear view across the entire space with its high, mirrored walls and opaque-glassed ceiling from which hung two elaborate birdcage chandeliers. At the centre of the room stood a huge, ornate floral display, and in the far corner a woman played the harp, barely audible across a sea of chattering guests. Erika had been taking it all in as Rowena and Mr Morell chatted.

'I do apologise, Row, I'm fine, just a little preoccupied, that's all.'

Mr Morell had a look of unbridled contentment on his face as he sat surrounded by tiers of cut finger sandwiches, teacakes, pastries and freshly baked scones. To his delight they had been able to serve him Caraway tea, a favourite. Between mouthfuls, he said: 'The harp makes a pleasant change from a piano, don't you agree?'

'It does indeed,' agreed Rowena.

'Pity we cannot hear it very well. I thought I recognised some Mozart just then.'

'You did … Sonata Facile in C major, first movement. It suits the harp well as it's mostly diatonic.'

Erika pulled a face. 'If you say so, Rowena, dear – whatever that means.'

'In simple terms, for heathens like you, it's rather like using only the white notes on the piano.'

'Now you're talking my language.'

'I say, I think I've drunk rather too much tea. Would you excuse me while I go and powder my nose?' Rowena stood up and, clutching her handbag, eased her way between the tables. As soon as she was out of earshot, Morell leaned forward towards Erika, speaking in German.

'Dear lady, I have been waiting all day for a moment to catch you alone.'

'Now is your chance.'

'I want to talk to you about Peter Yardley.'

'I would prefer not.'

'Frau Furse has told me of your suspicions – also what happened to your sister.'

'And what do you have to say about it?'

'I wish to apologise. Such behaviour towards a woman is totally unforgivable. If it is true and Bormann did that, I am truly sorry.'

'Thank you.'

'But you must not assume Yardley is responsible and that he is anyone other than Yardley. Naturally that is not his real name. He is German in all respects and I know his name, but it is not Bormann.'

'You're lying. Why should I believe you? It makes sense that he is Bormann, from what you have told us. He worked for you for years, and it is obvious you worked closely together. Bormann is the only high-ranking Nazi at large.'

'There are more than you might imagine. However, as I explained to Frau Furse, many people worked for me, thousands, not only National Socialist officials but ordinary people too, soldiers, airmen, sailors and civilians. You are jumping to conclusions by assuming this man is Bormann.'

'All right, Mr Morell, if Peter Yardley is *not* Martin Bormann and a perfectly innocuous individual – and ignoring the fact that he was intent on forcing himself on me the night I had dinner with him and only failed because I squeezed his balls so tight they nearly imploded, then please do tell me … who is he?'

'For all intents and purposes, he *is* Peter Yardley.'

'And is Peter Yardley a man who is prone to violence and not averse to the occasional murder as well as sexual aggression towards women?'

'Of course not.'

Erika's tone hardened. 'So how is it that on the night I had dinner at his house I saw a young man in the grounds, and that same young man was found dead the next morning – beaten and shot in the head? Are you telling me Peter Yardley had nothing to do with it?'

Morell was taken aback. Yardley had assured him that Erika had seen nothing. 'I'm sorry, I do not know what you are talking about.'

'It was in the local newspaper, the Surrey Mirror. Did you not see yesterday's edition, or the previous week's?'

'No, I did not.'

'The lad actually worked for them, as a junior reporter. Last week they reported the murder, and this week they followed up with an article about his funeral. This time they printed a photograph of the lad – and I recognised him. It was the same face I saw peering through the window at Peter Yardley's, watching us have dinner together.'

'I think you are mistaken, Erika.'

'Oh no, it was definitely him. And someone caught him there and smashed his face into the glass, which broke – and there was blood. I saw it with my own eyes. Yardley went out to see what had happened. When he came back he made light of it – said the boy was unharmed and had been sent on his way. That was a lie. Clearly, he was injured, badly. And lo and behold, the next morning he is found murdered.'

'If so, I think it must be a terrible coincidence. However, I am not convinced that it was the same person. Presumably it was dark?'

'There is no mistake. It was the same boy.'

'If Yardley was having dinner with you then he could not have attacked the boy.'

'Oh come on, Mr M, I wasn't born yesterday. He has a supposed chauffeur and a supposed valet, both of whom look as though they would strangle their grandmother for a packet of Woodbines. He may not have pulled the trigger, but he was to blame.'

'What are you going to do?'

'I am wondering about that – probably why I am quiet today. I'm meeting the boy's brother tomorrow to discuss it. He, too, is a reporter – on a national newspaper. I spoke to him by telephone yesterday. He is determined to find out who killed Ben, and he has asked for my help.'

'Ben, is that his name?' Morell sat pensively for a few moments. 'You know Yardley is out of the country. It would take little effort to warn him not to return, and if that was the case anything you do would be futile.'

Erika leaned forward towards Mr Morell until she was staring directly into his eyes. 'Now why would you do that if he's an innocent man?'

303

Morell stared back at her until his face broke into a smile and he began to giggle.

'I don't see anything remotely funny in this situation at all,' said Erika frostily.

'I do. I am finding it amusing that you are accusing Yardley of being Martin Bormann when I have so recently been accused of the same thing. It is becoming an epidemic. I wonder who next … Mr Furse perhaps?'

'You were accused of being Bormann? By whom?'

'Your friend Colonel Peregrine bloody Maxwell.'

'Maxwell? When, where?'

'Shh, here comes Frau Furse. I will tell you later if the opportunity presents itself.'

Rowena sat down and smiled amiably at her two friends.

'More tea?'

****

The St James's Theatre was in King Street, just a few minutes' walk from The Ritz. They were early so made their way into the bar and spent some time chatting and absorbing the surroundings. Gradually the room filled up and became noisy to the point that conversation was difficult, so they made their way to their seats. Esmond Knight had done them proud; they were sitting almost central to the stage in the fourth row of the stalls.

'Does this meet with your approval, Mr M?'

'Oh yes, thank you.'

They were the first to be seated in that row. As soon as they had settled – Erika in the centre, Mr Morell and Rowena on either side of her – Rowena decided they should all have programmes and set off to find some. Erika took the opportunity to resume her conversation with Morell.

'Quick now, Mr M, what has gone on between you and Colonel bloody Maxwell?'

'This is not really the place …'

'You must tell me!'

'Very well. He came to the house, Yardley's house. I am staying inside while he is away.'

'How the hell did Maxwell know where to find you?'

'I do not know, but I rather imagine he is quite a resourceful fellow.'

'Did you let him in?'

'He let himself in.'

'With a key?'

'A crowbar I think, judging by the state of the back door.'

'A crowbar!' Erika sounded suitably shocked.

'That is beside the point. He came in and confronted me, accusing me of being Bormann.'

'And what did you say?'

'I told him I was not.'

'And what did he say?'

'Oh, a lot of nonsense about Bormann, dead comrades, the Jews … I seem to remember he mentioned Freemasons at one point. And you of course. He wanted me to keep away from you. *My woman* is how he referred to you. I put him straight on that, but he didn't like it one bit. He is confused. He believes I am Bormann, and he has seen us together, so assumes you and I are …'

'Copulating?'

Mr Morell winced. 'I would not have put it so crudely, but that is what he believes, yes.'

'Did he harm you?'

'No, but he did threaten to shoot me.'

'Did he have a gun with him?'

'Yes.'

'Fucking hell.'

Rowena reappeared. 'Here we are – programmes. What are you two chatting about?'

'Nothing in particular,' said Erika. 'Just admiring this magnificent auditorium.'

'It's lovely, isn't it? Filling up quite a bit now. Look here in the programme. Esmond Knight, the man we met in The Old Wheel who kindly let us have tickets, is playing a character called Belzanor. There are some wonderful actors in other parts. Robert Helpmann – he was in *The Red Shoes* too. I wonder if he'll dance, ha ha! And some others I've never heard of. Desmond Llewelyn – who's he? I wouldn't queue for his autograph. I say, something to look forward to … Orson Welles will be here in October, producing, directing and starring in *Othello*. How exciting.'

'We must come and see him,' said Erika.

'That would be wonderful, this could become a regular outing, depending on how long you stay with us, Mr Morell.'

'That I cannot say,' he replied.

They browsed through their programmes and passed comment occasionally until minutes before the play was due to start. Every seat in the theatre was taken apart from three to the right of Mr Morell. Moments before curtain up, a rotund, elderly man with a babyish face accompanied by a younger woman made his way awkwardly along the row towards them. The man threw his hat and coat onto the seat next to Morell and sat down heavily into his own, the woman to his right. He turned and looked at Morell, inspecting him as if to determine whether or not they were known to each other.

'Good evening,' said Mr Morell politely.

'Good evening,' replied Winston Churchill. The two men held eye contact for a brief moment. 'Do I know you?'

'We have never met, but you know me.'

'You are enigmatic, sir.'

The house lights faded and the curtain rose. Throughout the first prologue the audience were mesmerised. Then, minutes into Act One, as Cleopatra was awoken by Caesar from her sleep between the paws of a Sphinx, a voice familiar to the entire English speaking world floated up from the fourth row of the stalls and was clearly audible on stage.

'By Jove – what a corker!'

****

At the interval, Erika and Rowena ventured off to powder their noses while Mr Morell stayed in his seat, as did Winston Churchill who spoke with his female companion for a while until she too stood up and wandered off. Churchill turned his attention to his neighbour.

'I have an excellent memory for faces, but I am struggling with yours. You say I know you, but we have never met. Pray, enlighten me?'

'I am Adolf Hitler.'

'Remarkable. Rather like Lazarus, risen from the dead?'

'Something along those lines.'

'We meet at last. I'm not convinced that your sense of humour is in good taste, sir. On the other hand, if you are who you say you are I must declare the loss of that ludicrous moustache to be a blessing. I never reconciled myself to the fact that someone was able to accrue such extraordinary power and personal loyalty in his ascendancy whilst resembling Mr Charles Chaplin, and still managed to be taken seriously. Additionally, I am delighted, albeit from beyond the grave as it were, finally to have had the opportunity to say so to your face.'

'Excuse me,' responded Mr Morell. 'I cannot equal your grasp of the English language. In German, it would be easy. It is probably just as well, otherwise this unexpected meeting would end up as no more than an exchange of insults.'

'Understandably so.'

'Having said that, I know enough of your language to say you are fatter in real life than I imagined.'

'Enough!' Churchill declared. 'I do not respond well to flattery. Pray tell me, I have had it on good authority from our extremely well-informed intelligence services that you committed suicide in a bunker in Berlin – with a gun, or poison, or both. Your body was burned and there were numerous witnesses who have confirmed so. What have you to say to that?'

'If that is true, then I am not sitting here.'

'But you are.'

'Then you have been misinformed about my death. Was a body found and identified?'

'The Soviets claim to have what remains of one, but they are not forthcoming in terms of evidence. There may even be photographs, but we are not party to them.'

'Perhaps that will change when Stalin is replaced,' suggested Mr Morell.

'That will depend on who replaces him and in which direction the wind blows. Have you ever met him?'

'You know I have not.'

'I thought perhaps you might have, since your apparent demise.'

'Relations between us since forty-one have not been good, for obvious reasons. Nothing has changed. I have more sympathetic comrades elsewhere.'

'Where have you been hiding yourself away for the past six years?'

'Somewhere you would not expect.'

'Not in England surely?'

'No – though if I had I would not have been the only Nazi doing so.'

Churchill stared intensely at Morell, as if trying to read his thoughts. 'That is debatable. And what have you been doing with yourself?'

'All manner of things, including learning a foreign language. Your language.'

'Your English is decidedly better than my German.'

'And like you, no doubt, I have been enjoying some leisure time. Painting, for example.'

'Ah yes, I adore painting. It has come to my rescue more than once in troubled times. Painting a picture is like fighting a battle, and as in battles you do not always win. You would know that only too well, Herr Hitler.'

'You also. May I mention Gallipoli?'

'No, you may not,' stated Churchill emphatically. 'The difference of course is that you can always correct oil paint if you make a mistake – scrape it off with a pallet knife and start again. And if you lose, there is not much harm done. You can always go out and kill some animal or humiliate some rival on the golf course. I know of nothing which more entirely absorbs the mind. Once the picture begins to flow there is no room for the worries of the hour or the threats of the future. All one's mental light becomes concentrated on the task. Don't you agree?'

'Yes indeed,' said Mr Morell. 'Do you paint portraits, or do you prefer landscapes and buildings?'

'I have painted a few portraits, including of myself, but mostly landscapes.'

'We have that in common. I have no great wish to paint people. They do not interest me as subjects.'

'A psychoanalyst might read much into that statement.'

'To no great purpose. It is merely a preference. I have often thought that I should have persevered with painting and made my mark in life as an artist, or an architect, rather than in the field of politics.'

'I am of the same opinion. Millions, nay billions of others would agree. I must say I like bright colours. I rejoice with the brilliant ones and feel genuinely sorry for the poor browns. If I had formulated a private army of hoodlums and thugs, I would have chosen a far more brilliant colour for their shirts than brown. Prussian blue perhaps.'

'Money was tight in those early days of the struggle. We had to make do with what we could get.'

Erika and Rowena reappeared. Erika leaned across Morell.

'Mr Churchill, how do you do?'

'Frau Hitler, I presume?'

'Hardly! My name is Erika von Tirpitz.'

Winston Churchill looked up towards the heavens. 'Are the Gods playing tricks on me this evening?'

His companion also reappeared and said: 'Are you all right, Father?'

'No, Mary, I am not. I have been obliged to sit and converse with the Narzee leader, Herr Hitler no less. Additionally, I have just been introduced to the female embodiment of a German battleship. I pray that the curtain will rise again soon and take me back to the relative sanity of Mr Shaw's Ancient Egypt.'

'I have no idea what you are talking about,' said Mary. She peered across at Mr Morell. 'He looks nothing like Hitler. Besides, Hitler's dead.'

Churchill turned towards Morell again. 'It has been interesting talking to you, sir, whoever you are. I do not begin to understand what game you are playing, however, I most certainly did not expect this evening's interval to be as entertaining as the performance.'

310

'Likewise, Mr Churchill.'

The lights dimmed again and the play resumed, culminating in Cleopatra and Caesar's farewell on the gangplank of a ship that will take Caesar back to Rome and ultimately his assassination. The applause seemed endless and there were numerous curtain calls. When the adulation had fizzled out, the audience started its chatter as people made their way towards the exits. As Winston Churchill rose to leave, he turned again to Mr Morell.

'One final question, sir. If you are indeed Hitler, which I very much doubt, how did you manage to escape from your bunker when the Soviet army was virtually on top of you?'

'*Täuschung.*'

'By which you mean?'

'*Täuschung.*'

'Toy … toysh …'

Churchill tried to repeat it but was hampered by his speech impediment. 'Can you spell it for me?'

'Allow me, Mr Churchill,' said Erika.

He listened intently as she pronounced each letter, then nodded in appreciation.

'Thank you. And if I seek a translation, presumably it will answer my question?'

'It will help you to understand,' said Mr Morell.

Churchill nodded and bowed his head slightly.

'As a parting shot, I have something to say – something I heard recently that I wish to share with you. One of our finest secret operatives has summarised rather succinctly that the war was, firstly, *won* by intelligence. We had a most secret source virtually throughout, of which you had no knowledge. So secret that the vast majority of our own people didn't know about it, and still don't. We had to make sacrifices to ensure it remained secret, some of which will haunt me for the rest of my days.

311

Secondly, he wrote that the war was *lost* by the crass stupidity of Adolf, quite clearly contributing to the downfall of his own empire through atrocious decision making. I wholeheartedly agree. I wish you goodnight, and preferably goodbye … Herr Hitler.'

Mr Morell sat stone faced, stunned by this blanching verbal onslaught. The best he could manage in return was: 'Goodbye, former Prime Minister Churchill.'

Chapter 33

Saturday 28th July

'That's just about all I can tell you, Storm Grimshaw,' said Erika as she sat on her sofa, a cigarette in one hand and a gin in the other, looking across at the young journalist who was sipping a beer. One thought was uppermost in her mind – she simply had to have sex with him. He was gorgeous.

'Thank you, Mrs von Tirpitz. That's been very helpful.'

'My friends call me Erika. You and I are friends now.'

'Thank you, Erika. Now can I ask you again – are you absolutely certain, beyond the shadow of a doubt, that the face you saw at the window was the same as the one of my brother in the photo in the Surrey Mirror?'

'Absolutely.'

'One hundred percent certain?'

'Two hundred percent.'

'Ben's facial injuries appear consistent with what you say, that his face was pushed through a pane of glass.'

'It was him, I have no doubt. You look very alike, same hair colour, same features.'

'We are often told that … *were* I should say. And Yardley claimed Ben wasn't injured at all?'

'He lied to me. He told me the boy wasn't hurt, but it was patently untrue. There was blood around the broken window, and drops on the carpet for God's sake!'

'When you left did you see or hear anything? Did you see the two men who work for Yardley?'

'Nothing and no one. Yardley was occupied nursing his balls, so I let myself out.'

'A lady who can look after herself, clearly.'

'I am far more approachable if I find a man attractive, Storm, I can assure you.'

Their eyes met and in her look Storm understood precisely what she was implying and what doors of opportunity were open to him. Erika von Tirpitz was a sexual woman, and she would be pleased to accommodate him. He looked down at his notepad and tried to concentrate on his investigation.

'You haven't told any of this to the police?'

'Not yet. I went straight to the Surrey Mirror, as Ben was one of theirs, and the nice man there advised me not to until I had spoken with you. Perhaps I should have, but as you are the poor boy's brother and clearly intent on getting to the bottom of this terrible business it seemed to me the right thing to do.'

'I appreciate that, Erika, if I can just have a head start on this lead. But you must tell them soon, otherwise you might be accused of perverting their course of justice.'

'When?'

'Tomorrow perhaps – give me a day.'

'One good turn deserves another, young man.'

Storm again looked down at his notepad.

'Shall I tell them everything?' she asked. 'Shall I say who we believe Yardley and Morell to be? They are only suspicions, despite Morell being freely adamant he is Adolf Hitler. Rowena and I are not convinced and are more inclined to believe he's a crackpot. Yardley is more likely to be Bormann in my view.'

'What you tell them is up to you,' replied Storm. 'Though you might find it difficult giving only part of the story. When I spoke to Inspector Thorne the other day, he knew nothing about Nazis in Reigate, or if he did he kept it to himself. That might still be the case, so it may come as a surprise to him. From my perspective, there are two stories here – my brother's murder and the Nazi angle that Ben cottoned on to. They're almost certainly connected. There doesn't seem to be any other reason to explain such a brutal killing. The first story is personal for me, obviously, and I want to find out who's responsible for Ben's murder. I'd like to see them hang. The second, speaking as a journalist, would make a national headline, international even. The police aren't fools … well, not all of them. They will pick up on the Nazi suspicions, so you might as well come clean. I'll still be ahead of the game.'

'I think you're probably right.'

'They'll be more interested in Yardley than Morell. He'll be their prime suspect.'

'Even if they think they have Hitler within their grasp?'

'They're just as likely to believe he's a crackpot, as you do. They'll be looking first and foremost to solve the crime, taking an interest in Yardley and his thugs as murder suspects more than possible Nazis on the run.'

'Whereas you will want to focus on both aspects?'

'That's right.'

'And if Yardley really is Bormann, then I want him to suffer too.'

'Because of what he did to your sister?'

'Precisely. Ben's murder is personal to you. Pinning down Yardley, if he is Bormann, for raping my sister and being responsible for her suicide, is personal to me.' Erika leaned forward and put her hand on his knee. 'We have something in common, Storm.'

315

'We do, and we must work together on this.' He placed his hand over hers.

'As closely as you like. Come for dinner tonight and we can talk some more. If you are free.'

'Yes, I am, thank you, that's kind of you. I may have some more questions to put to you.'

****

Mr Wells vaguely remembered Storm.

They had met a few times during his Surrey Mirror days, once to discuss some advertising, they recalled as they sat in Mr Wells' office, and another whilst arranging a charity event. There had no doubt been other times.

Storm explained that he was investigating his brother's death and knew Ben had been in Knight's during the weeks leading up to the murder. He wondered if there was any connection, or if Mr Wells could remember anything that might be of relevance.

'I'm sorry, no,' said Wells. 'He came in to glean the facts about some shoplifting incidents, asked a few questions, then left. That's the long and the short of it. We caught the woman eventually, but your brother wouldn't have known that because it was after …'

'After he was killed?'

'Precisely.'

'Did anyone else talk to him?'

'Only my wife. She works here too – one of my staff.'

'May I have a word?'

'She won't be able to tell you anything more.'

'Even so, I'd like to speak to her, if I may.' Storm's only purpose in being there was to speak to Mrs Wells.

'All right, but please don't keep her long. It's Saturday and a busy day for trade.'

Mr Wells went to fetch Barb and when he returned, to Storm's relief, he said: 'I'll leave you to it. Please don't keep her long.'

Mrs Wells looked nervous. She would not sit down, so Storm stood up too.

'Mrs Wells, I'll come straight to the point. Ben told me about you. I know that you were … becoming close.'

Barb looked shocked. She checked that the door was closed properly then moved closer to Storm so she could speak in a whisper. 'Please don't tell anyone,' she said anxiously, failing to keep a pleading note from her voice.

'I promise I won't.'

'Do the police know?'

'I don't think so. I certainly haven't said anything to them, but I can't be sure.'

'Please don't tell them.'

'I won't. It's no one's business but your own.'

'Thank you. That's a huge relief.'

'All I know is what Ben told me,' said Storm. 'That you'd been flirting with each other and that you were planning to do more than that. I don't even know if anything happened.'

'It did. Just the once.'

'When?'

'The night he was killed.'

'Where?'

'On my kitchen table.'

Storm tried to stifle a grin. 'I didn't mean you to be that precise.'

'Oops, sorry.' Barb looked at him coyly. He could see what had appealed about her to Ben.

'Then what?'

317

'He left, and I never saw him again.'

'How long was he with you and what time did he leave?'

'Less than an hour, he left around seven-fifty.'

'Not long then.'

'My husband came home early and nearly caught us.'

'Nearly?'

'But not quite.'

'So, no jealous husband as a suspect for murder then?'

'Oh no, you can rule that out. Tun ... Mr Wells isn't the jealous type. And he never knew.'

'Is there any connection between yourself and Ben's murder? Anything at all you can tell me?'

Barb shook her head. She could feel tears welling up and took out a handkerchief to wipe her eyes. 'Nothing. I was growing very fond of him.'

Storm believed her. He put his hand on her shoulder, thanked her and left.

It was ten minutes on foot from Bell Street via the tunnel to Alders Road. He walked past Rowena's house and ticked his notebook to confirm that the address Erika had given him coincided with the one he had gleaned from the telephone directory, that of a Howard Furse. He wandered around the corner into Wray Park Road and approached the Yardley house. It looked unoccupied and had that stillness about it that instinctively suggests there is no one at home. He walked confidently up to the front door and pressed the bell. He heard it ringing loud and clear inside. When there was no response, he pressed again, keeping his finger on longer.

He knocked firmly on the door with his knuckles. 'Hello, is there anyone there? Mr Yardley – are you there?'

When it was clear no one would answer, he walked from the porch along the front of the house and peered in through the windows, but it was difficult to see anything. He could make out the hallway, a coat stand, a grandfather clock and some stairs; that was all.

He came to a wooden gate that led into the back garden. He lifted the latch and pushed, but it didn't open. It was bolted on the other side. Storm glanced around him. The road was empty; no one in view. He grabbed the top of the gatepost with both hands, walked his feet up the wall of the house and vaulted over the top of the gate, landing with practised ease. He undid the bolt in case he needed to get out faster than he had got in.

The path led into a large garden, mostly lawn, with flowerbeds on either side and a stone patio that ran along the rear of the house. At the far end was a small pond, beyond which he could see a sizeable summer house.

'Is anyone there? Hello?'

He wandered across the lawn towards the summer house, looking around all the time. In his jacket pocket, his right hand clenched a set of keys, with a Chubb protruding from between two fingers, as a makeshift weapon. The summer house, too, looked deserted and having tried the lock and looked through the windows he made his way back towards the house.

'Anyone at home? Hello there?'

As he approached the house, his attention focused on one of the upstairs windows. A curtain rippled slightly. Not his imagination; it definitely moved. As he came nearer, it moved again. Someone was at home after all.

Do what you have to do and then get out of this place – fast, he said to himself.

He walked up to the patio to a point where it was overlooked by some French windows. He bent down and examined the panes of glass close to the ground. It was easy to see that one of them had been replaced recently; the putty was new and the glass cleaner than the surrounding panes. He peered closely at the ground beneath. It had been swept, but there were still some tiny fragments of broken glass to be seen. He took a small brown envelope from his pocket and scooped them up. Some had a dark stain on them which to Storm looked like congealed blood. Inside, through the French windows, he could see a mahogany dining table and matching Windsor chairs.

Calling out once more to make his presence known, he made his way back through the side gate and out onto the road. With a final glance towards the upstairs windows, he started walking away. Well, he thought, if that was Peter Yardley in the house he had no intention of making his presence known.

Why would he do that?

He was walking slowly. As he passed a house further down the road, he came to a halt, deep in thought. The house was set back slightly and hidden from view by a row of bushes. He stared at them, concentrating hard on his recent findings and not really taking in his surroundings. Then he noticed something that changed his focus of attention. Between the last two bushes, poking out slightly and barely visible, he saw what looked like the rear of a bicycle, the rim of a wheel with a mudguard and the back of a saddle. He grabbed hold of it and pulled it out, leaning forward to keep the handlebars straight. As soon as it was clear of the bush, he recognised it immediately. Ben's bike.

Curiously, between the next two bushes he noticed the rear wheel of another bicycle. Leaning Ben's against a fence he pulled the second bike out and examined it thoroughly. It was painted dark blue. Storm knew the style – he'd seen policemen riding them for years. He pushed it back where he had found it.

Mounting Ben's cycle, he set off down the road. He knew he should take it straight to the police station, but instead he headed towards his parents' house to wash and change ready for dinner with Erika von Tirpitz.

He'd come clean with the police tomorrow and, not for the first time, suffer Inspector Thorne's wrath for tampering with evidence and threats of being hauled over the coals for perverting the course of justice.

Just like old times.

****

Storm lay on his back on the bed with Erika straddling him. She was riding him, at a hefty gallop, thrusting up and down, her back arched and her ample breasts dancing in front of his eyes. She was screaming at him in German. He had no idea what she was saying but he didn't care; he was focused on keeping control and not coming too soon because this was just too good to end too soon. He was using a trick given to him one boozy evening by a fellow journalist and was currently imagining himself confronted naked by the notoriously unattractive Member of Parliament for Liverpool Exchange, Bessie Braddock. It was working and Erika was reaping the benefits of his staying power as she squirmed, seemingly endlessly, on top of him.

'Keep it up, Storm!' she yelled in English. 'This is working together at its best!'

'You're making a lot of noise, Erika. I hope your neighbours are tolerant.'

'FUCK THE NEIGHBOURS!' she screamed. 'When I'm taking pleasure, they can share it with me and if they don't like it they can go to hell.' Abruptly she lifted herself off him and leaned over the edge of the bed, thrusting her backside in the air and wiggling it. 'Now do it to me from behind.'

Storm did as he was told, gripping a buttock with each hand and thrusting as hard and as deep as he could manage.

'Oh, this is good. This is the best!' She then reverted into German again.

321

When eventually they had both come, Erika several times at full volume, they lay in bed smoking and talking.

'My God that was remarkable,' purred Erika salaciously. 'You know how to satisfy a woman.'

'Thank you.'

'I haven't had it as good in a long time. Better even that F for Freddie.'

'Who's he?'

'He comes around occasionally to keep me satisfied. He's good but not in your league.'

'That's good to know.'

'Changing the subject, we'll nail those bastards, Storm, for killing my sister and your brother. We'll nail them.'

'I went round to Yardley's house this afternoon. It was quiet. I didn't see much.'

'He is out of the country.'

Storm sat up. 'What? You didn't tell me.'

'Didn't I? I thought I had.'

'No, you didn't. Where has he gone?'

'I don't know.'

'When will he be back?'

'I don't know that either.'

'So how do you know he's away?'

'Mr Morell told me.'

'Shit, this puts a different perspective on things.'

Erika looked puzzled. 'Why?'

'Well for a start, our number one suspect has flown the nest and can't be interviewed.'

'He'll be back.'

'Not necessarily. If he gets wind of the fact that he's been linked with Ben's murder, he'll stay out of the country. I would if I was him.'

Erika took a final draw from her cigarette and crushed it into an ashtray. 'That's what Morell said … that he could warn Yardley to stay away.'

'There was someone in the house when I was round there. Upstairs. I saw them behind the curtains. Whoever it was didn't respond when I knocked. If not Yardley, then Morell?'

'Probably. He's moved in from the summer house while Yardley is away.'

'I need to speak with your Mr Morell.'

'That can easily be arranged.'

'Also,' said Storm, 'I found Ben's bike. It was hidden in some bushes along the road from Yardley's. I think he must have put it there before he made his way into the garden the night he was killed. That would explain why it's still there. No one knew about it.'

'Are you sure it's Ben's?'

'I'd know it anywhere.'

'What did you do with it?'

'Rode it home. It's at my parents' house.'

'I think we must both report to the police tomorrow.'

'You're right. Neither of us can put it off any longer.'

Erika ran her fingers across his chest. 'We'll go together.'

'Better not. We don't want to appear to be in league with each other. Oh, and I found another bike in the same bushes. A police bike of all things.'

'How unusual. I wonder how it got there.'

'I wonder too.'

'Did you take that bicycle away?'

'Hardly. Have you tried riding two bicycles at once?'

'I take your point.'

'I left it where I found it. I can't imagine there's any connection. Must be a coincidence. Hopefully the coppers will be pleased enough about its return to take the edge off my purloining the other one.'

'You know, Storm, has it occurred to you that we don't have to pin Ben's murder or Maxine's rape on this man Yardley, if he is Bormann?'

He looked at her with interest. 'How do you mean?'

'At the Nuremburg trials Bormann was sentenced to death in his absence. All we have to do is prove his identity beyond any doubt, and the noose will be round his neck without the need for any further evidence of further crimes.'

'True, but it would be satisfying to see him hang for Ben, and for your sister. Besides, whether he's Martin Bormann or not, Yardley is clearly culpable for Ben's death in my view. Whoever he is, I'm after him.'

'Changing the subject again, have you noticed the time?'

'No, what about it?'

'It's been an hour since you did it to me. Again please.'

'Must I?' groaned Storm teasingly.

'You have no choice. That is an order.'

'My God, woman, you are … I can't think of the appropriate word.'

'That is disappointing. Unimpressive, too, for a journalist, a man who supposedly uses words to earn himself a living. In German, I am almost certain you would choose *unersättlich*.'

'And what would that be in English?'

'Insatiable.'

Storm nodded approvingly. 'That's the word I was looking for.'

Chapter 34

Sunday 29th July

The clock on the mantelpiece had a gentle, soporific, almost hypnotic tick that cut through the silence in the living room. It was made of walnut, with a wide base, a silver face, Roman numerals and ornate hands. It had belonged to Beth Angel's grandmother who had given it to Beth's mother the day she got married. Beth had taken notional ownership when she married Terry, though not immediately; they had lived with her parents for two years until they could afford a place of their own, and the clock had moved with them.

Terry was familiar with the chime – a watered down version of Big Ben. In truth, he'd never before been aware to any great extent that the clock *had* a tick. In all the time they had lived together, there had never been silence enough to hear it. He sat in his armchair, looking across at his wife who sat opposite him in a similar chair, gazing into the empty hearth, saying nothing.

Terry was finding it very unnerving. 'I never thought I'd ever say this, Beth,' he said, 'but you're quiet.'

'I've got nothing to say,' she replied curtly.

'Not like you.'

'Are you complaining?'

'No, I like it. Just remarking.'

They slipped back into silence. Terry took a sip of stout, then lit a cigarette and smoked it too quickly. He was feeling on edge.

'What's bothering you?' he asked.

'How many guesses do you need?'

'Is it the court hearing?'

She turned a steely gaze towards him. 'What do *you* think?'

'Thought so. Tuesday ain't it?'

'You know very well it is.'

'Nothing to worry about. It's only a bit of thieving from a shop. The magistrate will probably give you a ticking off and bind you over. So long as you don't go nicking in Knight's again, you've nothing to worry about. Or if you do, just don't get caught.'

'I have no intention of nicking anything from anywhere ever again.'

'What made you do it?'

'I could ask you the same question. You do it all the time, and a lot more than nicking from shops. You're a professional thief. Maybe I thought if you can get away with it I could too.'

'Only you didn't.'

'Your track record isn't exactly snow white.'

'I haven't been banged up for a long time. Years.'

'Why do *you* do it?' she asked inquisitively. 'What makes you steal for a living, instead of getting a proper job?'

'It puts food on the table.'

'That's no answer. There are loads of other ways of doing that.' Beth stared into the hearth again and turned her thoughts back to herself. 'I don't know why I did it. First time it was on the spur of the moment. I didn't intend doing it at all. I was in there, in Knight's, and saw these lovely things and wanted them. I just did it. And I got away with it … so I did it again. It was really foolish.'

'Foolish to go back to the same place. You need to vary your location.'

'Listen to the expert talking! You're right of course. Though I did vary my appearance and wore different clothes, so I'd look different.'

'Didn't work though, did it.'

'No,' she said despondently. 'It didn't.' She reverted back into silence, her thoughts focusing on what might happen at the court hearing. 'Will it get into the papers?'

'Doubt it. Not juicy enough. Depends if there's anything more exciting happening.'

'Terry, can I ask you something?'

'You can ask. You might not get a reply.'

'Terry, will you pack it up, the thieving? Will you go straight … for me?'

He spread his arms wide. 'And do what? I've got no trade, no skills. I can't do nothing else, only thieve.'

'You can learn. There's loads of things you could do if you set your mind to it.'

'Like what?'

'You can drive.'

'Bit rusty.'

'But you've got a licence; you've passed your test. There's all sorts of opportunities – deliveries, the buses, milk, all sorts of things.'

'The money's no good.'

'Well we're not exactly minted now, are we! You may put food on the table but that's about all. If it weren't for my cleaning jobs, I don't know how we'd get by.' She could feel herself becoming tearful. 'Things have got to change. We can't go on like this … and we're not getting any younger.'

She fell silent again.

That's what really bothered Terry; the silence. Normally Beth talked so incessantly he could switch off and let it all flow over his head. But the silences meant that he found himself actually listening to what she was saying in between; and taking it in. It was usually one long moan. She was happy when she was moaning. But this was different. She meant what she said and it was important to her. Go straight? It was an idea. He'd tried it before a couple of times, usually when he'd just done time. It never lasted. He got bored and slipped back into his old ways. It peeved him to be asked outright like that. She'd married him knowing full well what he got up to and here she was trying to change him. Typical woman. On the other hand, she had a point about not getting any younger. He was the wrong side of forty, and getting long in the tooth for shinning over walls, hiding in bushes and getting pissed on by dogs. Perhaps he should give it a try. Driving sounded like an idea. Long distance lorries appealed. He could get out of the house for days at a time, weeks even. He was just about to say something conciliatory when Beth beat him to it.

'Actually, Terry, it's not just the court hearing itself that's bothering me, and I'm sorry I've given you that impression.'

'What else then?'

'It's what people will think, and how they are going to react. What if the children get teased about it at school? Bullied even.'

'It's probable no one will even know, especially if it don't get into the papers. If we keep quiet about it, there's no way it will get out. It's not as if you'll have a sign pinned to your back saying *Convicted Thief*.'

'And then there's …'

'There's what?'

'The Women's Institute.'

'Ah, is that what's really bothering you – what the W.I. will think?'

'I'm worried what they will say.'

'Do they bar people? Can you get chucked out for having a criminal record, no matter how good your jam is?'

'I don't know. Maybe. I could very well get thrown off of the committee.'

'Well same applies, there's a good chance no one will ever know. Are there any magistrates in the W.I.?'

'Not that I'm aware.'

'You're worrying over nothing, wife.' He paused to light another cigarette, blowing smoke out up towards the ceiling. 'Whatever happens we'll stand by each other. If anyone takes it out on you, they'll have me to deal with.'

Beth looked at her husband, awed by the first supportive thing he'd said to her since … she couldn't remember when. 'Do you mean it, Terry?'

'Of course I do. And here's another thing. I think I'll do what you say and have a try at going straight. See if you *can* teach an old dog new tricks. It's Monday tomorrow. In the morning, I'll do some knocking on doors. See if anyone needs a driver.'

'Are you serious?'

'Why not? As you said, things got to change round here.'

'Well I'll be … I don't know what's come over you, but I feel better already.'

'It's give and take, mind. Change ain't necessarily a one-way street.'

'Fair enough. What can I do?'

'I want you to do something we haven't done together for a long while.'

Beth looked at him askance. 'You're not talking about …'

'I am indeed. We're going dancing.'

329

'Oh, good heavens, for a minute I thought you mean, you know, the other.'

'That would be nice an 'all. Otherwise I'm leaving you for Diana Dors.'

'Ha! Fine chance. Diana Dors indeed. Anything else while we're at it?'

'There is actually. I want you to promise me something.'

'Go on.'

'If I go straight, I want you …'

'Come on, out with it.'

'I want you to as well!'

'Ooh you cheeky monkey!' Beth picked up a piece of kindling from the side of the hearth and threw it across the room. It bounced off his head. She chuckled, and he chuckled back – the first time they had laughed together since … they couldn't remember when.

Chapter 35

On the terrace overlooking Rowena's immaculate garden sat Mr Morell, Erika, Storm, Howard and Rowena herself. On the low table, they were seated around were cakes, sandwiches and a huge pot of tea. The atmosphere was tense.

Only Morell was eating. He picked at the last few crumbs on his plate, slotted some into his mouth and washed them down with a sip of tea. He looked around, conscious that all eyes were on him.

'Is this a tea party or an interrogation?' he asked, his tone calm but with a curtness about it.

'Good heavens, a gathering of friends, no more,' said Rowena, adding an artificial 'ha ha' as an afterthought.

'We are all friends here,' said Erika.

Storm leaned forward towards Mr Morell, his body language implying anything but friendship. 'I'm here for a purpose. I need to understand precisely what's going on,' he said. 'My brother has been murdered and I want to find out why and who is responsible.'

'I am sorry for you,' replied Morell.

'Thank you.'

'Do you wish to find out for yourself or for a good story in your newspaper?'

Storm's face reddened. 'Both, but for myself mostly, and you can help. We know there's a clear connection between Ben's death and your Mr Yardley.'

'My Mr Yardley? He is not mine. He is neither my property nor am I his keeper.'

'But you live in his house and are his friend and I'm told you have known him for many years. Mrs von Tirpitz …'

'Erika, please,' said Erika.

'Erika … saw Ben in the grounds of Yardley's house the night before his body was found. He was apprehended, brutally, and he was injured. That was the last anyone saw of him. Yardley lied to Erika, saying he wasn't hurt and had been sent on his way. But there is proof. Blood stains by the window where Erika saw him. He was clearly culpable in some way.'

'Why are you talking to me? I had nothing to do with this. I am not Yardley. You need to speak to him.'

'You know as well as I do he has left the country.'

Morell shrugged. 'I'm sorry but I cannot help you.'

'And his two thugs, have they gone too?'

'Where Yardley goes, they follow.'

'Yardley would not have beaten up Ben or pulled the trigger himself. It would have been them. Where have they gone, Mr Morell?'

'I do not know.'

'I think you do,' said Storm.

'I cannot help what you think.'

'Do you have any information at all that might be of help to me?'

'No, I do not.'

'Has he ever killed anyone before?'

Morell did not reply.

Erika smiled benevolently towards him. 'No one is accusing you of anything, Mr Morell, or even implying complicity. As Mr Grimshaw …'

'Storm,' said Storm.

'As Storm explained, he merely wants to get to the bottom of what happened.'

'I understand, however there is nothing I can do to help. You must talk to Yardley.'

'Is it possible that Mr Yardley knows he is under suspicion? Or that he might be made aware so that he does not return to this country?'

Mr Morell sipped his tea but said nothing.

Storm was becoming impatient. 'Listen, I have been snooping around for a while now, fact finding and putting two and two together. I've learned a lot from talking to people who perhaps know more than you imagine, and I'm ready to hand it all over to the police. You claim you had nothing to do with Ben's death, and yet there is circumstantial evidence connecting you through Yardley that might prove very difficult to explain away.'

Morell sat stone faced. 'For example?'

'Ben was in Yardley's garden the night he was killed – there is no doubt of that. You were living in the summer house at the time, so you were a matter of a few yards away. It could easily have been you who pushed his face through the French windows and directed Yardley's men to kill him. Or at the very least you could have alerted Yardley's men, which makes you an accessory. The police will look for opportunity and motive. You had both.'

'Motive? What possible motive could I have for killing a young boy?'

'Ben had cottoned onto your true identity. Yardley's also. You wanted to stop him from going any further. You wanted to silence him.'

'These true identities … say what you mean, young man.'

'You are Adolf Hitler and Yardley is Martin Bormann.'

'I am no such person.'

'But Mr Morell,' interjected Rowena. 'You have said many times …'

'And do you believe me when I say it?'

'Well now, that's a different matter.'

'Be frank, Frau Furse, do you believe I am Adolf Hitler?'

'Actually, no,' stated Rowena with conviction. 'I don't.'

'And you, Frau von Tirpitz, do you believe it?'

'I don't know.' She sounded confused. 'I'm not sure.'

'So, I am an eccentric old man who fantasizes about being Hitler – a game, no more. And if you choose to believe otherwise, Herr Grimshaw, there is not a shred of evidence to support it. And without proof, there ends your argument and my apparent motive.'

'But Yardley is Bormann – that we all believe,' said Storm. 'Don't we, ladies?'

Erika and Rowena nodded in mutual agreement.

'Again, you have no evidence,' responded Morell. 'I have never said so, and if you were to accuse Yardley he would deny it. So, what evidence are you left with? Your brother was caught trespassing on private property, caught red handed and escorted off the premises. Granted, he may have sustained an injury in the process, but there it ends. There is nothing whatsoever to connect those events with what happened to him later that night.'

Storm sat back in his seat, at a loss for words. Howard Furse, who had sat passively throughout, broke the silence.

'You know, Mr Grimshaw, having heard everything both you and Mr Morell have to say, I would suggest that the best course of events is to take your suspicions – by which I mean your evidence – to the police, lay it before them and let them investigate. Let the professionals take over and decide. That would be preferable to tackling Mr Morell in this way.'

'That's exactly what I intend doing, Mr Furse. I'm going to speak to them this afternoon.' Storm stood up. 'Thank you for tea, Mrs Furse. Goodbye.' He smiled at Erika and left hastily via the side gate.

'I must leave also,' said Morell. 'I cannot say I have enjoyed myself, but thank you nevertheless.' He made his way down the garden and disappeared though the gate in the hedge. When he was out of sight, Erika looked across at Rowena and Howard.

'I must go to the police, too,' she said. 'I have information they need to know, and not indirectly from a journalist who seems to relish in breaking all the rules. I'm fond of Mr Morell, but that bastard Yardley I have no sympathy for whatsoever. I'm convinced he is Bormann and that he's responsible for Ben's death. I have no choice.'

Rowena looked close to tears. Howard put his hand on her shoulder and said: 'We understand, Erika. I would do the same if I were in your shoes.'

****

Inspector Thorne glared at Storm from behind his desk. He listened intently, neither interrupting nor commenting until he had heard everything the young man seated opposite had to say. Then his attention turned to the objects in front of him. He picked up the brown envelope containing the glass fragments

335

and peered inside, then flicked through the pages of Ben's notebook.

'Fascinating, Storm. I ought to have you arrested.'

'What for?'

'Interfering with police business, removing evidence from the scene of a crime, possibly contaminating it. Perverting the course of justice even. I could throw the book at you. And your old boss at the Mirror as well for that matter, for not handing over Ben's notebook.'

'But you won't, will you? I'm working with you, not against you. I told you what I was going to do when we talked in the pub, and you gave me information. Confidential information. You encouraged me. Now I'm reciprocating and telling you everything I've learned.'

'And I'm most grateful, make no mistake. But you seem to have bitten off more than you can chew this time.'

'What do you mean?'

'Nazis living in Reigate? And not just any old run of the mill Nazi – Adolf bleeding Hitler and Martin sodding Bormann! I thought you were supposed to be trying to find out who killed your brother, not stirring up an international hornets' nest.'

'They are connected, Inspector, surely you can see that, from what I have just told you.'

'You know, this isn't the first time today – a Sunday I might hasten to add – that I've had to listen to this. I had Betty von Bismarck in here earlier telling me the same nonsense. No coincidence either, that you both happen to darken my doorstep within hours of each other. Some collusion going on here for certain. I am no fool, Teacup Grimshaw.'

'I know you're not. I'm simply passing on information I have gathered. It sounds preposterous, but whatever is going on with these Germans, there is a definite connection between them and Ben's murder. Peter Yardley, or whoever he is, and his two thugs are your prime suspects.'

'Perhaps.'

'Do you have anyone else in the frame?'

'Not at this precise moment. Do you have names for these two thugs?'

'Not so far. Does Erika … Mrs von Tirpitz I mean?'

'No, and only vague descriptions. Erika eh? On first name terms. You're not by any chance slipping her a torpedo?'

'That's none of your business.'

'You dirty dog. Wouldn't mind trying my luck – she oozes something, that woman. She sat where you're sitting right now an hour ago, crossing and uncrossing her legs. I almost caught a glimpse of paradise a couple of times.'

'How is Mrs Thorne these days?' asked Storm pointedly.

'Shut your mouth. Right, where were we?'

'Yardley's thugs.'

'Ah yes.' Inspector Thorne's tone hardened. 'Now listen carefully, Grimshaw. I've got something very important to say to you. Thank you for your assistance in providing evidence that is pertinent to the murder of your brother. It is appreciated, and we'll of course pursue our enquiries and take over from here. You can go back up to London now and carry on with your day job. By all means write a story about Ben's murder – though it's old news now I would imagine.'

'Not the story I intend writing.'

'Hold your horses, there is a but … a great big one. Under no circumstances will you mention anything about Adolf Hitler, Martin Bormann or any other references to Nazis, alive or otherwise, having anything to do with this. In fact, you will not mention anything about Nazis at all. You see, somewhere in high places feathers have been ruffled, and we, too, have been instructed to ignore any such lines of enquiry. It's come down

337

the line from Guildford. Steer clear. Investigate as a local murder enquiry but discard and ignore any nonsense about links with Nazis.'

Storm appeared stunned. 'When did you hear this?'

'Yesterday. As you can imagine, I hadn't a clue what the hell I was being told until Betty Bismarck and you came in here today. First I'd heard of it.'

'And what does that suggest to you?'

'That I do as I'm told. I shall be following up on your leads with a Mr Yardley and a Mr Morell, *not* senior ex-Nazi war criminals, nor indeed the flaming *Führer* himself. He's dead for God's sake, everyone knows that. Surprised at you, Teacup, being led off on a wild goose chase.'

'I need to talk to my boss. My Fleet Street boss.'

'He'll know all about it. He'll have had a D-notice slapped on him by now. Publish at your peril.'

Storm made sniffing noises. 'This whole thing stinks.'

'What I can tell you – and this is strictly between ourselves, just as it was between Detective Chief Inspector Hastilow and Chief Inspector Crimond, and then Chief Inspector Crimond and myself – is that a certain former prime minister who once encourage us to fight them on the beaches had something to do with it.'

'Well, well, well. Still influential with the security services. I wonder what he knows.'

'More than you or I have forgotten a hundred times over. That's it for the time being. Keep your mouth shut about Nazis and all shall be well. Now, where's PC Bent … thanks to you I can tell him where to find his sodding bike.'

Chapter 36

Monday 30th July

Rowena parked the Rover at the top of Reigate Hill. She and Mr Morell sat looking out across the valley with Reigate to the right, Redhill to the left and an uninterrupted view beyond across open countryside. It was a bright, crisp morning and the faint outline of the South Downs was visible in the distance. No words were spoken for a while.

Then Rowena said sheepishly: 'Mr Morell, I would like to apologise for yesterday.'

'Apologise for what?'

'I feel as though I let you down as your host in my house, and as a friend.'

'Think nothing of it. You have no cause to blame yourself. That journalist was doing his job, and seeking the truth about his brother. I bore the brunt because Yardley was not there to defend himself. Without his presence, my position has become noticeably vulnerable.'

'Do you think he will come back – Yardley I mean?'

'Perhaps, eventually. He likes it here. But not for a while. He has influential friends.'

'And what will you do?'

'I do not know. I must move on, but where and how I cannot say.'

'Shall we walk? Along the ridge there's an even lovelier view which I'd like to show you.'

They crossed a footbridge over the road into Reigate and along a path through woodland. On the left they came to what appeared to be some abandoned buildings within a large oval hill fort.

'What is this?' enquired Morell.

'I'm not sure, to be honest. I know it was built in Victorian times as a defence of some sort, but quite what for I have no idea. I believe it was used by Canadian troops during the war and probably had some connection with South East Command. Their headquarters were just below – in caves halfway up Reigate Hill.'

'21st Army Group. Erika pointed out the location to me.'

'Monty was based there.'

'That man again. Our paths crossed not long ago.'

'Ha ha, how will I ever forget! I'm talking about the real one of course, not his double.'

'May we look inside?'

'By all means. I don't think it's under lock and key.'

They pushed open the iron gates and wandered into the centre of the oval-shaped earthworks that sheltered some functional brick buildings.

'Not very effective as a defence,' said Morell, clearly unimpressed. 'Our Panzers would simply have gone around.'

'I'm sure you are right. However, it never came to that, thank goodness.'

'I had bigger fish to fry.'

'You ended up hooking a whale that wouldn't fit in your frying pan, I think.'

Morell frowned at the unwelcome analogy. On the edge of a central open space they came to some stone steps leading down to a tiny courtyard. He started making his way down.

'Do you think we should?' said Rowena.

'Why not, I am curious.' Holding on to a metal handrail, he made his way down. Rowena followed. At the bottom, to the right, was a solid-looking door with a round handle and latch. Morell turned it and the door creaked open. The interior was dark, but just inside the doorway his hand found a light switch that appeared to be a recent addition. He flicked the switch. Two naked bulbs gave out a feeble orange light, enough to make out a large concrete bunker; a single room about twenty feet square. It smelled of damp and the walls were trickling with water. A constant dripping sound could be heard. In the far corner was a doorway with steps beyond leading up to ground level; another means of access.

On the far wall was a noticeboard with some mildewed papers attached by rusty drawing pins. The only furniture was, somewhat incongruously, a pair of battered old sofas positioned roughly in the centre.

'Ooh yuck!' said Erika as she peered in over Mr Morell's shoulder.

They wandered inside and could hear their feet squelching through pools of stagnant water. Morell made his way over to the noticeboard and scrutinised the scraps of paper. One in particular caught his attention.

'Here is a poem about me,' he said. 'According to the author I only have one testicle – and the other can be found in London's Royal Albert Hall. It would seem that my mother removed it with a knife when I was in my infancy.'

Rowena came over and read the poem. 'Pay no attention to such vulgarity. It's all nonsense.'

'I think they are confusing me with Göring. He suffered a groin injury during the Munich Putsch in twenty-three. He was shot below the belt, though I believe it is a myth that he actually lost … anything.' He stumbled with embarrassment. 'Our troops had similar rhymes about Churchill and his alcoholism, though I cannot recall any of them.'

'Thank goodness.' Rowena shivered. 'This place is very unwholesome. Needs a jolly good clean.'

Morell looked around him, taking in every detail, turning full circle in the process. 'It is indeed unwholesome. But in a strange way I feel a sense of being at home here. It is not unlike the *Führerbunker*, though wetter. I spent months there, also in similar constructions during the war. I feel an affinity with places such as this.'

'Well I don't, so may we return to the surface now?'

Morell turned towards her. To Rowena's surprise he had a look of anxiety on his face that she had not seen before. Fear almost. 'What am I to do, Frau Furse? What am I to do?'

'Mr Morell, I …'

'I think I made a terrible mistake coming here. Yardley advised against it, and he was right. He very often is when it comes to such things. When I left Fuerteventura, I should have gone straight to South America.'

'If you had we would never have met, and I would not have had the pleasure of your friendship.'

'And that journalist boy would still be alive. I don't know what to do. This is madness. Please help me.'

Rowena took his arm but Morell pulled away sharply.

'Dear Mr Morell, would you like me to arrange for you to see a doctor? Perhaps you need some medical help.'

'You could be right. I was in good hands in Fuerteventura. I found a doctor who corrected many of the prescribing errors made by the man whose name I have taken – Theodor Morell. I see now that he was a quack and injected me with all manner of unnecessary concoctions, some of them bordering on poison. Physically I was a wreck, but my Spanish doctor improved my health greatly. He was also highly skilled in psychiatry and we had many long discussions together which for me were illuminating … often challenging. I learnt a great deal about myself and the decisions I have made during my lifetime. I see things more in perspective now. He talked of megalomania, and he was right. I allowed success – and in truth I was a supremely successful leader – to go to my head. That all seems like a lifetime ago, and I am no longer that person. But I have few regrets. I am still convinced that others were to blame for the downfall of the Reich. If they had listened to me and carried out my orders to the letter without fail, we would have been victorious beyond the shadow of a doubt.' He stood silent, the only sound the occasional dripping of water from the ceiling onto the floor. 'But now, here without Yardley, I feel weak and I feel vulnerable. I sense people surrounding me, waiting their turn to take their revenge. The young journalist's brother, Storm, Colonel bloody Maxwell, soon the police. Do you know someone who might help?'

'I don't know … I will need to find out. I can make some enquiries.'

'Discreetly please.'

'Of course. I might speak to Howard. He may know someone in London.'

'Money is no object. Please consider only the best.'

'I understand.'

They slammed the metal door shut and climbed up the stone steps, meandered around the ramparts of the fort and then back out onto the pathway, heading towards Colley Hill.

'In truth, I could not have gone straight to South America. It was not possible. I had Eva to consider, and there were problems with funds. I had to come somewhere until the circumstances were right. But the way is clear now. Funds are released in abundance, loose ends tidied up. I just need Yardley to tell me what he has arranged.'

'And he has fled.'

'I sincerely hope not. He has gone anyway, to oversee some business for me. But complications have arisen.'

'Are you in touch and can you warn him not to return?'

'That is possible, yes. But he is extremely well informed and may not need me to make him aware of his predicament.'

'If I were in his shoes, I wouldn't come back.'

Morell seemed disturbed by this comment and his head lowered, deep in thought.

Rowena pointed to their left at a gap in the tree line and a patch of barren earth. 'You see this scar in the landscape. A plane crashed here in the last few weeks of the war. Smashed straight into the hillside in bad weather. The entire crew was killed. Americans, on their way home from … well, you can imagine where. Howard and I weren't living in Reigate then but lots of people at church heard it fly overhead, and moments later the crash. Terrible. It was about teatime.'

Mr Morell glanced momentarily at the site and then away again, indifferent to Rowena's commentary. 'He will be back,' he muttered. 'He is resourceful and would never desert me.'

'Are you certain of that?'

'It is impossible to be certain of anything.' His tone was dark. 'Meanwhile I need to make some plans of my own. Seek some protection from men of power like myself.'

'Would you say you are a powerful man … still?'

Morell didn't answer. He appeared to have withdrawn into himself, talking to himself. Thinking aloud. 'Churchill. I need to speak with Churchill.'

'I seem to recall that you did just that the other evening, at the St. James's Theatre.'

'We talked about trivia. I need to speak to him on more serious matters. Come to terms. I seem to remember being told that he lives near here.'

'That's right. His home is called Chartwell and it's near Westerham.'

'How would I find it?'

'Just follow the A25. It's virtually a straight line eastwards from here. But surely, Mr Morell, I don't see the point. What good will talking to Winston do? He's in opposition now, not in government.'

'He is a man of influence. Someone like him always was and always will be, as long as he has breath in his body. May we please go home now? I need to give this some serious consideration.'

'But we haven't reached Colley Hill yet. You haven't seen the magnificent view.'

Mr Morell wasn't listening. He had turned around and was heading back towards the lane where the car was parked at the top of Reigate Hill. His pace had quickened; he was, all of a sudden, a man with a purpose and a mission. Rowena had difficulty keeping up with him.

****

'Storm, this is Erika calling.' She was sitting on her sofa with legs curled up in front of her, Mr Chips by her side. 'I thought you should know that Rowena – Mrs Furse – came to see me earlier. She's been talking to Morell and is very worried about him.'

'In what way?'

'He is behaving oddly. She thinks you have scared him, you and others. She tells me he is very anxious, thinks he made a mistake coming to England and that there are people after him. Yourself included.'

'Is he talking as Adolf Hitler or as a nondescript German refugee living in a fantasy world and an accessory to murder?'

'I cannot say. Possibly he cannot either. He must be confused, mixing fantasy with reality even.'

'If you have anything of interest relating to Ben's murder then I want to hear it. If it relates to the Adolf Hitler story then I cannot help.'

'Then what I am about to tell you will be of no interest.'

There was a brief silence before Storm answered. 'Tell me anyway?'

She told him about Rowena's trip to the fort on Reigate Hill with Mr Morell. 'He was asking where Winston Churchill lives, saying he needs to talk to him.'

'Have the police spoken to him yet?'

'When Rowena was with him they had not done so, but I wouldn't be at all surprised if they weren't knocking on his door as we speak.'

'You're probably right.'

'Storm, come and see me again soon?'

'As soon as I can. I might be able to come down on Wednesday after work.'

'There will be a warm welcome for you – and an even warmer bed.'

****

Inspector Thorne knocked on Yardley's front door and waited. Next to him stood Sergeant Baldwin. The bell had failed to generate any response and so he rapped on the door just as Storm Grimshaw had done two days earlier.

'No one at home, sir,' said Baldwin.

'I wouldn't bet on it.' Thorne filled his lungs and bellowed: 'This is the police! Open the door!'

There was no immediate response and he was about to call out again when he heard a rustling and then the sound of a bolt being slid to one side. The door opened a fraction.

'Mr Yardley?'

'No.'

'Is Mr Yardley at home?'

'He is away at the moment.'

'And you are?'

'My name is Morell.'

'In which case can we have a word with you, Mr Morell? I'm Inspector Thorne and this is Sergeant Baldwin.'

'What do you want?'

'We'd like to talk to you about the murder of Ben Grimshaw. May we come in?'

****

Tuesday 31st July

'Goodbye Howie.'

'Cheerio Flossie, old girl.'

Rowena Furse pecked her husband on the cheek and watched him saunter down the drive, struggling to light a pipe whilst juggling a briefcase, as she had a hundred times before. But today, instead of disappearing along Alders Road towards Reigate station, he stopped in his tracks and glanced down the side of the house. He turned and looked back towards his wife, a puzzled look on his face.

'Garage door's ajar, Floss. I shut it last night, I remember doing it. Have you been in there this morning for any reason?'

'No, I haven't been outside yet.'

Howard walked up the drive and Rowena followed. He examined the door.

'No damage.' He opened the door wide and peered inside. The garage was empty. 'The Rover's gone! I'm calling the police. Don't go in there or touch anything.'

Rowena stared into the garage, then looked at her husband, her face pale.

'While you do that, I will nip next door and see if Mr Morell is at home. I have a nasty suspicion he might not be.'

Chapter 37

Police Constable Bent was at the Old Town Hall police box when the call came in; to investigate the report of a car theft in Alders Road. Some excitement at last, he thought as he hopped on his bike. He arrived at the Furse house just a few minutes later. Howard was waiting for him in the driveway.

'A Rover 75 P4 Saloon,' repeated PC Bent as he stood in the centre of the garage and scribbled on a notepad. 'Colour?'

'Black.'

'I see. Registration number?'

Howard gave it. PC Bent dutifully wrote it down.

'I know how you feel, sir,' said the young policeman with an air of mutual loss. 'I recently had a vehicle stolen and it left a most unpleasant taste in my mouth I must say.'

'A car?' asked Howard Furse.

'No but just as serious. A police bicycle.' He pointed proudly towards said bike leaning against the garden gate.

'I hardly think the two compare,' remarked Howard with more than a hint of sarcasm.

'Be that as it may, you'll be pleased to know that my bicycle was retrieved and I have no doubt we will find your car in due course.'

'That's very reassuring to hear.'

'Now, have you any idea who might have took it?'

'Took it?'

'Sorry … taken.'

'A thief perhaps?'

'Hmm. And the door into the garage was shut?'

'I remember closing it last night.'

'And did you lock it?'

'I never lock it.'

'And no sign of a break in?'

'Why should there be? The door was unlocked.'

PC Bent nodded in understanding and made notes.

'There is another door,' added Howard helpfully. 'At the back there, leading into the garden. That was unlocked, too.'

'That must have been how the thief gained entry.'

'We're getting somewhere,' said Howard.

Any idea who might have pinched it?'

'None.'

'May I use your telephone, sir? I'd like to get a description of the stolen vehicle distributed as soon as I possibly can.'

'Yes of course.' They walked through the rear garage door and into the house via the patio. Rowena was on the phone and they stood patiently waiting for her to finish her call.

'Yes Erika, I know, all rather worrying. I don't quite know what's to be done. Lunch would be fine, and we can have a good talk about it. Howard is still here but I imagine he'll be off to town shortly now it's been reported. Talking of which, my dear, I'll have to ring off. There's a policeman standing next to me and I rather think he would like to use the telephone. Yes … yes that's fine. See you there at one.'

PC Bent took over the phone and Rowena and Howard made a tactical withdrawal into the hallway.

'Any sign of Morell?' whispered Howard.

'None. I tried the house and the summer house. I rang the bell and banged as hard as I could on the doors. In fact, the summer house was unlocked and I went inside.'

'It's looking rather suspicious.'

'Oh Lord,' said Rowena. 'What shall we do? Do you think we ought to tell the police?'

'Not just yet. You never know, we might be jumping to conclusions here.'

'I think he's gone to Chartwell.'

'What!' Howard sounded genuinely shocked. Rowena told him about her conversation with Morell the day before.

'Why didn't you tell me?' said Howard testily.

'I didn't imagine for one moment he was serious about it.'

'Does he know how to drive?'

'I don't know. He must do – or the car would still be here, surely. He knows a good deal about cars and loves being driven, but I can't honestly remember him saying he's able to drive himself.'

'Look, Flossie, I have to get to work. I'm terribly late. Can I leave you to sort all this out with PC Plod in there? There's nothing more I can do. I'll catch up with the latest when I get home this evening.'

'All right, off you pop.'

Howard gathered up his briefcase and raincoat and headed off down the road. At the station, instead of walking onto the platform, he squeezed into the telephone box next to the entrance and lifted the handset. He fed some coins into the holding slot and dialled a number. A voice answered and he pressed Button A.

'Hewson? This is Perriam, sir.'

There was a grunt by way of an acknowledgment at the other end of the line. 'Hewson, we have a problem.'

****

'Fucking hell!'

Heads turned, eyebrows rose and frowns stretched from one oak-beamed wall to the other in The Old Wheel Luncheon and Tea Rooms.

'Erika, mind your language, please,' said Rowena.

'Well fucking hell,' repeated Erika, reducing her volume to merely loud. 'What are we to do? Poor Mr Morell is off on some wild goose chase in a stolen car, making God knows what mischief, stalking Winston Churchill for all we know … and we can't do a thing to help him.' Then for good measure she added another 'Fucking hell'.

Rowena glanced across the tea room and noticed Jane Robinson standing within earshot, her face puce. 'I rather think you've just expanded young Jane's vocabulary over there,' she observed.

'About time I should imagine. She looks as though she could do with having her horizons broadened.'

Rowena's mind wandering back to Reigate Heath on carnival evening. 'I wouldn't be so sure,' she said. 'Bit of a dark horse, Jane Robinson.'

'Seriously, Row, what are we going to do? We can't go to the police with some cock and bull story about a nutcase who thinks he's Hitler stealing your car to go and visit Winston Churchill. Besides, I'm very worried about Mr Morell and the last thing I want is to get him into trouble. What do you say to jumping in my Alvis and driving over to Chartwell – see if we can find him and talk some sense into him?'

'That's if he's found the place. He could be anywhere by now. His knowledge of the area can't be very good.'

'He'd only need a map, or to ask a few directions. It's a straight road along the A25 from here.'

'I don't know, Erika, perhaps we should leave well alone.'

'We can't. We can't leave well alone. We haven't told the police about him and no one knows apart from us two.'

'And Howie.'

'And Howard, yes of course. We may have put Morell at risk in some way by not telling anyone. We have a duty to try and find him.'

'Perhaps you're right.'

'I know I am. Come on, drink your tea, we're off.'

The Alvis was parked directly outside the tearooms and minutes later they were heading out of Reigate. Soon they were through Redhill and on high ground speeding towards Godstone. The canopy was down and the throaty sound of the engine filled the air. Erika was driving fast; the only speed she knew.

'I say, this thing really can shift,' chirped Rowena, somewhat anxiously.

'Top speed of ninety-five. When we hit a straight patch I'll see if I can get there.'

'No need – I believe you.'

'Pass the gin, dear.'

'What!'

'In the glove compartment. There's a flask.'

'Oh Lord. Must I?'

'You must. I drive better when I'm half cut.'

They skirted the village green at Godstone, then on through Oxted and before long were pulling into Westerham where they stopped to ask directions to Chartwell. Erika nipped into the butcher's shop, flirted outrageously with the man behind the counter and five minutes later reappeared, triumphant. As she got back in the car, she handed a brown parcel to Rowena.

'Next turning on the right, up the hill, left and we're there. We're looking for Mapleton Road. Lovely man.'

'What's in the parcel?'

'Pork chops.'

'Why?'

'A gift. I massaged his ego.'

'If I'd tried that I'd have probably come out with a bit of scrag-end.'

'You underestimate the power of your own femininity, Row, darling.'

The last few miles were along narrow country lanes. They nearly missed the final left turn and Erika overshot it. She screeched to a halt, swore, reversed wildly and sped into Mapleton Road.

'What are we going to do when we get there?' asked Rowena. 'We haven't actually got a plan.'

'Leave it to me,' grinned Erika. They were approaching a high brick wall on their left, behind which they glimpsed the tall chimneys and tiles of a sizeable house. 'This has to be it.'

Erika slowed down marginally as they reached some gates and turned into the gravelled drive, almost knocking over a policeman who was barring their way. The facade of the house stretched ahead of them, reddish brickwork and neat rows of windows on two floors. The drive curved round to a large central porch and further round to another gate that exited back onto the road. The policeman approached them.

'I'm sorry, ladies, I'm afraid you can't come in here, this is a private residence.'

'I do apologise, officer,' said Erika, adopting her most alluring smile and tone. 'I'm afraid we're lost – I'm looking for Freddie Partridge's place. It's along here somewhere.'

'Well this isn't it I'm afraid. Now can you please follow the drive and out of the other gate, thank you.'

'I say isn't this Chartwell … Mr Churchill's home?'

'It is.'

'How exciting. Is he at home?'

'He is not. He's up in London.'

'Thank heavens.'

The policeman's eyebrows rose in curiosity. 'What makes you say that?'

'No reason,' grinned Erika. 'Does he usually have policemen looking after him?'

'Not as many as this, no, but there's a bit of a flap on.'

'What sort of a flap? There are more police over there, and a police car. Must be a big one. I hope no one is trying to harm Mr Churchill.'

'I can't tell you anything. Now would you drive on round and out as quickly as you can, please?'

Erika did as she was bid, driving as slowly as she could manage past the house. They both stared like sightseers, absorbing as much as possible. The front door was open and just inside they saw another policeman talking to what looked like a butler. Then they were at the other gate and heading back onto the road towards Westerham.

'Who's Freddie Partridge?' asked Rowena.

'My odd job man in Reigate. It was just a name that came into my head at random.'

'I need someone to do odd jobs for me. You must give me his details.'

'I'd recommend him. He can turn his hand to most things and has helped me out a number of times, especially when I've been let down by someone. Always gives satisfaction.' She winked at Rowena but the innuendo was entirely lost on her friend. 'I wonder what the flap is all about. Do you think it's Mr Morell? Do you think he managed to reach Chartwell and tried to get inside?'

'I don't know. It's possible I suppose. Perhaps we ought to go back and tell them the truth. Mr Morell might be being held

355

in the house for all we know. We might be able to help get him released.'

'I'm not sure about that. We don't know for certain he's there, or even that's what the flap is about. And if he is there we might make matters worse.'

They drove in silence for a while and before they knew it were back in Westerham. Erika pulled off the main road and parked the car by the side of the village green. She reached across for the flask, unscrewed the top and took a large swig. 'To be quite honest, Row, I simply don't know what to do now, or have any notion of what is best. Do you? Surely this isn't a coincidence. We're worried Mr M is intent on finding Chartwell to try and speak with Winston Churchill, and when we arrive, there are policemen everywhere and we're shooed away. Put two and two together and what do you have?'

'More than four, I'd say.'

'So would I. We can't drive away now and leave it. We have to do something. I think our only option is to go back to Chartwell and own up. If he's there, they will want to hear from us. If we're barking up the wrong tree, they'll simply send us on our way again. What do you say?'

Rowena was staring across the green towards main road. 'I don't think we need to.'

'What do you mean?'

'Look – over there!' She was pointing towards a familiar looking car.

'What?'

'Look at that car.'

Erika followed her line of sight and saw a black Rover driving past them, a policeman at the wheel.

'That's yours isn't it, Row?'

'It certainly is, and look what's behind it.' Following the Rover was a police car, an Austin A70. In the back, they could see the profile of a man.

'It's him,' cried Erika. 'It's Mr Morell!'

'It is indeed. Fucking hell.'

'Rowena!'

'Oops, sorry … it just slipped out. Please don't tell Howard.'

'He wouldn't believe me if I did.'

'Quick, Erika, go after them.'

Erika passed the flask over to Rowena and gunned the engine. She sped round the green onto the main road, cutting in front of another car with barely inches to spare. Rowena looked at the flask and took a huge gulp. She licked her lips and screwed the top back on.

'They're turning off ahead. I imagine they're heading for the police station.'

'That would make sense if he's been arrested. Oh dear, poor man, I hope he hasn't done something regrettable.'

They followed in convoy to the edge of the town where the Rover and Austin pulled into the forecourt of an austere looking, functional building with a blue lamp above the doorway that left no doubt as to its function. Erika parked next to them. They got out just as Mr Morell was being led into the building.

'Excuse me,' called Erika. 'May I have a word?'

Mr Morell turned at the sound of a familiar voice. His face reflected a cocktail of emotions; he looked confused, distant, defiant and resentful all at once.

'Frau von Tirpitz. What are you doing here? Please tell these people to leave me alone. They won't let me see Churchill. They tell me he is not at home but I don't believe them. He is there, I know it.'

357

The more senior policeman, an inspector, said: 'You know this gentleman?'

'We do indeed,' replied Erika. 'We are friends of his.'

'And that's my car you have there,' added Rowena.

'Might I ask his name?'

'Theodor Morell.'

'That's not the name he has given us.'

'He may be using a different name. Initials A.H. perhaps?'

The inspector nodded almost imperceptibly. 'Would you mind stepping inside with us, ladies? There's something strange going on here and you may be able to help us resolve the matter.'

****

The Alvis sped along the A25 heading away from Westerham back towards Reigate. Rowena followed behind in her reclaimed Rover. Next to Erika sat Mr Morell; silent, brooding, his face like thunder.

'Cheer up, Mr M. You're a free man thanks to Rowena and yours truly. Without us you'd probably have spent the night in a police cell.'

Morell said nothing; he stared at the road ahead as if in a world of his own.

'How are you feeling? I'm concerned about you. Are you all right?'

'I am feeling down,' he replied. 'They should have allowed me to see Churchill.'

'He wasn't there – he's up in London.'

'That is not true. I am certain he was there. If they had told him I had come, he would have seen me. They had no right to treat me like that.'

'The inspector made it quite clear that Winston is in London,' said Erika. 'Besides, don't you think it was a little foolish, turning up unannounced like that? I'm not quite sure what you were trying to achieve.'

'I wanted to meet him again, leader to leader, to discuss ways of dealing with this situation.'

'What situation?'

'My situation. I need to get away from here. I have been in this country too long and it is time to continue my journey. I have overstayed my welcome. People are plotting against me … again. I cannot trust anyone, not even Bormann it would appear.'

'Don't you mean Yardley?'

'Yardley, Bormann, what does it matter!' said Morell with venom. 'It makes no difference what you call him. He appears to have abandoned his *Führer*. And this business with the young boy, the murder. And your Colonel bloody Maxwell. It is getting out of hand. Churchill can make arrangements for me. I know he can. He did it for Bormann.'

'I doubt that very much.'

'I know it. He helped Bormann to escape from Berlin in forty-five. He sanctioned the military operation. I made my own arrangements, but Bormann was given help. I even know the code name the British used. Operation J.B.'

'That's curious. What does J.B. stand for?'

'I do not know.'

'You know, Mr M, I don't think it was the best approach to arrive at Chartwell unannounced, in a stolen car, claiming to be Adolf Hitler and demanding to see Churchill. How did you imagine they would react? You're supposed to be dead and buried long ago. No wonder they thought you were a lunatic.'

'Is that what they thought of me?'

359

'Well, yes. The inspector told me as much. He said they believe you are not in your right mind.'

'He is a fool – they are all fools!'

'But they regarded you as harmless. That's why they let you come away with me. I gave assurance that we would take care of you, and that there would be no repetition.'

'Take care of me? I don't need taking care of. I just need help to get out of this country and on my way to South America, as I should have done six years ago had it not been for Eva and her foolish anxieties. She would not get in to the U-boat!'

'Mr M, stop it. You are talking nonsense.'

'I am not. She claimed she suffered from claustrophobia and would not get on board. That's why we were stuck in Fuerteventura for six years. Six years! Then she deserts me for Delgado. After everything we had been through together she goes off with a slimy Spanish piece of shit.'

Erika glanced at him. 'You're scaring me now, Mr M.'

'I am sorry, Eva.'

'My name is Erika.'

Morell seemed oblivious to his mistake. 'But Bormann has dealt with them now. Both of them. I will not tolerate disloyalty or betrayal. There is only one outcome for those who try to stab me in the back. Bormann will take his turn to discover this.'

'Please stop.'

Morell slumped back into his seat and was silent. Erika had been genuinely frightened by his outburst but moved by the passion that had welled up from within.

'Be that as it may, I am taking it on myself to look after you. I have become very fond of you, Mr M, and hate to see you so disturbed. If Yardley has let you down and can no longer be trusted, then let me take over. And the first thing you're going to do is move in with me. I have plenty of room and you'll be safe at mine. No one will know where you are, apart from me and Rowena.'

Morell stared vacantly through the windscreen and eventually said: 'Thank you.'

'That's settled then. We'll stop at Yardley's, collect your things, then I'll take you to Smoke Lane.'

'Please, only you and Rowena must know. No one else.'

'I promise.'

'I knew about the boy, Erika. I knew he had been killed. But only afterwards. I was not involved. I did not sanction what happened to him. It was Bormann's doing.'

Erika stared at him for as long as she could take her eyes off the road, then smiled and nodded. 'I believe you.'

****

From his vantage point in the road that ran parallel with Smoke Lane, Colonel Maxwell could see clearly the entrance to Erika's private parking space at the rear of her house. He was seated in the back of his car, slumped sideways so that he was barely visible from outside, and had been there most of the afternoon, ever since he'd lost Erika when she sped off from The Old Wheel at lunchtime. He'd failed miserably to keep up, and his only option had been to turn back and wait. He was stiff and had pins and needles in both legs, which he rubbed vigorously every now and again.

Shortly after the distant sound of the bells of St Mary's Church struck six, he heard a car approaching and peered out of the window. The distinctive shape of Erika's Alvis loomed large and then turned, without slowing down it seemed, into the parking area.

361

She was not alone, Maxwell realised with a heavy heart. Next to her sat that old hunched up bastard with a stick, Martin Bormann.

Maxwell watched in disbelief as Erika opened the boot and between them they carried a suitcase and a number of bags into the house. Then the car was locked and they disappeared inside together, talking, smiling, her arm in his.

He's moving in! Nothing between them? Just good friends? That lying cheating Kraut was moving in!

Maxwell could feel his heart pumping wildly; it felt as if it would burst through his ribcage at any second. The veins in his temples were throbbing and when he stepped out of the car and stood upright, the head rush was so strong he almost fainted. He leaned against the side of the car until it passed. There followed a powerful urge to vomit, but he managed to resist, climbed into the driver's seat and headed for the solitude of his home on Reigate Hill.

'I should have killed him when I had the chance,' he hissed through gritted teeth. 'I should have pulled the trigger. You lying cheating old Nazi German bastard. This time I'll nail you once and for all.'

Chapter 38

Wednesday 1st August

By late morning, with several hours of concentrated work on the herbaceous borders behind her, Rowena was ready for some opera. She brushed soil from her front, removed her gardening gloves and went indoors to fetch the Fidelity. As she carried it out, she passed the door at the rear of the garage and opened it slightly, to check that the Rover was still there. It was.

Howard had been relieved to see it back where it belonged when he returned home, later than usual, the evening before. Rowena related to him the day's events; lunch with Erika, the trip to Chartwell, Mr Morell's arrest, their intervention, his release into Erika's care and Morell's move to Smoke Lane.

Howard seemed to take it all in his stride. 'Probably the best place for him,' he commented from behind his newspaper. 'They can keep each other out of mischief in future. And away from our Rover preferably.'

'He doesn't want anyone to know where he is. You won't tell anyone, will you?'

'Not a living soul,' he reassured her.

'He's very shaken,' Rowena said. 'Erika is worried about him. She thinks he's going crazy.'

'I rather think the horse has already bolted in that respect, Flossie old girl.'

'I'm worried about him too.'

'It's Erika you ought to be concerned about, using that sort of language in The Old Wheel.'

Rowena looked coy. She had missed out any reference to her own language when she'd spied Mr Morell in the back of a police car.

She knew her Howard and could tell he wasn't quite as unperturbed as he liked to appear. As she waved him goodbye that morning, he too had checked in the garage to make sure the Rover was still there.

Rowena set the Fidelity down on the terrace table and plugged it in. From a handful of Long Play records, she chose Kirsten Flagstad singing Richard Strauss's *Four Last Songs*, which Flagstad herself had premiered the previous year, shortly after Strauss's death. Rowena resumed her gardening.

The first day of August, and everything was in high bloom. The summer was moving on and although it had been warm so far, hot on some days, the lawns were not yet showing hints of yellow to indicate they were past their best. In truth, there wasn't much to be done, little maintenance was necessary, and Rowena could as easily have sat and enjoyed her garden as knelt beside the borders tinkering for hours.

Shortly after midday, and two playings of *Four Last Songs* later, Rowena heard Ethel calling out. She'd finished her chores, there was a light salad and some cake in the kitchen for Mrs Eff's lunch and she'd be off if there wasn't anything else. Rowena called out that was fine and decided to rest for a while.

She sat on the terrace and ate her lunch. Over a pot of tea, she sat back and listened again to the songs, her eyes half closed. Such beautiful writing, and so sublimely performed. What a pity Strauss hadn't lived to hear them. Hadn't Mr Morell mentioned that he'd met Strauss? She felt certain he had. Rowena would have liked to meet him too, to thank him for these gorgeous songs alone, not to mention all the wonderful operas.

What an extraordinary man, she mused; Morell, not Strauss. After all that had happened over the summer months, she was still confused as to his true identity. Sometimes she was convinced he was Adolf Hitler and had escaped death in Berlin to live another day, and at other times she was certain he was nothing of the sort; a deluded old man, eccentric at best, insane more likely. Would they ever know the truth? Did she really care one way or the other? If she had to choose, she of course wanted him to be Mr Morell, the eccentric, mild-mannered old man who was her friend; a fellow lover of opera, enjoyable company. Not a tyrant in hiding; not a war criminal responsible for a world war and a bottomless pit of pain and suffering.

She wondered what Neville Skepper, the vicar of St Mark's, would make of it all. Perhaps she'd consult him about it. In his sermons he frequently emphasised Christ's teachings on forgiveness and reconciliation, which in those post-war times was often a bitter pill to swallow. What would he make of an hour or so chatting over tea with Adolf Hitler?

She cared about Mr Morell, as she knew Erika did, and was concerned for his wellbeing. She was pleased he'd gone to Smoke Lane. It was a strange existence he had led next door, living in the summer house, with Peter Yardley coming and going. She'd miss him appearing at the fence and popping over for tea. But he wasn't far away and she could go and see him at Erika's whenever she chose.

The sun was warm on her face and soon she felt her eyelids starting to droop. She could hear the bees at the end of the garden buzzing faintly. Mr Morell had said his father kept bees; she wondered if Hitler's father had too. Then she wondered how Mr Morell had come to meet Richard Strauss; under what circumstances. It made more sense if he was Hitler; a great composer coming head to head with his country's leader. Nor had Strauss exactly distanced himself from the Nazi regime, and he'd been criticised for it – so had Kirsten Flagstad for that matter. Rowena remembered reading somewhere that someone had once said: *To Strauss the composer I take off my hat; to Strauss the man I put it back on again.* She chuckled to herself. She could say something similar of Mr Morell, depending on his true identity.

She dozed off.

When she awoke, the music had stopped. She stood up slowly, stretched her arms and ambled down the garden, admiring the fruits of her labours. When she reached the gate in the fence, to her surprise, she heard a voice on the other side. A man's voice. It was faint, too faint to hear what was being said, but the timbre of the voice was not unfamiliar. Then another man was speaking, muffled and indistinct. Curious. Mr Morell had moved away and Peter Yardley was out of the country with his thugs. To her knowledge, the place was deserted.

Silently, Rowena opened the gate and, with some difficulty, squeezed her way along the back of the summer house, listening intently. The first voice was talking again, speaking English with a marked German accent.

'What do you mean, you cannot tell me where he has gone? I am responsible for him. You must.'

She recognised the voice now. It was Yardley. Back from abroad, obviously, and asking someone about Mr Morell's whereabouts. There came a reply, too vague and unclear to make sense of. Yet the rhythms of speech, the inflections, were known to her. Then Yardley spoke again.

'It was a risk bringing him here, but he insisted … and it was only meant to be for a short time.' Another muffled response from the other voice. 'Yes, yes, but what is done is done and now I must get him away from here. All arrangements

366

are in place. Please tell me where he is, I will have him away from here immediately and there will be an end to it. Where is he? I must insist.'

The conversation was clearly taking place in front of the summer house. By the time the other voice spoke again, Rowena had crept as far as she could around the side without showing herself, and this time she heard precisely what was being said.

'And as for you, will you go too? I think it would be wise under the circumstances.'

'I tend to agree.'

'We have contingency plans, as you know. They can be put into place very quickly.'

Rowena's jaw dropped. There was no mistaking the voice now. She was so shocked that any sense of wishing to remain hidden vanished and she rounded the corner of the summer house. The two men were standing close to each other, both smoking, their body language oozing tension.

'Howard!'

'Flossie!'

'What on earth are you doing here?'

It was the turn of Howard's jaw to drop. He stared at his wife, his mouth opening and closing like a fish under water. But no words emerged other than, 'Flossie, I ...' Peter Yardley was quicker to respond.

'Good afternoon, Mrs Furse. I have just returned home and your husband was kindly bringing me up to date with events, the thoughtful neighbour that he is.'

Rowena ignored him and addressed Howard again. 'What *is* going on, and why are you here next door talking to Mr Yardley? Why aren't you at work?'

'Flossie, I can explain ... but not just at this precise moment.'

'What do you mean? I think you need to explain to me right now. Why are you talking to Peter Yardley in his garden? You hardly know each other.'

'Frau Furse,' said Yardley, 'do you know where Morell has gone?'

'He's staying with Erika, where he is safe.'

'Thank you! See, Perriam, not so difficult.'

'Perriam?' exclaimed Rowena. 'Who's Perriam?'

'And where exactly does Frau von Tirpitz live, please?' asked Yardley.

'Don't tell him, Floss,' said Howard firmly. 'It would not benefit Mr Morell for anyone to know where he is just at the moment, including Yardley here.'

'Nonsense,' said Yardley. 'I am merely trying to help him, isn't that obvious? And to help you, too. You have just told me quite clearly that his being here has been nothing but a foolish embarrassment.'

'Nevertheless …' began Howard.

'Very well, I shall look her up in the telephone directory.'

Howard's tone hardened. 'I really would not do that if I were you.'

Rowena moved forward until she was standing immediately between the two men. 'Stop! I am very confused about what is happening here. If neither of you will explain to me what's going on this minute, I shall phone the police. They want to talk to you, Mr Yardley, about a very unpleasant incident that you appear to have been involved in. The murder of a young boy.'

'Flossie, no …' said her husband.

'Well talk to me then!'

Yardley's body tensed and his face drained of all colour. 'I don't know what you mean.' He started to back away, towards the house. 'I will leave you now. Keep the police away from

368

me, Perriam. You know how unwise it would be to confuse matters at this time. Pull the necessary strings.' He turned and made his way up the garden towards the house, a squat, almost toad-like figure in a hurry. Rowena could see the outline of someone hovering inside the kitchen door as Yardley reached it and slammed it shut.

Howard looked at his wife; her face was dark with suspicion and distrust. He took her arm but she pulled away from him.

'Why did he call you Perriam?'

'It's a sort of nickname. You know, like Flossie.'

'A nickname? Strangers don't give each other nicknames.'

'They do sometimes. Let's go back home and I'll try and explain as best I can. But it will be difficult.'

'I think you had better try.'

'First I must make a very important phone call.' They squeezed round the summer house and back through the gate into their own garden. 'You get some tea ready and I'll make that call.'

Before he could disappear into the house, Rowena tugged at his arm and said: 'Why aren't you at work?'

Howard paused for a moment, as if weighing up how to respond to his wife. Then he shrugged his shoulders and replied simply: 'I am.'

Chapter 39

'Much obliged, Jack,' said Inspector Thorne. 'Do the same for you one day.' He slammed the handset down onto the base unit with unnecessary force and yelled out of his office door. 'Baldwin! In here – now!'

Baldwin appeared with almost guilty haste. 'Sir?'

'I've just had a very interesting call from my friend Inspector Dougal at Westerham nick. Apparently, they had a nutter trying to break his way into Chartwell, Winston Churchill's place, yesterday, wanting to speak to him.'

'Blimey, did he succeed?'

'No, but it wouldn't have made any difference if he had. Winston wasn't there.'

'So why of interest?'

'Because, Baldwin, the nutter was none other than …'

'I'm all ears.'

'Our very own local resident Kraut fruitcake, Mr Theodor Morell. Also known as …'

'Adolf Hitler!'

'The very same.'

'Well, well. What was he doing over there, I wonder?'

'According to Jack, he wanted to talk to Churchill to try and sort something out with him – leader to leader.'

'Hardly,' said Baldwin. 'Churchill hasn't led this country for years, and Hitler's dead.'

'Concisely put. Forget the Hitler rubbish, we've been told to back off. But we still have a domestic murder to solve, and in Yardley's absence, Mr Theodor sodding Morell remains our number one suspect for interview.'

'If we can find him again. I don't suppose Westerham have him in custody?'

'They let him go.'

'Not good.'

'Do not despair. They released him into the care of, wait for it … a Mrs Erika von Tirpitz of Smoke Lane, Reigate.'

'That's better. Shall we pay him another visit?'

'We shall indeed,' replied Thorne. 'And there's no time like the present.'

****

The bell rang long and loud and was immediately followed by a solid knock. Mr Chips ran to the door barking loudly. When Erika had opened it wide enough to realise who was there, she immediately tried to slam it shut again. But Peter Yardley had his booted foot wedged against the jamb and the combined force of him and the thug standing next to him, despite the bandage around his hand, forced the door open with ease. Yardley strutted into the hallway.

'Where is Morell?'

'Get out of my house this instant or I will call the police.'

'Everyone wants to call the police today. Where is he?'

'Fuck off!'

Yardley grabbed her savagely by the collar of her blouse which tore in his fist. Mr Chips growled and tried to bite his leg but Yardley kicked him away viciously.

371

'If you choose to behave like a whore, I will treat you like one and finish what I started once before.' He pushed her against the wall until his body was crushing hers and their faces were almost touching. 'Do you understand?'

Mr Morell appeared from the living room. 'Enough, Yardley. Do as Erika wishes and leave.'

Yardley let go his grip and stepped away. 'I need to speak with you. We have much to discuss.'

'What are you doing back here? You deserted me … and betrayed me. I no longer trust you. Kindly leave.'

'*Mein Führer*, please, that is not fair. I do not know what you mean.'

'You lied to me then deserted me, leaving me at the mercy of the police and the authorities. That is unforgivable.'

'Lied to you? I did no such thing.'

'You told me that Erika here saw and heard nothing the evening the boy was killed.'

'That is correct.'

Morell looked towards Erika. 'Frau von Tirpitz?'

Erika stood rigidly, arms folded. 'I saw the boy while we were having dinner – and you know very well I did. He was at the French windows. He was pushed through the glass and there was blood on his cut face.'

'That proves nothing,' sneered Yardley.

'You fool,' retorted Morell. 'It links the boy with your house, being assaulted there on the night he was murdered.'

After the slightest pause, Yardley said: 'That was not the same boy.'

'Erika has told the police otherwise.'

Erika nodded. 'It was the dead boy without a doubt. I saw his photograph in the newspaper, and I'm willing to stand up in court and swear that it was him.'

'There, Yardley. Now the police want to talk to you about it. And I am implicated.'

'Why did you not warn me?' said Yardley. 'If I'd known I would have stayed away – stayed in Spain.'

'I did not imagine you would return. I thought you had deserted me to save your own skin.'

'I would never do that. I have always been loyal, when all others deserted you. I went to complete a job for you, in Fuerteventura, as agreed.'

'And did you?'

'Partially, though we were not entirely successful. Eva is dead. Unfortunately, we were not able to deal with Delgado. But we will. I shall go back and track him down for you. That is a promise. I can report in detail if you wish.'

Morell sat down on a chair, his hands on his cheeks, staring at the floor. 'No, I do not wish. What now? What now?'

Yardley held out his doughy hands in a pleading motion. '*Mein Führer*, come away with me. You are not safe here. There was a break-in at the Villa Winter. Delgado for certain. Papers were stolen that could be used to track us down, here in Reigate. Come away now. The plans are all made. The funds are organised and in place. I have been to Switzerland, also to Malmö in Sweden, and arranged the transfer of all assets to South America. There is enough to keep us rich and comfortable for the rest of our lives. Transport is ready. I can have you out of England by morning en route for Spain. Then a ship to Argentina, just as you would have gone by U-boat in forty-five. President Perón was ready to welcome you then and he is ready still. You will be in Buenos Aires in under a month, and soon afterwards lost to the world in deepest Patagonia. The mansion on Lake Nahuel Huapi is ready for you. You will be reunited with some familiar faces – Gestapo Müller for one. You remember him, of course?'

373

Morell gave no hint of recognition. 'And you, will you be joining me?'

'Not immediately. I must return to Fuerteventura. Unfinished business with Delgado.'

'If he hasn't followed you here already.'

From the open doorway came an anxious call from one of the thugs. 'Police! Coming down the road.'

'Quick,' said Yardley. 'Come with me now!'

'No,' replied Morell.

''Come, please, there isn't a moment to lose.'

'You go. I will be in touch. How can I contact you, at Wray Park Road?'

'Never again – unsafe. Here.' Yardley handed Morell a card with a phone number written on it. 'Phone me. Soon.'

The thug said: 'Quick, round the back and through the garden. We'll have to abandon the car.'

Yardley was out of the door and gone.

****

Erika was upstairs changing her blouse when the front door bell rang again, so it was Mr Morell who opened the door. When she came back down, he was sitting in the living room talking to two men; one she knew by name and the other by sight from the police station.

'Inspector Thorne,' she said. 'What an unexpected pleasure. Drink?'

'No thank you, Mrs von B … Tirpitz.'

'Well I think I will. G and T, Mr Morell?'

'No, thank you. These gentlemen are interrogating me again about the death of the boy journalist. They think I am responsible for his death and that I murdered him.'

'Not quite, sir,' remarked Thorne. 'As I explained when we spoke with you at Mr Yardley's house, I think you can help us with our enquiries and shed some light on what happened that night. Following on from our initial meeting, we need to go into more detail.'

Morell stirred uncomfortably. 'Is that the only reason you are here – to talk to me about the murder?'

'Why, what else could there be?'

No one spoke. Both policemen stared at Mr Morell who watched Erika finish making her drink and sit down next to him. Mr Chips jumped onto her lap.

Eventually Morell said: 'I do not think I can be of any help to you. Besides, I have told everything I know to the boy's brother. Erika, what is his name?'

'Storm Grimshaw.'

'I know,' said Thorne. 'We've spoken to him. To Mrs von Tirpitz also.'

'Please call me Erika.'

'Erika. But you will have to tell *me* now. Let's see, shall we? Erika here kindly made a positive identification for us that the murdered lad, Ben Grimshaw, was in Yardley's garden on the evening he was killed, and was in fact injured when his head was forced up against a glass window. She saw it happen and has given a very clear and precise description. Yardley was with her at the time, having dinner, so we're to assume Ben was accosted by the two men employed by Yardley.'

'Have you asked them?'

'They've disappeared. So has Mr Yardley, as you well know, living in his empty house.'

Morell shrugged noncommittally. 'Have they?'

'Of course there was someone else in the garden at the time Ben was injured.'

'And who might that be?'

375

'You.'

'Ah yes, I would have been in my summer house, reading or writing probably.'

'Were you alone?'

'Yes.'

'So we only have your word for it.'

Morell shrugged again.

'You could have easily been involved,' said Inspector Thorne. 'My guess is Ben was caught trying to spy on Peter Yardley – caught red-handed – beaten up, taken away to the Hearthstone quarry, and shot. You and Yardley may not have pulled the trigger, but I believe you knew about it, and in all probability ordered the killing.'

'You have not a shred of evidence.'

'Not yet. Tell me, Mr Morell, why would an ambitious young journalist spy on your Peter Yardley? What interested him enough to want to sneak around in his garden at night?'

'You'd have to ask him.'

'I'm asking you. What is it about Yardley that made Ben so curious? Is there more to him than meets the eye? You're his friend – if anyone would know, you would.'

'I cannot help you.'

'Come to that, is there more to *you* than meets the eye? I've heard some remarkable stories about you of late.'

'*Zum Beispiel?*'

'Do what?'

'For example – what stories have you heard?'

Sergeant Baldwin leaned forward: 'Sir, I don't think …'

Thorne ignored him. 'Am I talking to Mr Theodor Morell or to Adolf Hitler?'

'My name is Morell.'

'And would I be trying to find one Peter Yardley or one Martin Bormann?'

Baldwin tried again. 'Sir, you're off limits.'

'Quiet! You see, what I don't understand is why an ordinary little German refugee called Morell would be wanting to speak to Mr Winston Churchill – *leader to leader.*'

'You are well informed.'

'Inspector Thorne,' said Erika. 'This was all sorted out yesterday with the police at Westerham. Mr Morell is not well. He is confused and made a misguided attempt to speak to Mr Churchill. He suffers from delusions. He has been released into my care and I intend to look after him. I will be seeking some medical attention as soon as it can be arranged. No harm has been done.'

'Would you say no harm has been done to Ben Grimshaw, and his family?'

'That is a different matter entirely.'

'Well now,' said Thorne smugly, 'that is where I have to disagree. I think the two are most definitely connected. You see, Mr Morell here is not being cooperative in trying to help us solve a nasty murder – not cooperative at all. I would say he is being very defensive in fact. Why is that? Why would an innocent refugee behave like that? On the other hand, a war criminal in hiding would think nothing of it. Just another life snuffed out. Barely worth a thought. The same would apply to Peter Yardley. Why would a well-off man living a quiet life in a Surrey town want a young man murdered? On the other hand, if he too is a war criminal with a track record of being responsible for killing on a massive scale – and for some reason I can't begin to imagine happens to be living in bloody Reigate of all places – then I think we are getting much closer to the truth.'

Erika said: 'Of Yardley I think you could be right. I too believe he is Martin Bormann and, together with his thugs, is responsible for Ben's death. But with Mr Morell, you have the wrong end of the stick.'

'Have you any idea where we might find Yardley?'

'He was here not fifteen minutes ago,' said Morell.

'What!'

'He left – just as you arrived. The back way.'

'Why didn't you tell us?'

'You did not ask.'

'Where's he gone? Will we find him at his home in Wray Park Road?'

Erika shook her head. 'He won't go back there. We have no idea where he will be.'

'Shall I raise an alert, sir?' said Sergeant Baldwin.

'Not yet, let's get back to Chart Lane first. Mr Morell, do you have any way of contacting him?'

Erika glanced at Mr Morell who sat motionless. 'None.'

Inspector Thorne stood up. 'We'll find him, with or without your help. I don't know the ins and outs of all this, but my gut instinct is not to share Erika's opinion about you. I'd be inclined to think that if you have two apples left at the bottom of a barrel, they'll both be rotten. My job is to try and solve a murder, but should my prime suspects turn out to be culpable of far greater crimes, then my efforts will no longer be required. In other words, Mr Morell, if Yardley is Bormann and I am in fact staring into the eyes of Adolf Hitler, then it's only a matter of time for you both. You're dead men. There will be no parley *leader to leader* with anyone – just a couple of hangings, and a very long line of people queuing up to pull the lever. I can't arrest you at the moment because I don't have enough evidence – yet. But I'll be back for you, that's a promise. Please do not leave Reigate in the foreseeable future.'

Thorne strode across the room with Baldwin in tow and the front door slammed.

'Mr Morell,' said Erika. 'You really ought to have handed over the number that Yardley gave you to Inspector Thorne.'

Morell stood up and walked across to the telephone, picked up the handset and dialled the number. He waited a few moments, listening, then put it down again.

'The number does not exist.'

He sat back down, put his hands over his face and started to rock backwards and forwards.

****

Barely minutes after the police had left, the doorbell rang for a third time.

Her head spinning and not caring who the hell it was this time, Erika strode up to the front door and opened it wide. There in front of her, in high dudgeon, stood Colonel Peregrine bloody Maxwell.

'All right, where is he? I know he's living with you now. Where is Martin Bormann, the bastard who stole my woman from me?'

'OH, FUCK OFF!' screamed Erika and slammed the door so hard that the frame shook.

Chapter 40

Sir Thomas Beecham looked up at the stage from his podium, observed Rowena with a critical eye, and raised both hands to shoulder height. He paused for a second, glanced momentarily towards the lower strings in the orchestra pit to his right, then back to Rowena, and brought his baton down in a slow, precisely measured beat.

Exactly on cue, she began to sing: *Mild und lies wie er lächelt, wie das Auge hold er öffnet, seht ihr, Freunde?*

The auditorium was open air, and enormous, with seats panning out in an ever-widening arc that stretched farther than the eye could see. Every seat was taken. It reminded her of the celestial courtroom in *A Matter of Life and Death*; in fact, it was identical apart from the fact that 'God' wasn't sitting on a throne or a bench but standing in an orchestra pit.

Rowena felt elated and overwhelmingly confident as the melodic line of the *Liebestod* flowed out of her, beautifully alliterated and ... pitch perfect! Sir Thomas looked up at her, his face melting with the effect of her truly sublime voice.

A phone started to ring, faintly at first then rising in a rapid crescendo until it was so loud and shrill that it swamped the music. The orchestra ground to a halt and Rowena's voice croaked into silence. Beecham's face reddened and he smacked his baton down onto the music stand.

'Who the bloody hell is telephoning at this time of night!' he yelled. Only it wasn't the brusque, assertive voice of the maestro. It was Howard's voice.

A spotlight suddenly shone into Rowena's eyes and she blinked wildly for a few moments before turning away from the bedside lamp.

'Hello? Goodness, this is a surprise, I can hardly hear you. That's quite all right. Hang on. Flossie, it's for you. Erika … and she's talking very quietly for some reason.'

Rowena sat herself up in bed and took the handset, her dream of operatic stardom already a fading memory. 'What's up, Erika?'

The voice at the end of the line was barely audible.

'Row, listen, help me please. I'm in my bedroom. Morell has gone totally bonkers now. Absolutely crazy. He just woke me up and is insisting that I take him out. He is waiting downstairs while I get dressed.'

'Out?' Rowena glanced at the bedside clock. 'It's nearly midnight. Out where?'

'You'll never believe it.'

'Not Chartwell again?'

'Worse.'

'Tell me, for goodness sake.'

'The bunker.'

'The bunker?'

'The one at the top of Reigate Hill. You took him there.'

'Oh, the old fort. Why would he want to go back up there I wonder?'

'He keeps saying he must return to the *Führerbunker* … that it's all over and time to journey to Valhalla and join those who died in combat to save the Fatherland. He's scaring me, Row. I really think he is going to kill himself. He has a gun.'

'Good Lord! What can we do to help?'

'Shh, he's coming back. I must go. Meet us at the bunker.'

The line went dead. Rowena stared at the handset.

'Howie, she's in trouble. Mr Morell has flipped. He has a gun and is taking Erika up to the bunker.'

'What bunker?'

'The fort at the top of Reigate Hill. I took him there earlier in the week and we went inside. He said it reminded him of his bunker in Berlin. I think that may have triggered something in him. What shall we do?'

'Does she think he will harm her?'

'No, yes, possibly – I don't know! She's terrified and wants us to go there.'

'Right, put some clothes on. But I'm phoning the police first. If there's a gun involved they need to know.'

Ten minutes later Howard was easing the Rover out of the garage so Rowena could climb in. He turned right and headed up Alma Road to cut through onto the main road halfway up Reigate Hill.

'Hurry, please,' begged Rowena. 'Hurry!'

****

Thursday 2nd August

'Come on, pick up the bloody phone,' mumbled Sergeant Baldwin impatiently. It had been ringing for an age. He guessed that when an answer eventually came it would be a mixed blessing; and he was right.

He heard a click and then a very drowsy voice: 'Thorne.'

'Baldwin here, sir. Sorry to disturb you.'

'Do you know what the sodding time is?'

'Twelve oh five. Sorry, sir, but it's important.'

'It had flaming well better be.'

Baldwin heard a woman's voice in the background: 'Not now, Len, please.' Then Thorne: 'Don't be ridiculous, Shirley … it's the phone.'

Baldwin suppressed a snigger. 'This is important, sir, most definitely.'

'Well, tell me then. Get on with it.'

'Our friend Adolf. We've had a report that he's kidnapped Mrs von Bismarck at gunpoint and has taken her with him up to Reigate Fort.'

'What!' Thorne's voice instantly shifted from drowsy to fully alert. 'Tell me more.'

'That's it, sir. She managed to alert her friend, Rowena Furse, whose husband telephoned us. We need to get after them. I thought you might want to be involved.'

'Too bloody right I do. Anyone else heading their way?'

'PC Bent. I've just briefed him at the Old Town Hall. He's on his way up the hill as we speak.'

'On his bike?'

'That's right.'

'Reigate's finest – Hitler won't stand a chance.'

'I'll be over in a car to pick you up in ten minutes.'

'I'll be ready in five.'

****

There was no traffic at all on the road when PC Bent set off through Reigate tunnel and along the Broadway towards the hill. Then, shortly after cycling over the level crossing at the station, a sports car passed him at speed and shot up the hill. Even though it was dark, the roof was down and he caught a glimpse of a woman in the driving seat. More clearly, he saw the passenger next to her; an elderly man, almost bald and wearing steel-rimmed glasses. The view was fleeting, but Bent recognised him instantly. The man who'd cycled away from him in the middle of Redhill on a stolen bike. His bike!

He puffed and grunted after them. It was a steep climb and by the time he reached The Yew Tree pub, half way up the hill, his legs were beginning to feel the strain, so he dismounted and started to walk. Behind him he heard a car pull out of a side road. When it passed him, he thought he recognised Mr and Mrs Furse, the couple from Alders Road whose Rover had been stolen earlier in the week. He'd heard that it had been found and returned to them. What on earth were they doing driving up Reigate Hill at this time of night, he wondered.

Not long after the Rover had disappeared round the bend ahead, Bent heard the sound of another car approaching from behind, changing down into a low gear as the gradient of the hill became steeper. When it drew level with him, he saw the Police sign on the roof. The car came to a halt, the passenger window wound down and Inspector Thorpe stuck his head out.

'While you're off that thing you might as well try milking it, my lad.'

'If you say so, sir.'

'Seen anyone pass you?'

'Two cars in the last few minutes, sir. Firstly, a sporty job with a female driving and a male passenger.'

'That'll be Hitler and Mrs Battleship.'

'Did you say Hitler, sir … as in Adolf Hitler?'

'That's right. His name is Morell but there's a strong possibility he is in fact Hitler.'

'But Hitler's dead.'

'That's what we all thought. Anyway, he's our man, and the woman he's with has been abducted.'

'I recognised him. He stole my bike.'

'Well now, did he indeed …'

'And you say he's actually Hitler?'

'There's a distinct possibility. What about the second car, did you see who was driving it?'

'It looked to me like the couple from Alders Road whose car was pinched – Mr and Mrs Furse.'

'All right, Bent. Now hurry up to the top because that woman with your bike thief is in danger. Make your way to the fort. That's where they're heading. So are we. See you there.'

'Right you are, sir.'

The police car sped off. PC Bent had barely walked a further hundred yards when another car passed him, driven by a young man in his twenties with a shock of ginger hair. The car disappeared round a bend. As he reached the top of the hill where a footpath led off towards the footbridge, yet another sped past. This time he made out the figure of a dark-haired man, slightly older. He didn't recognise either of them.

By now Bent was sweating profusely, so he stopped briefly on the bridge to smoke a cigarette. As he stood looking down towards Reigate, a fifth and final car chugged its way up the hill, under the bridge and out of sight where the road levelled out on top of the North Downs. Another male; older this time, with dishevelled white hair and sitting bolt upright in the driver's seat. Bent scratched his head in wonder, then continued across the bridge. On the far side, he cycled precariously along the footpath which was rough, shaded by trees and very dark. He had lights on the bike but at such a snail's pace the dynamo could barely produce a beam at all, let alone one of benefit.

Shortly he reached a metalled lane and passed a couple of houses on his left. He knew the fort was situated just beyond them. As he cycled along the lane approaching the entrance, he saw a line of cars parked at random. There was no one in sight.

He propped his bike against the fence and shone his torch ahead of him towards the fort entrance. There was a gate. It was open.

****

The orange glow from the naked bulbs cast an eerie light upon the two occupants of the sofa. Mr Morell sat at one end, the gun resting on the arm next to him, Erika sat at the other. The space mirrored the tension between them. The constant dripping of water was the only sound until Erika spoke for the first time since Morell had led the way into the bunker.

'Dear Mr Morell, please talk to me. Tell me what is going on. Why are we here and what *is* going through your head? You're frightening me and I'm confused. If I understood better, I may be able to help.'

'There is nothing to be done, Eva, this is the end. I have been betrayed yet again and there is no way out.'

'Do you intend killing us both – is that what you have in mind? Is that what the gun is for?'

Morell put his hand into his jacket pocket and pulled out two small cylindrical metal objects which at first, in the poor light, looked to Erika like bullets. He unscrewed the top of one and tipped out an oval-shaped capsule. 'I'm afraid there is no choice. However, you can use this if you prefer. Bite down on it and the liquid inside will provide a very quick death ... instantaneous I am told. I will do likewise and shoot myself at the same moment.'

'But I don't want to die,' said Erika. 'I'm not ready. You called me Eva again just now ... I think you are confusing me with your wife.'

'It makes no difference. We are here together, destiny has decreed it so and we will die here in the bunker as it should have been six years ago. You are my Eva now. Do not fear, this was ordained. It was meant to be.'

'It was not,' said Erika, keeping her voice as calm as she could manage. 'You are my friend, Mr Morell, not Hitler. I

386

believe you're imagining all this and for some reason you have associated yourself with the *Führer* to the extent that you are convinced you're the man himself. I think you were meant to stay alive and continue being our friend – going to the opera with Rowena, having lunch and dinner with me. Stay with us. You do not have to go anywhere.'

'It cannot be,' said Morell with an air of finality. 'I am being hunted by too many people. The boy's death changed everything. That fool Bormann thought he could behave as he did at home in the Fatherland, and now he has left me to face the music. Whether I am Morell or Hitler makes no difference. I am a marked man.'

Her voice shaking, Erika said: 'Let me smoke first, please.' She pulled out a cigarette case from her handbag and lit up, inhaling deeply and allowing a long slow jet of smoke to spread across the room, black against the orange light. 'All right, so once and for all, if you are Adolf Hitler, will you please tell me your story? If I am to die with you in this place, at least I have a right to know how our paths eventually crossed and what led us here.'

'Where would you like me to start?'

'In the *Führerbunker* in Berlin. All I ask is that you tell the absolute truth. Nothing less.'

'So,' said Mr Morell. 'The truth you shall have.'

'The war is lost; the Russians are knocking on your door. You marry Eva Braun … you did marry her I assume?'

'Oh yes, we were married. She had been my true and loyal companion for many years but I had refused to marry her. It would have interfered with my career – my destiny. I said many times that I was married to Germany. By then that argument no longer carried any weight, so we married, in the map room. It was her reward. The ceremony was witnessed by Goebbels and Bormann.'

'Then the next day you supposedly both committed suicide. But that was sleight of hand, so you said. You told Mr Churchill as much.'

Morell nodded. 'That is exactly how it was done. Bormann arranged everything, with the help of Gestapo Müller. Bormann could be cruel and extremely ruthless, but at his best he was a remarkably efficient organiser. I could absolutely rely on my orders being carried out by him immediately and despite all obstacles. Everyone else came to me with problems. Bormann brought me solutions. His proposals were so precisely worked out that I had only to say yes or no. With him I dealt in ten minutes with a pile of documents for which with any other man, including my generals, I needed hours.'

'How did he manage to fake your death, and that of Eva?'

Morell nodded his head gently, implying a sense of self-satisfaction. '*Doppelgänger*,' he announced with obvious pride. 'We used doubles.'

****

When the police car came to a halt in the lane, Inspector Thorne got out first and led the way towards the entrance of the fort, torch in hand.

'What do you think he'll do?' asked Sergeant Baldwin. 'Will he really harm Betty Bismarck?'

'It's possible. If we were dealing with an insignificant German refugee I'd say not, but if we've got Adolf Hitler to contend with, who knows what he's capable of! Having said that, he may be responsible for the deaths of millions, but did he ever actually kill anyone in person?'

'I don't know, sir.'

'Nor do I. Probably not is my guess. He may not be able.'

They approached the first of the brick buildings. Baldwin clutched Thorne's arm and stopped dead.

'Did you hear that, sir?'

'Yes. Sounded like a car on the lane out there.'

Thorne switched off his torch. They edged around the corner of the building and stood in silence, looking back towards the gates. Watching. A pinprick of light appeared and slowly danced its way down the path towards them. The sound of shoes on gravel sounded very loud, exaggerated by the otherwise total silence. When the light was level with them, Thorne stretched out his hands and seized the arm. There was a scuffle in which the other arm was bent behind the man's back. Thorne flicked his torch on again and shone it into the stranger's face.

'Grimshaw! What the sodding hell are you doing here?'

'Same as you, I imagine,' replied Storm. I'm concerned about Erika's safety.'

'How did you know to come here?'

'I went over to Smoke Lane tonight to visit Erika – she was expecting me.'

'At close to midnight? To play cribbage I suppose.'

'Something like that. Anyway, just as I was approaching the house, out came Morell, with Erika in tow. There was something not right. Not a word was spoken but I could tell. Tension in the air. They got in Erika's car and drove off. So I followed them. Thought I'd lost them on the hill, then saw your car ahead of me and followed you instead. I had a hunch the police might be involved in some way. Is she here?'

'I think so. Are you on your own?'

'Funny but I don't think I am. Got a feeling I wasn't the only one outside her house, and I'm fairly certain another car followed me through Reigate and up the hill. I think it pulled up further down the lane. Unless it's one of your lot.'

'I doubt it. PC Bent is on his way but he's on his bike. Whoever it is will have to wait. Come on, we're looking for a bunker – so presumably we need to find steps down.'

They spread out and searched around the buildings.

'Over here, sir,' called out Baldwin after a while. 'Look.'

Thorne and Storm Grimshaw hurried over as best they could in the dark. Thorne shone his torch downwards, illuminating a longish row of stone steps that ended in a small courtyard next to a door that was slightly ajar. Outside the door, with their ears pressed against it, were a man and a woman. Caught in the torch beam, they stared upwards, blinking and squinting in the sudden light. Thorne led the way down, treading gently.

'Who are you and what are you doing here?' he said when he reached the courtyard.

'Shh,' said the man. 'Keep your voice down.'

'Mr and Mrs Furse – is that you?' said Storm.

'Mr Grimshaw,' replied Rowena *sotto voce*, recognising the voice. 'Who are these men with you?'

'Police. What's happening?'

'Police – thank goodness! Erika's inside, with Mr Morell. We're very worried about her. We think he might harm her. He's got a gun.'

'Let us through, please,' said Inspector Thorne.

'No wait,' whispered Howard Furse. 'Not yet. He's explaining how Bormann faked his and Eva Braun's death using doubles. I want to hear this.'

'So do I,' whispered Storm. 'Budge over.'

'Me too,' said Sergeant Baldwin, pressing forward.

Thorne elbowed Baldwin in the ribs. 'Join the queue.' He listened for a moment. 'They're speaking German – I can't understand a sodding word.'

'Rowena will translate,' said Howard. 'Now shush.'

Sergeant Baldwin waited patiently for a while, then, peeved to be at the back, pushed forward again, this time pressing against Storm, who shunted into Inspector Thorne, who lost his balance and stepped on Rowena's foot.

'Ow!' she cried and toppled against the door, which moved a few inches, creaking loudly.

****

'What was that?' said Mr Morell. He stood up, grabbed the gun and pointed it towards the doorway. 'Who is there? Show yourself. Show yourself now!'

'Mr Morell, is that you?' came a sheepish voice. 'It's Rowena … and Howard is with me.' She appeared in the doorway, behind her the burly figure of her husband.

'What are you doing here?' said Morell sharply. 'How did you know where to find us?' He turned to Erika. '*You* warned them – you must have done.'

I did,' she replied. 'And I'm glad I did.'

Rowena said: 'Mr Morell, please don't hurt Erika … or yourself for that matter. We're here now, so perhaps we can talk about it?'

'Come in,' ordered Morell. He indicated the sofa opposite the one Erika was occupying. 'Sit. Do you have a weapon?'

'Of course not.'

'Keep your hands where I can see them. Do not speak.'

They did as they were told. Morell also sat down, holding the gun out in front of him, panning gradually, wavering his aim between the Furses and Erika.

'You're just in time, Row,' said Erika. 'Mr Morell is telling the truth at last and explaining how he cheated death in the *Führerbunker* using doubles. Mr M, I know Howard's German isn't very good. Could you manage in English?'

391

'I will try.'

'Thank you.'

'I had several over the years,' said Morell. 'I am talking about doubles. The one we used at the end was a man called Weber … the likeness was remarkable and he stood in for me often during the last year of the war. He had an illness that made him shake, especially his left arm. Parkinson's disease. I found it amusing to read this has been attributed to me. Eva's double was even better – identical in fact. She was an actress, one of Goebbels' many mistresses. With makeup and the same hair styling you could not tell them apart. I never knew her name. It was they who were killed in the bunker and their bodies carried outside, doused with petrol and burned.'

'And you?' asked Erika.

'We left the bunker and made our way up to my private quarters in the Old Reich Chancellery building.'

'Who precisely?'

'Myself, Eva, Bormann, and some soldiers from my personal bodyguards, *SS Liebestandarte Adolf Hitler*. And my beloved Blondi of course.'

'You took your dog?'

'She was a loyal and devoted companion. I could not leave her behind.'

'Go on.'

'From there a secret tunnel led to the *U-bahn* system near *Kaiserhof* station. We walked along the tracks for miles, to *Fehrbelliner Platz* where some Tiger tanks and other armoured vehicles took us to *Hohenzollerndamm*. They had turned the avenue into a makeshift airstrip. A Junkers 52 was waiting for us. We flew out. There were Russian shells raining down on us. I did not think we were going to make it.'

'All of you?'

'Not Bormann. He stayed behind in the Old Reich Chancellery to tie up loose ends. Then he made his own way out, with help from British military intelligence, and the personal approval of Winston Churchill, so I discovered later. I told you this on the way back from Chartwell.'

'How? How did Bormann get out?'

Morell shrugged slightly. 'You will need to ask him. You wouldn't believe me if I told you. It involved canoes of all things. Ask him about Operation J.B. if you ever have the opportunity. British military intelligence organised it.'

'Canoes?' exclaimed Erika. 'This is bonkers!'

'Bonkers it may sound, but you asked for the truth and that is what you are getting.'

'What did J.B. stand for?' asked Rowena gingerly, conscious that she had been ordered not to speak. But Mr Morell seemed to have forgotten.

'Frau von Tirpitz asked me that. I do not know. It was the name of the operation to get Bormann out of Berlin. If it has any significance, it is unknown to me.'

'Where did you fly to?'

'Our ultimate destination was to be Argentina. As it turned out, we never got further than Fuerteventura. We took a convoluted route to reach there for security reasons, by way of Denmark and Spain, courtesy of my old friend General Franco. The entire journey was pitted with danger. More than once we were nearly shot down, and the plane was hit on numerous occasions. Blondi was scared stiff – Eva also. Eventually we reached Reus in the Catalan region, not far from Barcelona, and from there flew on to Fuerteventura.'

'Why Fuerte …?' Erika stumbled over the name. 'I can't say it. Why there in particular?'

'We had a secret base. The Villa Winter. The *Abwehr* had it built a few years before at Bormann's suggestion. It was

393

manned by the SS and a key link in the escape route. Hundreds got out this way.'

'But you didn't. You stayed. Why?'

Morell stirred on the sofa and became more animated as he recalled the reason. The gun was shaking in his hand. 'Because Eva would not get in the U-boat!'

'Why not?'

'We were only supposed to stay overnight at the Villa Winter. There was a U-boat waiting offshore to take us to South America. But when it came to climbing inside, she panicked. Claustrophobia. I tried everything to persuade her. Even Blondi went in without any difficulty. But Eva could not … and would not. So, we returned to the island.'

'Where you remained?' said Rowena cautiously.

'It was pleasant enough. The climate is good there, the villa was luxurious, and we were safe under Franco's governance. I received some excellent medical care which I was in need of, and we lived a comfortable life. I even learned to speak English.'

Rowena again. 'Then one day you upped and left and came over to England. So, what changed? What made you decide to come here all of a sudden?'

'Eva again.' His voice sounded tired now, as if drained of energy.

'I remember you telling me you're estranged. Didn't your relationship stand the test of time?'

Mr Morell breathed in deeply, then exhaled as if to calm himself. 'She was unfaithful to me.'

****

Colonel Maxwell was on familiar territory wandering around the fort. He'd been up there often during the war for one reason or another; liaising with the Canadians mainly. He crept stealthily around the various buildings, but there was nothing and no one to be seen. They must be inside one of the rooms below ground level. Nowhere else they could be.

He made his way to the steps leading down to the large space which he remembered had been used as a recreation area. He was about to descend when he heard faint voices below. He stopped in his tracks and peered into the gloom. Gradually he made out the shapes of three men, tucked behind a half open door … listening intently.

'Bloody rush hour up here,' he murmured. 'Better use the other entrance.' He made his way round the mound that covered the ceiling of the underground room below and found another set of stairs, less obvious than the first.

Moments later, a tall, dark-haired figure, who had been close behind Maxwell and mirroring his route, also decided against the main steps and followed this man who clearly knew his way and no doubt had the same intent, or similar.

As he approached the second set of stairs, he heard a loud thud from some way off, in a distant corner of the fort, the sound of a body hitting the ground. It was followed by a pained voice: 'Oof!'

PC Bent was having trouble finding the bunker.

****

Mr Morell spoke quietly, as if the memory was hurting him. His tone had developed a sinister edge. The gun stopped wavering and focused deliberately on Erika. He spoke to her as if addressing Eva.

'I found out about you six months ago. I knew for some time something was wrong. You had changed. You became critical of me, commenting on my appearance, my eating habits, my moods. You never used to do those things. You shunned my music – told me Wagner was boring. How could anyone say such a thing! Then one day I was walking in the dunes with Blondi and I stopped beside the hut used for changing into swimming costumes. I heard noises inside so peered through the window. There you were … fornicating. He had you over a table and was behind you, like two dogs. It disgusted me. We never did such things. Then I heard you say his name and that you loved him and that, that …'

'Mr Morell,' said Erika. She was now very scared. 'Don't continue if you don't want to. I'm not Eva. Put the gun down.'

Morell seemed oblivious to her words. 'You said it was so good to have a real man at last, after being unsatisfied for so many years.' He lulled into silence for a while, then continued. 'I was never very interested in sex.'

'You and me alike,' muttered Rowena. Howard stirred uncomfortably on the sofa next to her.

'Morell – the real one – used to give me injections. They helped, but not much.'

'She is younger than you I believe.'

'Was!' shouted Morell. He half stood up and stretched his arm out so that the gun was almost in Erika's face. She instinctively backed up against the side of the sofa. He stared at her. 'You are not Eva. Eva is dead. I'm a widow.' He swayed a little, as if about to faint, and looked confused as the illogicality of the situation seemed to sink home.

'Widower,' corrected Rowena without thinking. 'I'm sorry to hear that.'

'She paid the price for betraying me. Bormann arranged it. Her lover was also meant to die, but he escaped. Bormann said he would go back and finish the job. I doubt it. I can trust no one. That is why the end has come.'

'Don't say that, please,' said Rowena. 'What did you do when you found out about Eva and this man?'

'Nothing at first. I pretended all was well.' Morell grew silent again.

'And then?' prompted Rowena.

'Then.' He sighed deeply. 'Then Blondi died. Quite suddenly. I felt very lonely at the Villa Winter and decided I had had enough. I tracked down Bormann here in England and came to visit. I asked him to arrange my passage to Argentina – and to deal with Eva. That was in May. Here I am … still.'

Rowena said: 'Did you have anything to do with Ben Grimshaw's death?'

'I have already told Eva. I knew about it only after the event. I had no knowledge beforehand.'

'To be absolutely clear, Yardley and Bormann … they are one and the same?'

Morell said nothing, but nodded his head.

Howard Furse took advantage of this lull to contribute. 'Are you saying you're responsible for murdering Eva Braun?'

'I ordered her to be killed.' Mr Morell moved closer to Erika and held out his other hand towards her. 'Here, take this. Just bite down on the capsule and it will be over in seconds. I will do the same. Join me in Valhalla.'

'I don't think so,' said Erika.

'Do it for me. For your *Führer.*'

'I will not.'

'You must!' he yelled. '*DO IT!*' He pressed the gun against her forehead and with his other hand tried to force her head back and push the capsule into her mouth.

'No!' she cried.

At the far side of the bunker a figure appeared in the second entrance; a spectre-like orange silhouette. He stood for a few seconds, as if familiarising himself with the scene before him,

397

then moved into the room, slowly yet purposefully, until he was standing in front of Morell. He pointed a gun at his head, his arm ramrod straight.

'Harm a hair on her head and I'll blow you to kingdom come,' said Colonel Maxwell.

Morell did not move an inch.

'So, I got it wrong. I thought you were Bormann, when in fact I had the biggest Nazi thug of them all in my sights! How the hell did you escape death in forty-five?'

'Doubles,' said Rowena. 'You must have missed that bit.'

'*Dummkopf*,' hissed Morell.

'Don't call me that!' yelled Maxwell. He pushed the gun against Morell's head and squeezed the trigger. The gun produced a puny clicking sound, but no bullet. 'Bloody thing!' He started to fiddle with the mechanism. 'Hang on …'

Another figure, taller and younger, emerged from the second entrance and ran across the room. He too had a gun. He barged Maxwell out of the way, knocking him to the floor, and took his place pointing a gun at Morell.

'Who are you?' said Morell.

The man flicked on a torch and shone it into his own face so that his features were clearly illuminated. His eyes gleamed beneath dark hair, and in the artificial light his olive skin looked sallow.

'You know me.'

Morell nodded submissively. His gun hand wilted.

'This is for Eva.'

The crack of the shot was deafening in the confined space of the concrete bunker, the brilliant light from the barrel blinding for a split second. Morell's head jerked sideways and backwards in a shocking, violent movement. He fell back onto the sofa. Caught in the torch beam, his eyes stared lifelessly towards the ceiling. A small fountain of blood spurted from his temple.

Suddenly the bunker was a cauldron of noise and movement. Erika and Rowena screamed. Howard leapt to his feet with uncharacteristic agility that astonished even his wife. He lunged at the assassin, pushing him forwards and down until he was pinned to the floor. The gun that had killed Mr Morell spun out of reach. From the main entrance ran more men. One, in police uniform, rushed forward to help Howard; another moved to the centre of the room, surveying everyone and everything; a third remained just inside the doorway.

'We heard most of that,' said Inspector Thorne. 'Mrs von Tirpitz, are you all right?'

Erika had a hand over her mouth and was gazing at Mr Morell's body next to her on the sofa. There was blood spattered on her clothes and in her hair. She couldn't speak, so she nodded her head.

Thorne moved closer to the man pinned to the ground beneath Howard and Sergeant Baldwin.

'Who the bloody hell are you?'

The man's head was pushed flat against the wet floor and there was water in his mouth. He gurgled something. Howard lifted his head up slightly.

The voice had a rich Spanish accent. 'Mateo Delgado.'

Damp and dishevelled, Colonel Maxwell clambered up off the floor. He looked down at the body on the sofa. 'Pipped at the post,' he sneered from between gritted teeth. 'Was just about to finish the bastard off myself. Damned unfair.'

The third figure at the main entrance moved forward.

'I have no gun,' said Storm Grimshaw. 'But if I had I'd have gladly shot him too.'

399

Erika stood up and put her arms around him. 'Oh Storm,' she said. 'He denied having anything to do with Ben's death. Bormann's men did it.'

'I heard, but he was responsible. Without him there would have been no need for any of this.'

Erika started to cry. Storm embraced her in return and stroked her hair, oblivious to the flecks of blood.

Maxwell observed them. His eyes glazed over and he lifted his gun towards them in a feeble gesture, held it there briefly then let it drop. He turned, walked away towards the far entrance and disappeared.

From the main entrance, heavy footsteps could be heard clumping down the steps. PC Bent appeared, torch in hand, and looked around eagerly. He picked out Inspector Thorne, then Sergeant Baldwin, and finally focused on Mr Morell lying on the sofa.

'That's him, sir!' he announced. 'I'd recognise him anywhere.' He strode across to the sofa. 'Adolf Hitler, I'm arresting you on suspicion of stealing a police bicycle. You do not have to say anything unless you wish to do so, but ...'

'Bent!' interrupted Thorne. 'Idiot. You're wasting your sodding breath, lad. There really isn't much point in arresting a stiff.'

Chapter 41

Two hours later the bunker was empty of people and the body had been removed. Under normal police procedure, it would have taken much longer, with the scene secured and gone over with a fine toothcomb. But this was not a normal situation. Inspector Thorne had been instructed by radio to clear the bunker as quickly as possible and take the body away while a decision was made as to how it would be processed. It ended up overnight in a cell in Reigate police station.

When all the noise had ceased, and another half an hour had passed, to be on the safe side, a door at the side of the bunker scraped open and out peered Terry Angel.

'Blimey,' he muttered, slamming the door shut and locking it. 'Half Surrey Constabulary up here tonight.' He made his way up the stairs to where his bicycle was hidden. Beth would wonder where the hell he'd got to.

After tonight, going straight would be a walk in the park.

****

A while later, from a door to another side room at the far side of the bunker that even Terry Angel didn't know about, out stepped a young woman and a young man, oblivious to what had gone on in the bunker all evening.

'That was amazing, bishy,' said the girl, sighing contentedly. 'The best yet. No wonder we dozed off afterwards … you wore me out! Mind you, that mattress you brought up here doesn't help. It's so cosy. Here, have you seen the time – it's the middle of the night! Mum'll be sending out a search party.' She squeezed his hand. 'I do like it up here. Bit damp but fewer creepy-crawlies than on Reigate Heath. They get everywhere!' She giggled. 'Quieter too – apart from that loud bang earlier. I wonder what it was. Much quieter – don't you agree?'

The Bishop of Reigate nodded in silent ecumenical acquiescence.

Chapter 42

Sunday 5th August

Rowena brought out the tea tray and placed it carefully on the table. Erika and Howard were sitting in silence on the terrace. Mr Chips lay on the paving stones, luxuriating on his back. It was a warm day but overcast. The mood was sombre.

'Shall I be mother?'

'Please, Flossie,' said Howard.

'Ethel's made a lemon drizzle cake. I had a slice earlier – it's to die for.'

She poured out tea for them all, then offered around slices of cake, but there were no takers, so she sat down.

Four days had passed since the events in the fort on top of Reigate Hill. They had all taken their turn to make statements at the police station in Chart Lane, but other than that nothing much had happened. Rowena had buried herself away in the garden, Erika had spent most of her time sitting on her sofa, smoking and drinking gin, and they hadn't seen each other until Howard suggested inviting Erika over for tea. There was an overall atmosphere of shock at Mr Morell's violent death that cast a veil across the story he'd told just before he was killed; and the revelations about his escape from Berlin and subsequent life were generally forgotten.

Howard flitted between home and London. He had been very protective towards the two women, and done most of the talking with the police. Some senior police officers from Guildford had overseen the interviews. Howard underplayed the whole business of Hitler and Bormann and explained events away in terms of an eccentric old German refugee who had come to stay with his friend, made some bizarre claims, clearly had some kind of nervous breakdown, then been shot by his wife's lover. There didn't seem to be any real evidence linking him with Ben Grimshaw's murder.

This all sounded odd to Rowena and Erika, but they didn't question it; they were too stunned by their friend's death. The police officers seemed to accept Howard's interpretation, nor did Inspector Thorne or Sergeant Baldwin contradict him. One of the Guildford officers, Chief Inspector Crimond, had said dismissively: 'Hitler and Bormann here in Surrey? Utter balderdash!'

The sun was making attempts to break through the clouds and when it did for a few moments the temperature rose markedly, much to Mr Chips' delight. Rowena made a couple of attempts at polite conversation, but mostly they sat quietly. Presently they heard a man's voice calling from somewhere up the garden.

'Hello … Mr and Mrs Furse, are you there?'

'Ah,' said Howard. 'Here he is.' He stood up and wandered down to the gate in the fence. Rowena and Erika looked at each other, puzzled. They could see him engaged in conversation, but it wasn't until he opened the gate and the other man entered the garden that they could see who he was talking to. They walked down towards the terrace, chatting together.

'It's Mr Yardley,' called Howard. 'Back from his travels. Would you mind fetching another cup, Flossie? You'd like some tea I assume, Peter?'

'Thank you, yes.'

Rowena did as she was asked and when everyone was settled with tea again, Howard led the conversation.

'So how was your trip?'

'Good, thank you. I was in Switzerland for a while and then Spain.'

'You missed all the excitement.'

'Ah yes, poor Morell – what a terrible business. The police have the man who did it I gather?'

'They detained him, yes.'

Rowena and Erika remained silent, both staring at the man and exchanging glances with each other. Howard sensed their hostility.

'The police are keen to speak to you, Peter.'

'They have done so already. I had a long talk with them yesterday afternoon.'

'And what was the outcome?'

'With regard to the death of the boy Grimshaw, they have – as they put it – eliminated me from their enquiries.'

Erika leaned towards him. 'Are you saying that you had nothing to do with it?'

'I am.'

'Do you know who did?'

'No.'

'Did you rape my sister in Berlin in 1940?'

'I did not.'

Erika stared at him intensely for some considerable time then sat back in her chair and looked down towards the ground. 'No, I don't believe you did.'

'I was not in Berlin in 1940.'

'No, I don't suppose you were.'

'Erika …' Rowena began, but she didn't follow through, too confused to construct a sentence.

'And your fiancée,' said Howard. 'Is she well?'

'Fiancée?' exclaimed Rowena.

'Yes, I am to be married. She is well, in fact she is waiting for me next door, so this is a brief visit.' He drained his cup, placed it firmly back on its saucer and stood up to leave. 'I must go now. Thank you for the tea and for your very kind hospitality. I hope to see you all again soon. You must come over for tea ... and meet Hildegard.'

Howard stood up and shook his hand. 'Cheerio, Peter.'

As Yardley turned to leave, he paused. 'Do you know anything about funeral arrangements ... for Morell?'

'There will be no funeral.'

'I see. Thank you.' He meandered down the garden and disappeared through the gate.

They watched him go. With the click of the gate latch closing into place, Erika's attention turned to Howard. She seemed to him rather like a kettle about to boil over. 'What the fucking hell is going on?'

'To what, precisely, are you referring?'

'You know very well. That is not Peter Yardley.'

'Yes it is.'

'It's not the same man, Howie,' said Rowena.

'And you know it,' added Erika, 'so stop playing games. What *is* going on?'

'All right, all right. Now listen to me, both of you. I need to explain some things because I think you have a right to know – and a need to know. I don't intend asking you to sign the Official Secrets Act, but I must impress upon you that what I am about to tell you *must* remain absolutely confidential between the three of us. Do you understand?'

'Howie,' said Rowena, sounding very confused. 'What are you talking about?'

406

'You must answer my question or I cannot say any more. Do you understand?'

'I understand,' said Erika mechanically.

'So do I,' said Rowena. 'But not really.'

Howard took out his pipe, padded some tobacco into the bowl and lit it, puffing away until it was well alight. 'That's good enough for me. The first thing you need to know is what I do for a living.'

'You're in the Civil Service,' said Rowena plainly.

'Sort of. I have to come clean. I work for the security service. You've probably heard of MI5.'

'You're a spy?' gasped Erika.

Howard chuckled. 'Good Lord no. Our job is to keep the country safe from spies – other people's. We spy on the spies. But I'm purely an administrator. A pen pusher.'

'Well I'm blowed!' gasped Rowena. 'I hadn't a clue.'

'It's been easy to keep secret from you, Floss, because you've never asked, never pried. Some of my colleagues have a devil of a job with their spouses – being accused of having affairs, leading double lives, all sorts, because they don't know the truth and can't be told.'

'Well I'm blowed,' repeated Rowena.

'Why are you telling us this, if it's so secret?' asked Erika. 'And what has this to do with Peter Yardley?'

'I'm coming to that. I'm going to tell you a story – a true story – and as I do you will see how the parts of the jigsaw fit together and who in the story you recognise.'

'You have our undivided attention,' said Rowena.

'It begins on familiar territory – in that Berlin bunker at the end of April 1945 where Hitler has been holed up for months. He's run out of options, lost touch with reality … he's depressed and close to suicide. Others are making the decisions. He's finally admitting defeat to the small number of cronies

407

remaining down there with him. Himmler has cleared off, Göring is up a mountain in Berchtesgarten. Goebbels is the most senior Nazi present other than Hitler ... but he isn't the one in charge. It's Martin Bormann – Hitler's right hand man. He holds the power, not to mention the purse strings, and by this stage is running the Third Reich. Hitler isn't the only one contemplating suicide, and those who aren't are planning their personal escapes. What no one wants is to be captured by the Russians. They've heard horror stories of atrocities against German soldiers and civilians alike as they fought their way west – torture, rape, murder. Reprisals for the atrocities the German army had been inflicting on Russians for almost three years. Who can blame them, some might say.'

'Not I,' said Rowena.

Howard smiled sympathetically. 'No doubt Hitler has heard what Italian partisans did to his friend Mussolini a few days earlier – shot him, and his lover, and strung them up on a metal girder, upside down, to be ridiculed and their bodies abused. Hitler is determined that will not happen to him, or to Eva, at the hands of the Russians. So, what is his solution to the problem? Does Eva take cyanide, does Hitler shoot himself, and are their bodies doused with petrol and burned, as he ordered? That's what you'll read in books and papers on the subject ... Trevor-Roper's book, for one. And there's a chap called Bullock currently working on a biography of Hitler which will no doubt say the same.' He paused for effect. 'Or did he escape, as Mr Morell described the other night?'

'Rather convincingly, I thought,' said Rowena.

'I agree, Flossie.' He puffed on his pipe for a moment. 'But let's leave Hitler for the moment and focus on Bormann. Here's a man who's a highly skilled planner, a forward thinker, a resourceful administrator with great influence and power. He's been pulling the strings behind the scenes for years as Hitler's secretary – his gatekeeper. Since 1943 Bormann has seen the writing on the wall, when the tide began to turn for Germany. Even earlier perhaps. He knew there was only one way it would end. It's unimaginable that he would have allowed himself to end up in the bunker without an escape strategy. So far, I've said nothing that you could not read in a book, but what I am about to tell you now is absolutely top secret. Morell alluded to it the other night.'

'About British military intelligence helping Bormann escape?' said Erika. 'Operation something or other.'

'That's it, Operation J.B. – I seem to recall you said at the time it was bonkers.'

'It sounded bonkers to me.'

'Perhaps. But that's what happened. Morell didn't have the facts quite right … it was a naval operation, not military, and they used kayaks, not canoes. You see, naval intelligence had a chap working for them who had personal connections with Ribbentrop, Hitler's Foreign Minister. His godson no less. His name is of no consequence, but he was one of our top operatives. Ribbentrop was also looking for a way out by early forty-five. The plan was to turn a blind eye to Ribbentrop vanishing in exchange for his putting us in contact with Bormann. He was the one we wanted to get our hands on at the time.'

'Why, what was so important about him?' asked Rowena.

'Money, Floss. Money pure and simple. We knew the Nazis had been stashing away massive fortunes. They not only looted the art galleries and museums in every city they captured, they also stole vast amounts of cash, not to mention huge fortunes from German Jews. They'd been squirrelling millions away for years – *tens* of millions. Martin Bormann knew where it all was – the bank locations, account numbers. Most importantly of all, he was the signatory. He signed all the cheques! We'd barely even heard of him until then. He wasn't a public figure like the others, he was a backroom boy. We've since learned that he virtually controlled access to Hitler. If Bormann didn't approve of something, it didn't happen. All the other senior Nazi leaders hated him. He was known as the man with the hedge clippers – if anyone rose above a certain level, he cut them down to size. Göring once said he hoped the bastard fried in hell, pardon my French.'

'Tell us about the operation.'

'Right. Naval intelligence managed to get in touch with Bormann via Ribbentrop. Incredibly, they even arranged a meeting with him in March of forty-five … in Berlin of all places. That's a story in itself. The man in charge of the project was a naval commander called Fleming, Ian Fleming. A remarkable chap, with a highly creative mind. He christened it Operation J.B. Stands for James Bond. He pinched the name from the author of a book about birds apparently. Anyway, they set up the whole thing. It was meticulously planned. They decided roads and air routes were too dangerous, so used the rivers instead, and rowed Bormann out. Simple but brilliant, Bormann waited until Hitler had flown out – we'll come back to him shortly – then as all the remaining occupants of the bunker fled in all directions, Bormann slipped away to the banks of the River Spree and floated off in the company of a small group of very brave men indeed … Ribbentrop's godson amongst them.'

'No qualms about aiding and abetting a ruthless Nazi war criminal escape justice?' asked Erika. 'The man who raped my sister and was responsible for her death?'

'I'm sorry, Erika. We perceived him then as a mere administrator, a desk bound official not directly involved in atrocities of war. Ultimately, they delivered him to England and to a safe house, here in Reigate, very near to where we're sitting in fact. Bormann was debriefed and proved extremely cooperative. We took him on trips to Switzerland and Sweden, and emptied some bank accounts. Just turned up with the correct account number and the right signature. No questions asked.'

'All that just to get your hands on some money. Why?'

'Absolute necessity. By the end of the war this country was totally bankrupt. The coffers were empty. We only survived thanks to a huge loan from the USA which we will be paying off, if my memory serves me well, until the year 2006. Without the money Bormann gave us access to, it would have been infinitely worse. In exchange, we offered him a new identity and a fresh start anywhere he chose. He liked Reigate … so here he stayed.'

'We moved here about the same time,' said Rowena. 'Just after the war ended. I preferred East Grinstead, but you insisted on Reigate.'

'It was no coincidence, Flossie. I was entrusted with keeping an eye on him and have been doing so ever since, from a casual arm's length. Over the garden fence, so to speak. He's been no trouble at all – good as gold. We knew about his two ruffians, but they'd been checked out by the boys in Special Branch and given the all clear.'

'Until recently.'

'Quite. Until his friend Mr Morell popped up out of the blue. I thought nothing of it at first, even when you told me you'd had drinks with Hitler, Floss. There had been rumblings in the halls of power that he may have managed a disappearing act somehow. But overall Trevor-Roper's findings convinced most of us that the newlyweds Eva and Adolf Hitler had committed suicide and their bodies burned. Most people wanted it that way. Like you both, I rather imagined Morell as a harmless old crank. I asked Bormann about him and he assured me he was an old business acquaintance from the early days, no more.'

'Do you still think that?' asked Erika.

'Do you?'

'It's rude to answer one question with another.'

'As you said, Erika, what Morell told us in the bunker was convincing. The escape from Berlin, the flight out of Germany to Spain, then on to Fuerteventura and the Villa Winter ... which does exist by the way. I had our friends in the other service check for me. All very feasible.'

'I thought it was convincing,' said Rowena.

'Or was it the imaginings of a deluded, fantasising, senile old man?'

'Howie, you lied to me,' said Rowena. 'You told me all the top Nazis were either dead or in prison.'

I'm sorry about that ... I had no choice. You were getting too close to the truth. I very nearly gave the game away by muttering that there was one exception. Foolish, and I had to lie my way out of it.'

'Not very convincingly. I heard you and it got me thinking and I worked it out for myself.'

'You did indeed, much to my embarrassment. You know, this reminds me of one of Agatha Christie's mystery stories – *Murder on the Orient Express*. Having heard all the evidence from the passengers in the railway carriage where the man Ratchet has been stabbed to death, the detective, Hercule Poirot, proposes two solutions. A very simple one of murder by a mysterious intruder who subsequently escapes, or a more convoluted plot that seems improbable but fits the facts like a glove, and implicates ... well I won't say in case you've never read it. Personally, I prefer simplicity, and so do the powers that be. They've made that abundantly clear. A harmless old crank wandering around declaring he's Adolf Hitler is one thing – the

412

Führer turning up alive and well in Reigate enjoying afternoon tea in The Old Wheel is another. Can you imagine the furore if that got into the newspapers!'

Erika thought for a moment. 'What about Delgado – how do you explain his appearance from nowhere? After all, he put a bullet in Mr M's head. That was no fantasy.'

'Reminding you again of the Official Secrets Act, Delgado has been thoroughly debriefed. We know now he's employed by an organisation called Mossad, the intelligence service of Israel. They're new but extremely efficient, and if they got wind that Adolf Hitler was alive and well, they would hardly hesitate in following it up. Who could blame them.'

'But how did they know about him?'

'According to Delgado, Mossad managed to track their suspect down to Fuerteventura – we don't know how – and Delgado, a local man, was tasked with infiltrating their base, the Villa Winter. He managed to get a job there as a handyman. They weren't sure for some time if it was indeed Hitler living there. Meanwhile Delgado fell for his wife, and she for him. Not part of the plan, but ironically it was this that gave them the proof they needed. She told Delgado everything – spilled the beans.' He sighed wistfully. 'Pillow talk I imagine.'

'Don't be vulgar, Howard,' said Rowena sternly.

'And when Eva was killed,' said Erika, 'this Delgado man came over to England to seek revenge on Mr Morell for the death of his lover?'

'Or on Yardley … or both if he had the opportunity.'

'How did he know where to find them?'

'After Eva was killed, he broke into the Villa Winter and stole some papers containing Yardley's address. Yardley was on his way back to England by then. His thugs followed a few days later once one of them had been treated for a badly injured hand. Delgado did that to him. They bit off more than they could

413

chew trying to kill him. Thought they were dealing with a local peasant, but unwittingly found themselves taking on a trained agent.' He chuckled. 'Must have been quite a surprise.'

'What will happen to him now – do you think he'll be tried for murder?'

'I doubt it. I suspect he'll be packed off home and told to forget about everything. Let's face it, if he killed Adolf Hitler, it's hardly a crime anyone will want to bring to trial. Perhaps we should be giving him a medal instead.'

The discussion reached a natural conclusion. There didn't seem to be anything more to understand.

'I shall say no more on the subject,' said Howard. 'What I will tell you, however, is that the man who now lives next door to us, Flossie, and with whom you have just taken tea, is Peter Roderick Yardley. He was chosen by us because of his close resemblance to someone we've just been discussing. He has been handsomely rewarded for the loan of his identity, plus other subterfuge, not least of all making random appearances in various parts of the world thousands of miles away from Reigate.' He broke off to chuckle to himself. 'A kind of human decoy duck if you will. Anyone who may have resembled him and with whom you may have been acquainted, will never be seen again.'

'En route for South America?'

'Possibly.' He puffed on his pipe 'Have you heard of Albert Speer?'

'Of course,' said Erika. 'Hitler's architect.'

'He was, and during the war he became Hitler's Armaments Minister. Speer is on record as saying: *Bormann was a born survivor – if anyone got out of the bunker alive, it would be he.* A born survivor is right. If he were on a plane or a boat to Buenos Aires as we speak, I wouldn't be at all surprised.'

'Erika,' said Rowena. 'Are you convinced now that our Mr Morell was Adolf Hitler?'

'Oh, I have protected him, because I was very fond of him, but I think I've known for a long time.'

'Since when?'

'Ever since we dined with him in the Dinner Gong and he said we had met before, at the Kaiserhof in Berlin.'

'But we discussed that and you said you were introduced to many men that evening, including other Nazi officials as well as Hitler.'

Erika pinched her nose with a thumb and forefinger. 'Yes, but only one who smelled quite like that. It really was very distinctive. I can assure you, once experienced, never forgotten. Mr Morell had that very same combination of personal aromas. The halitosis alone was a unique identifier, let alone the body odour.'

Rowena nodded as if in reluctant agreement. 'You do have a point. It was rather overpowering.'

Howard said: 'I believe one high-ranking Nazi wrote in his memoirs that at meetings held in the summer months, they used to dread Hitler taking off his jacket.'

'That would make sense,' agreed Rowena.

'You know,' said Erika contemplatively, 'the most bonkers part of this whole business for me is the notion of Martin Bormann escaping from Berlin by paddling up a river in a canoe.'

'A kayak,' corrected Howard.

'Are we really expected to believe that?'

'It does sound rather implausible,' agreed Howard. 'And yet that part – Operation James Bond – is the one part I can vouch for personally. I was aware of it at the time and had some small involvement in its planning. Most ingenious.'

415

'I like the name,' said Rowena. 'Top secret it may be now, but Commander Ian Fleming sounds like a very resourceful chap. Who knows, he might put it all down in a book one day. James Bond may become a household name.'

Howard chuckled, shook his head and relit his pipe.

'Unlikely, Flossie, old girl,' he said, puffing smoke out until he had all but disappeared from view. 'I would say that's highly unlikely.'